WITHDRAWN

POLITICAL WOMAN

For Shon and Dian

Political Woman

MELVILLE E. CURRELL

CROOM HELM LONDON

ROWMAN & LITTLEFIELD NEW JERSEY

54572

First published 1974
© 1974 Melville Currell

Croom Helm Ltd
2–10 St. Johns Road, London SW11

ISBN 0–85664–039–5

Rowman & Littlefield
81 Adams Drive, Totowa
New Jersey, 07512

ISBN 0–87471–564–4

Printed in Great Britain by
Biddles of Guildford

Contents

	Acknowledgements	
1.	Introduction	1
2.	The Late–Comers	22
3.	Women in Parliament, 1918–1970	53
4.	The Woman MP	74
5.	The Volunteers: Women as Prospective Parliamentary Candidates	93
6.	Women's Liberation	114
7.	Political Women: Cross National Comparisons	122
8.	The Changing Role of Women in Society	135
9.	Why so Few? Towards Explanation	158
	Appendices	186
	Select Bibliography	189
	Index	196

Acknowledgements

My primary debt of gratitude is to all those 'women in politics' who gave so generously of their time, experience and interest, in answering my questions. For their help in enabling me to contact women Prospective Parliamentary Candidates, I would particularly like to thank Mr. R. W. Elliott, MP, Vice-Chairman of the Conservative Party, and Miss Betty Lockwood, Chief Woman Officer of the Labour Party. To the many people, too numerous to mention individually, who helped to add details to the emerging patchwork of biographical data, basic to a study of this kind, I am extremely grateful.

For advice and encouragement especially in the initial stages of this work, I would like to thank Dr. A.H. Halsey of Nuffield College, Oxford. I am indebted, also, to Professor H.S. Ferns, Department of Political Science, University of Birmingham, for his ready encouragement and interest.

I would like to thank Mrs. J.E. Taylor for her work on calculations, and Miss Marjorie Davies for her meticulous typing assistance.

Chapter 1 Introduction

1. *The Problem Defined*

Probably at no time since the era of the militant suffragettes have the media and literature been so filled with material on the subject of women, as in the past five or so years.[1] As a bonus for feature writers, notable developments such as the Divorce Act in the latter part of 1969, followed in 1970 by the Equal Pay Act, plus the abortive Private Members' Anti-Discrimination Bill and the assurance of government legislation on the subject, have resulted in a rash of reports, analyses, and speculation. And all this has been set against the vivid backcloth of the Women's Liberation Movement.[2]

Included in this trend are to be found the articles, news reports and profiles of 'political women'.[3] Such writings, whatever else they suggest, at least provide some evidence in support of the proposition that for a woman to adopt a formal political role is still for her to adopt a newsworthy role, one unusual by the standards of her sex. In such articles, words like unfeminine may be implied but left unwritten, or, perhaps more significantly, the charge of unfemininity may be specifically denied. There is nothing particularly novel in this publicity, since it approximates to the degree of publicity accorded to women who are the first to attain positions previously occupied by men. Such 'newsworthiness' is typically (perhaps ironically?) expressed in emotive terms: bastions are stormed, dykes breached, fortresses fall.[4] The tone is reminiscent of Dr Johnson's much quoted dictum on women preachers, who, he maintained, resembled dogs walking on their hind legs. 'It is not done well, but you are surprised to find it done at all.'[5] This 'disproportionate publicity syndrome' will be discussed in greater detail later, as part of the characterisation of women as a minority group.[6]

The 'headline value' of those women in the political elite illustrates the paradox underlying this study. Despite women's majority in the electorate, their rate of political participation is very low. Nowhere in the political elite is reflected women's numerical strength in the population. Although women have been granted the parliamentary vote on equal terms with men for a little over forty years, the norm for women still seems to be non-participation in political leadership. The presence of an outstanding woman in the Cabinet from time to time seems to underline rather than invalidate this proposition.

Moreover, it may be suggested that both the low rate of participation and the 'special' position for women that seems to accompany it are, despite a certain amount of evidence to the contrary, very largely accepted, and regarded as a normal state of affairs. A quotation from a government publication in 1960 illustrates the second proposition particularly, or rather, suggests a double standard for rating male and female political activism. In the publication it is stated: 'the full participation of women in industry, the professions, *and in all kinds of public administration*, is today accepted as a normal feature of the national way of life.' . . . 'women have also played a prominent part in the organisation of the major political parties, *each of which has a woman's advisory committee or women's organisation* (emphasis added)'.[7]

2. *The Focus of the Study*

Essentially, the aim of this study is to attempt to evaluate factors relevant to women's participation in the political elite. In other words, it seeks to throw some light on the question 'Why are there so few women in politics?' Why, after enfranchisement, was it not a case of the flood-gates opening for 'political women' as suffragettes so hoped and the 'anti's' so dreaded. In 1909, Dicey was writing of women's political enfranchisement that 'a revolution of such boundless significance cannot be attempted without the greatest peril to England'.[8] Queen Victoria's fear of the consequences of the enfranchisement of women was very real to a substantial proportion of her subjects of both sexes.

> The Queen feels so strongly upon the dangerous and unchristian and unnatural cry and movement of 'women's rights' . . . that she is most anxious that Mr Gladstone and others should take some steps to check this alarming danger and to make whatever use they can of her name.[9]

Yet in numerical terms, the few women who have sat in Parliament (less than one hundred) are neither a very considerable dividend on the investment of the suffragettes, nor a very awesome harvest from sowing a whirlwind. This, then, was the paradox underlying and initiating this study.

Inevitably, wider issues are involved in a consideration of the basic paradox, so that the framework includes some treatment (necessarily attenuated) of the way in which women relate to politics generally, and the factors which influence this relationship. Further than this, in order to describe and evaluate women's political role, it is necessary to look at women's roles as a whole, of which her political role is, or in the majority of cases may not be, a part. If woman's political role is a departure, a deviance in one sense of that word, then it is essential to consider the norms from which she departs, the factors which influence or impinge on woman's role, and the images and models which that role may engender. This is by no means simple. It is a commonplace today that norms and values are in a state of transition and flux. A traditional pattern of male dominance and female subservience is no longer applicable. But the traditional norms of behaviour for men and women (as incidentally for young and old) have not been replaced by guide lines equally well defined and explicit. Rates of change are not the same in all sub-cultures and sections – the main support for the Women's Liberation Movement comes, it must be remembered, from sections of the middle and professional classes. Adaptive reaction to modification in values is both uneven and belated, generating new tensions and strains. As illustration of this pattern generally, we may cite the 'captive wife' syndrome, or the appearance of 'suburban neurosis'. It must be stressed that any exploration of women's changing role is for the purposes of the present study contextual only, the background not the whole canvas.

Except for certain comparative material, the study is focussed mainly on British politics in the period which runs from the first granting of the limited franchise to women to the present day. Clearly, basing a study of women's political role in the year of their first limited enfranchisement is open to objection on several counts.

The first and major objection hinges on the question of the definition of 'the political'. How is political activity to be distinguished from other human activity? Certainly beginning with 1918 suggests equating political activity with the legal privileges of voting and candidature. Defining 'the political' may almost be termed a growth industry for political scientists. For the purposes of this study, however, it seems sufficient to adopt a relatively simplistic approach namely in Easton's terminology that 'people may be said to be participating in political life when their activity relates in some way to the making and execution of policy for society'.[10] This is consonant with Easton's broad and seminal definition of politics as the process of the authoritative allocation of values in a society. Under this rubric, then, may be subsumed all kinds and all levels of activity, both voting, candidatures, party activism, pressure group membership. and extra-institutional informal activity of any kind aimed at influencing the policy makers.

On this definition, then, objections to the emphasis on the 1918–1970s period may be cogent. It may be maintained that enfranchisement does not mark the base-line of women's political activity, since it can be shown that women were active politically or para-politically before this date.[11] Women were involved in the early Radical movement, the early Trade Union movement, the agitation both for the Repeal of the Combination Acts and of the Corn Law, the Chartist Movement and the Co-operative Movement, and in left-wing political Associations. Women also acted as canvassers and propagandists for the Labour Party: they were in the invidious position of trying to persuade male voters to support a party for which the women canvassers themselves were ineligible to vote. In other words, even before the political emancipation of women, there appeared to be some indication that women might in the future play, if not a major part, at least a significant part in political life.

Another criticism of making 1918 the starting point for the major part of this work is that it dismisses as pure prologue the activities of women's suffrage organisations, activities which on our working definition may certainly be classified as political. The reasons for this exclusion are not only those of time and space, the fact that much history and analysis of the suffrage movement is readily available,[12] or the fact that women's suffrage organisations were not of themselves instrumental in attaining enfranchisement. The main reason is that the study concentrates on women in the political elite when they are competing on the same terms as men, i.e. investigation of the assimilation into political life of women unhampered by legal disabilities. In the history of the widening of the franchise, the sequence was characterised by two priorities, the one of sex, the other of class. Women entered at the end of the chapter, the latecomers, and it is these latecomers and their assimilation into politics on which this study concentrates. A major study of the relationship between feminism and political activity (a relationship obscured by the coincidence of timing between expressions of feminism in the late nineteenth and early twentieth century and the demands for woman suffrage) has yet to be made. This book makes no such contribution.

The material on which a significant part of this investigation is based is drawn primarily from empirical data, on and provided by women in the political elite. Details of the samples, etc. will be found in Appendix I. The study of women's political role which follows is, then, intended to record representation in the political elite at specific levels, in a manner somewhat analogous to the exploratory trial trenches of the archaeologist, determining the depths of the levels, and the boundaries. The levels are those of elected representatives, that is women MPs, and the women prospective Parliamentary candidates, the volunteers, the group which is at least to some extent self-selected, having accepted, as it were, a potential political role.

From the point of view of boundaries, briefly the study aims at investigating the women in these groups, in terms of (a) personal history, background and career patterns; (b) their motivations as reported by the women themselves; (c) the attitudes of this highly selective sample to the whole complex of factors operative in defining women's political role; and (d) their view of what women can contribute vis-à-vis men, that is whether they set limits to women's competence in terms of what Maurice Duverger has termed 'feminine ideology'.[13]

This study, in essence, then, attempts some discussions of the factors associated with the way in which women relate to politics. In seeking to explain under-representation of a particular group in a particular situation, disincentives, discrimination, anything construed as disadvantageous are usually cited. There are, however, countervailing forces which may mediate women's entry into politics rather than militate against it: these factors will also be considered here. Thus the overall strategy is that women in politics are considered from several different angles. Various aspects of the subject, various perspectives will be discussed, some factual, some descriptive, some basically explanatory and exploratory approaches. Corresponding to the various approaches are the various kinds of evidence used, the various types of quantitative and descriptive data. By using such a composite of approaches and evidence, it is not intended to give the impression that any one factor is a discrete entity which stands independently of the others: rather it should be clear that all such factors operate in a complex interaction. The bulk of this study, then, lies very much in an inter-disciplinary 'no man's land' between the frontiers of political science, history and sociology. While drawing on insights, generalisations and formulations from all these fields, the study does not attempt anything that might justifiably be termed a strictly theoretical orientation.

In the interpretation of data presented here certain caveats have to be entered. Basically it is necessary that these data are set both in the framework of the general situation of women's status in society and in the framework which the field of political sociology is developing, i.e. in terms of the way people relate to politics, voting behaviour, the processes of political socialisation.

Then the isolation of women as subjects from the mass of the male political elite brings problems. Since Namier's work on the personnel of Parliament, in which he adopted what we may now consider a broadly sociological approach to the interpretation of history,[14] the scholarly tradition focussed on the British political elite has been lengthy. The more recent of these studies included women when, rarely, they are members of the elites considered. Such studies, in general, investigate characteristics which may be objectively determined, not opinions and attitudes of those involved. There has, as yet, been no large scale study, based on interview techniques, of male Members of Parliament. With few exceptions, until the Maud Report[15] very little extensive research was done on the composition of local councils, and very little on the attitudes and opinions of councillors.[16] This is a trend now being reversed with the current academic interest in urban politics in Great Britain. Something has been written on women's political role,[17] again mainly in terms of the characteristics of those in the political elite, or in terms of voting behaviour.

In the long term, then, in attempting to probe women's place in the political elite, the ideal would be a study of that elite on a large scale, and in depth, within which elite women might, or less probably might not, form a sub-group. In the short term, though, there seems good reason for concentrating on women only, at this stage. Women in the political elite, it may be argued, 'deviate' from the more usual role of women in society: within the elite they seem, as will be shown, to play a part now approximating that of men. Moreover, in certain respects, there are ways in which a factor may operate differentially for men and women in the political elite. To take an obvious example, marital status and number of children in the family may be tabulated for a sample of men and women MPs. For a woman member, care of husband and a young family could be a strain, a limitation on her career. For her male colleague, a wife and children might enhance the image he was trying to project and his wife might play a valuable supplementary role in the constituency. In respect of the insecurity of a political career the advantages to each sex might well be reversed. Marriage for the woman MP could be an advantage in cushioning the effects of the sudden termination of a paid occupation. Family responsibilities for the male MP who loses his seat might be an additional hazard.

It has to be admitted, too, that confusion and ambiguities persist in much of our thinking on women's role. Most striking is the confusion between equality of the sexes and identity of the sexes. The more the homogeneity of women is stressed in such expressions as 'the status of women' the less it is likely to be clear that differences exist within each sex grouping as between them. The phrase, 'status of women', while a convenient shorthand expression, ignores or at least blurs significant divisions such as class. A similar ambiguity arises from ignoring the differences between demanding equal rights for women (identifiable as a group becuase they lack these rights) and imputing a common and identifiable point of view to women once these rights have been acquired. In other words, if it can be shown that women relate to politics in ways distinct from those of men, the question immediately arises whether the differences vary according to the social and economic situation of women, or whether they may be construed as modes of reaction characteristic of the sex itself.

Applying these considerations to the interpretation of the empirical evidence to be presented here, it must be made plain that the material presented on women's reported motivations, attitudes, etc., cannot be assumed to be applicable to women only and not to men, that is, relevant to women *qua* women. Only, as has been indicated, within the context of a wider study covering both sexes is there the possibility that such relevance might reasonably be validated. Such a conclusion cannot be drawn from this material, the limitation is inevitable.

In a study of this kind, focussed on the relatively minor political role of women compared with that of men, there is an important question of emphasis. To see the study in perspective, it has to be borne in mind that the majority of *men* is not politically activist.[18] Then the type of material used, and the relatively small numbers involved, do not lend themselves to sophisticated statistical analysis.

To conclude this section on limitations, a final point has to be made not so much in terms of interpretation of data as in its presentation. The empirical material was obtained by interview and questionnaire under the assurance to those good enough to participate, that information would be used anonymously, mainly on a quantitative basis. For this reason, quotations are not identified, nor, it is intended identifiable, and care has been taken to avoid citing material in association with a career pattern that might be well known. This has inevitably involved contraction of material presented and, sadly, the reduction of much striking, interesting and vivid raw material to a much less colourful form.

3. *Women's Political Activity before Enfranchisement*

The description of women as politically impotent before receiving the right to vote in a national election or stand for Parliament may be shown to be not completely accurate. The first obvious qualification to be made is that even before 1918 some few women were beginning to enter political life by voting for and serving on School Boards, and at local elections.[19]

In contrast, the 'power behind the throne' notion was one that had been widely canvassed over the years, and at various levels. The belief that women already had the means of expressing their political views by influencing male voters in their electoral decision was used as an argument against the enfranchisement of women. Gladstone, though not a supporter of woman suffrage yet addressed to women a somewhat sentimental appeal for their help in the General Election of 1880. There were two associations of women supporters of the Liberal Party, divided on the question of women's suffrage. Other evidence exists for women having a vicarious part in elections before 1918. Emmanuel Shinwell recalls two occasions when women's influence was crucial, before emancipation.

> ... In the trade unions many admitted women on sufferance, using the fact of their smaller wages as a reason to impose smaller dues and therefore to restrict the women members' influence on the management of union affairs.
>
> ... The result was that a formidable part of the campaign for female emancipation concerned women's right to vote on equal terms with men in the unions, and the matter of a Parliamentary vote sometimes took second place ....
>
> It was the campaigning of these two women (Miss Eva Gore-Booth and Esther Roper) which had helped to return David Shackleton as Labour MP for Clitheroe in 1902, the votes in the ballot of the local union which approved him being given by more women than men: Shackleton was pledged to press the claims for female emancipation, though his subsequent activities in this regard were not distinguished.
>
> More significant was the women's success at the Wigan by-election in the general election of 1906. [sic] It was the women who selected Thorley Smith to stand as 'Women's Candidate and Independent Labour', which automatically got him disapproved by the miners' union and the local trades council. To their credit the railwaymen's union protested at the decision but theirs was a minority view. Smith surrounded by women wherever he spoke and supported by an array of women speakers, including

> Mrs. Pankhurst, polled more votes than the Liberal although, as expected, he failed to gain a traditional Tory seat. He got some 2,200 votes which were virtually the votes of the 96,000 women trade unionists in the Lancashire area who had shown almost frenetic enthusiasm for a campaign in which they had nothing but indirect influence on husbands and other male relatives.[20]

It seems, then, that in the wider context of seeking to promote party political ends, women's contribution pre-enfranchisement has frequently been ignored or seriously underestimated. A few more examples may be added. Women canvassers in General Elections were not unknown even in the eighteenth century, when for example Georgiana, Duchess of Devonshire, campaigned for Charles James Fox in the 1784 Westminster campaign. Opposing her for the Tories was the Countess of Salisbury.[21]

In the latter half of the nineteenth century, women canvassers and women propagandists were more usual. The activities of Labour propogandists such as Mrs. Bruce Glasier (Kathleen St. John Conway) in the 1890s,[22] and the women of the Clarion Clubs who campaigned primarily for the Labour Party, and also for the vote, are interesting. These clubs were associated with a Socialist weekly paper, *The Clarion*. This paper also sent out a horse-drawn caravan to tour the countryside. The caravan was used as a base from which Socialist propagandists lectured and held meetings. The 'Clarion Vanners' seem to have included a sizeable proportion of women.[23] It is difficult to provide accurate figures. Certainly the figure of ten per cent for women among the 'principal social and political reformers in this country' at the turn of the century, seems likely to be an understatement.[24]

Kathleen Glasier was also connected with the Independent Labour Party, an organisation overtly in favour of women's suffrage. At its second Annual Conference, the party declared in its constitution for extending electoral reform to both men and women. In 1914 it was reported: 'There is pride for us in the fact that at a time when there was literally no public opinion in support of the women's claim, the I.L.P. by its declaration and its constitution and its advocacy of "Votes for Women" did very much towards creating that opinion which is now manifest.'[25] Paradoxically, in the period from its inception in 1893 to 1918 there were only nine women (national) members on the N.A.C., and of these only six had two or more years' service. The numbers involved are so small as to make anything but a few comments unrealistic. Middle-class origins and the 'communication' type of occupation link these women activists. 'Communication' in the sense of writing and lecturing was clearly basic to their lives.

Miss Caroline Martyn was an author, after having initially worked as a teacher in Church and Board schools. Miss Isabella Ford was also a professional writer.[26] Mrs. Kathleen Glasier, as already mentioned a lecturer and writer on socialist subjects, had also published two novels. Miss Mary McArthur (Mrs. W.C. Anderson), Miss Enid Stacy and Mrs. Pankhurst (of woman's suffrage fame) wrote and lectured on socialism and social reform. (Both Mrs. Anderson and Mrs. Glasier were married to Chairmen of the I.L.P.)

Work for Trade Unions links three of the six. Margaret Bondfield, later to become Minister of Labour, was one time chief woman organiser of the National Union of General and Municipal Workers, and was a founder of the Women's Labour League. Mary McArthur was one of the leading figures of women's Trade Unionism, but was unsuccessful in her later attempt to win election to Parliament. Miss Isabella Ford, a Quaker, came from a Yorkshire family well known for its Radical sympathies. With her sister, Miss Ford was instrumental in improving women's conditions in the clothing industries of Leeds, and helped women there to organise into a trade union. Miss Ford was also active in the suffrage movement but was later to refuse invitations to stand for Parliament.

Thus far, consideration of women's political activities before their enfranchisement has been confined to their work relative to, often marginal to, local elected bodies and political party organisations. It is now necessary to round out the picture by considering women's part in the context of what would now be termed the arena of pressure group politics. In this framework may be placed women's participation in such diverse phenomena of the nineteenth century English political scene as Chartism, the anti-Corn Law agitation, Trade Unionism, the agitation for the repeal of the Contagious Diseases Act.

Women took part in Chartist groups, around 8,000 signed the 1842 petition, and some all-women groups existed. There was at one time discussion of including woman suffrage in the Charter. Women played an important role in the chain of groups which covered the country in the move to obtain Repeal of the Corn Laws.[27] The Women's Trade Union League, founded in 1874, and with a membership at its peak of around 20,000, is well known. From its leadership came two of the earliest women MPs, Dr Ethel Bentham and Dr Marion Phillips. What is less well known is that women were also participating in Trade Unions not specifically for women, long before enfranchisement.[28]

In terms of pressure group politics the agitation for the repeal of the Contagious Diseases Acts absorbed the attention of a great many, mainly middle-class women. In the Victorian social climate this is particularly significant since the Acts to which they objected were intended to reduce the incidence of Venereal Disease by draconian measures taken against women who might be suspected of prostitution. The example of Mrs. Josephine Butler, who led the campaign for the Acts' repeal, merits some comment here. The Grey family into which she had been born had long been associated with the higher reaches of public life.[29] While Mrs. Butler's early activities could be described broadly as forms of welfare work (caring for the sick, setting up an Industrial Home for women and girls), her later work in national and international agitation against the Contagious Diseases Acts took on an essentially political character. Mrs. Butler, having made the personal decision that the Acts should be opposed, set about organising opposition, securing publicity, going on propaganda campaigns lecturing to working-class (predominantly male) audiences seeking signatures to a Manifesto, and forming a Ladies' National Association for Abolition. Despite the hostility of the press, the work went on, though this entailed the establishment of the Association's own paper, *The Shield*. The work, in fact, was the sustained attack of a well-organised and adequately financed pressure group. In 1886 the Acts were repealed as the culmination of about twenty years of agitation.

The agitation against the Acts had been a well planned, single-minded operation, led by a woman of considerable administrative skills. The pressure group to be considered next is in complete contrast. In the fascinating forms taken by the Social Democratic Federation,[30] changes in nomenclature were associated with the secession and coalescence which marked its history. In the period of the S.D.F. in particular, women were playing by no means a negligible role. The London members of the Executive always included one or two women, and there was also Eleanor Marx Aveling, whose prestige as a daughter of Karl Marx was to the S.D.F. particularly and to Socialist propaganda generally, a valuable asset.[31]

Similarly the Socialist League[32] founded by William Morris on secession from the S.D.F. always included a few women. Morris' daughter May Morris was active, and was joined in 1886 on the Executive by a second woman, Lena Wardle.

The numbers of women in these Associations are too small to permit of realistic comparisons, though it seems important to note that the influence of these women seems to be more considerable than either their numbers or their formal positions suggest.

The Fabian Society, which has now been in existence for over eighty years has always had a sizeable proportion of women in its membership. For the pre-enfranchisement period, the percentage of women in the total membership ranged from 17 per cent in 1893 to 33 per cent in 1918, with a peak of 43 per cent in 1912. It is interesting that this proportion is paralleled by the proportion of women members on the Fabian Executive over about the same period (17 per cent in 1888 and 33 per cent thirty years later).[33] From 1908 there also existed a Fabian Women's Group,[34] which did not seem to detract from women's service on the full Executive, as the women's group did not seem to attract many of the most influential Fabian women. It is interesting to consider in a little more detail the women who have served on the Executive in the years before women's enfranchisement.[35] Only those with a minimum of two years service are included, and the total is only twenty-eight. Coupled with the small numbers is the lack of comprehensive data for each member. Detailed analysis is, therefore, not attempted, though certain features emerge.

Just under one-third can be traced as graduates – a high proportion for that period.[36] The intellectual calibre revealed is exceptionally high, when one considers that one member was elected to a chair of English, another qualified both in medicine and as a barrister, and that Beatrice Webb and Annie Besant (neither educated at University) served at this period.

There is very little identity of personnel with other fields of 'formal' political activity. Miss Susan Lawrence, Dr Bentham, and Dr Marion Phillips were to serve later as Members of Parliament, and all three later served on the National Executive of the Labour Party. Otherwise, the majority of these women were to remain outside politics, though some served as Justices of the Peace, Poor Law Guardians and as members of School Boards. Social commitment was extensive.

One of the most interesting features of the women on the Fabian Executive, very obvious in this period, is the high proportion of 'wives and relations,' the Webbs, George Bernard Shaw and his wife, the wife of Snowden, and the daughter and son-in-law of William Morris. This is not, however, strict 'male equivalence' as described elsewhere in this study, as some of the husbands and wives served at the same time. Shaw preceded his wife on the Executive, and they then served together, as did the Webbs, since Sidney Webb was not joined on the Executive by his wife until 1912. Wells preceded his second wife Catherine, who then served for two years, but they did not serve together. This is probably a more exact example of male equivalence since Wells himself was much involved in controversy within the society, and at one stage resigned. Through his wife, he may well have maintained a watching brief.

The class background of this sample of Fabian women reflects educational standards. As far as can be ascertained, all of the sample were of at least middle-class backgrounds, as, of course, were the majority of the Fabian Society. In this, the Fabian women did not differ from women organising the various suffrage societies.

A factor which emerged from this consideration of women on the Fabian Executive was the proportion (just over half) who in this period had an occupational background of the 'communication' type, that is writers, teachers, lecturers. This proportion is not surprising in the context of the Fabian Society, and may be illustrated by a few examples of some of the lesser known women members of the Executive.

Miss Emma Brooke has been educated at Cambridge and at the London School of Economics, and was noted as a social and political reform lecturer. She had been a member of the New Life Fellowship ancestor of the Fabian Society, of which she was a founder member. Miss Brooke was also a succesful novelist. Dr Letitia Fairfield had been active in women's suffrage activity and later became a Lieutenant Colonel in the R.A.M.C. and was subsequently Senior Medical Officer to the L.C.C. A barrister, Dr Fairfield also acted at one time as assistant editor on a medico-legal journal. Dr Edith Morley was appointed to the chair of English language and literature at the University of Reading in 1908, as one of the first women Professors in this country. Professor Morley was, in addition, active in the women's Social and Political Union. All the influences of her professional home background were towards Conservatism, and she was converted to Liberalism and then, by reading Blatchford's works, to Socialism. Her subsequent activities included taking a major part in founding the British Federation of University Women, work as a Justice of the Peace, and she was largely responsible for the introduction of women police in Reading.[37] All this was in addition to considerable works of literary criticism. Miss Honor Morten, after training as a nurse, was warden of a London settlement for many years, at the same time working as a writer and journalist.[38] Mrs. Pember Reeves, whose husband was at one time Principal of the London School of Economics, had, under her maiden name of Magdalen Stuart Robison, written the book *Round About a Pound a Week*.

So far, we have discussed women's part in the political sector in the period when they were unenfranchised nationally, and on our definition of the 'political' the examples we have taken have been of women within a political party or a pressure group. But this is, as it were, only one side of the coin, there is a quite other category of women's political activism.

In the years before enfranchisement (judging mainly from anti-suffragist literature), support, influence, persuasion, as the basis for activity were usually regarded as much more readily compatible with women's role than were elements associated with manipulation, overt wielding of power. The difference in essence reflects that between what Talcott Parsons would term the expressive and the instrumental orientation of the female and male roles respectively.

Yet translated into the political sector, there have always been some few examples of women who have by some means assimilated manipulative power into their own feminine role, without appearing to arrogate to themselves any part of the masculine role. In a role apparently expressive, yet instrumental in quality, the political hostesses held real though not necessarily overt power. Their role encompassed far more than that of a wife entertaining for her husband, or a daughter for her father. What is significant is that a certain minority of upper class women, whose father, husband, or relatives were in the elite of the social and political world, were in a pivotal position of power, able to arrange meetings or engineer confrontations of male decision makers as they thought fit. Thompson's view which he applied to the nineteenth century would not be inappropriate applied to the previous century, or indeed to the early twentieth. 'Predominantly landed families revolved round their menfolk. Those gifted ladies who ventured into the man's world of politics . . . were careful to conceal their evident power and prowess beneath a veil of deferment to the male politician'.[39] Two examples from the early nineteenth century of the real power of women in this context are that of Lady Melbourne and that of the Duchess of Devonshire.[40]

Moving on to later periods, there are other names to be included in any consideration, however abbreviated, of the role of political hostesses. On the Liberal side, Margot Asquith was famous. Before her marriage, as Margot Tennant she had been a leading figure in 'The Souls', a group whose members included Arthur Balfour and George Curzon. In her opinion, 'since those days there has been no group in society of equal distinction, loyalty, and *influence*' (emphasis added).[41] Her circle of friends lay in the political elite and included

Rosebery, Salisbury, and Gladstone. After her marriage, her activities as hostess in her own right, and for her husband, continued.

The case of the Countess of Warwick (1861–1938) makes a fascinating story. A beauty in the 'Marlborough House Set', the circle of the Prince of Wales (later Edward VII) she entertained both Liberal and Conservatives. Years later, after her 'conversion' to Socialism, the Countess worked to promote Labour interests.[42]

In later periods, other names may be added to the list. The Marchioness of Crewe[43] was distinguished in this field among Liberals and the Marchioness of Londonderry among Tories. The Marchioness of Londonderry was the daughter of a Tory politician, and married Viscount Castlereagh, who sat as Tory member for Maidstone until he went to the Lords. In the 1914–18 war the Marchioness was the founder and director of the Women's Legion. After the war, her activities lay in the political field, and she is reported as having bridged party boundaries in being a personal friend of Ramsay MacDonald and his family, and acting as hostess on behalf of her husband. In Ulster with her husband, she is 'considered to have given powerful aid to the newly formed Northern Ireland Government.'[44]

Duff Cooper's autobiography is revealing on the subject of his wife's activities in the political milieu of their lives. One of the incidents he recalls refers to the way in which his wife arranged a meeting and prompted a reconciliation between a politician and a newspaper proprietor, thus ending a damaging campaign against the politician. The politician was Winston Churchill, the newspaper proprietor Beaverbrook. Duff Cooper wrote, 'I am under the impression that this dinner party produced results and that the press campaign against the Secretary of State for War was abandoned, but old men forget . . .[45]

The examples cited so far have been drawn from history or from the immediate past. But the exercise of manipulative power, together with supportive and persuasive activities continue as a supplement to, not as a substitute for, the political power achieved via the ballot box. The hey day of the Edwardian political hostess will probably never be approached, but in very different forms and not under the same name, some sort of similar activity persists. Fictional illustrations may be drawn from the work of Maurice Edelman,[46] or C.P. Snow's *Corridors of Power*.[47]

In terms of the continuation of the importance of the expressive supportive side of women's role in a political context, only a few of many illustrations and indicators may be cited here. These range from the 'vetting' of the wives of Tory parliamentary candidates,[48] to the fact that at least three women MPs have been on record as lamenting the lack of a wife.[49] Ellen Wilkinson, as reported by the former Dr Edith Summerskill, was one of the most explicit '. . . reminded me of Ellen Wilkinson coming into the Women Members' Room during my early days in the House, with a brief-case in one hand and a dozen letters which she had just collected at the House Post Office, sighing, "Oh! for a wife." I looked puzzled. She added, "If I had a wife, she might have collected these, drafted answers and finally typed them. She would help with the women's section, give a hand with the bazaar, and, when I get home fagged out, have a delicious meal ready for me".'[50]

The attitude implicit in the words which James Barrie gave to his heroine Maggie is not outdated, then, and perhaps in one sense never will be outdated. 'It's nothing unusual I've done, John. Every man who is high up loves to think that he has done it all by himself; and the wife smiles and lets it go at that. It's our only joke. Every woman knows that.'[51]

We cannot leave this section without reference to one of the most tantalising episodes of American history in this context. The situation is hardly classifiable on a straight instrumental-expressive dichotomy, as it seemed to combine something of manipulative influential and supportive elements. Suffice it to say that the episode provides the example *par excellence* of a woman's wielding of considerable power without holding any formal, authorised position. The wife of President Woodrow Wilson, in acting as intermediary between her sick husband and his cabinet (while he was almost completely incapacitated) virtually performed the duties of the President of the United States for some months. The press openly referred to this period as 'The Regency' and to Mrs. Wilson as the 'Acting President'.[52]

Thus far, the positive side of women's activity has been considered. But where women have, by supportive and manipulative activities helped to ensure male political success, women have also been indirectly responsible mainly via the divorce courts, for preventing a male politician from achieving higher office. The nineteenth century yields two clear examples, Parnell[53] and Dilke.[54] With a changed social climate, divorce is a less effective weapon of attack against opponents. In the days of mass circulation newspapers, however, discredit through scandal such as in the Profumo affair is still unlikely to be ignored.

What kind of conclusions may be drawn from this admittedly attenuated treatment of the manifold forms of the political activity of women before their formal enfranchisement? Certainly there can be no straightforward 'before' and 'after' comparisons, since as has been shewn, elements of women's participation in the realm of politics – indirect or vicarious – were present before enfranchisement, and have persisted since. It is, therefore, not realistic to consider women's political activity as developing steadily from zero in the year before enfranchisement, taking the right to vote as the *sine qua non*. The real question is rather, why, when women were so active in certain political activities and in some forms of public life before enfranchisement, has the impetus given by formal access to the locus of power been so slight?

Notes

1. The list may include a variety of approaches, e.g. M. Fogarty *et al. Women and Top Jobs*, London, 1967; E. Dahlstrom, (ed.), *The Changing Roles of Men and Women*, London, 1967; E. Gundry, *Jobs for Mothers*, London, 1967; Fabian Study Group, *Woman Power*, London, 1966; G.B. Social Survey, *A Survey of Women's Employment*, London, 1968; J. Kamm, *Hope Deferred: Girls' Education in English History*, London, 1965; M. Laing (ed.), *Woman on Woman*, London, 1971; R.J. Lifton, *The Woman in America*, Boston, 1964; A. Michel and G. Texier, *La Condition de la Femme d'aujourd'hui*, Geneva, 1964; E. Sullerot, *Woman Society and Change*, London, 1971. Relevant also in this connection are studies in the developing field of ethology, e.g. L. Tiger, *Men in Groups*, London, 1969. Insights from this field will be discussed in Chapter IX.
2. Of the many books and pamphlets recently published, the most notable include G. Greer, *The Female Eunuch*, London, 1971; K. Millet, *Sexual Politics*, London, 1971; and E. Figes, *Patriarchal Attitudes*, London, 1970.
3. e.g. 'The Political Female', *Sunday Times*, 9 September 1962; 'Women in politics: the useful sex?', *The Times*, 1 November 1967; 'Women in a Man's World: Member of Parliament', *Homes and Gardens*, September 1972. See also the articles on Mrs. Barbara Castle and Mrs. Margaret Thatcher, when they became Cabinet Ministers.
4. e.g. 'Another Female Assault', *Times Business Review*, 19 May 1969; 'Miss Bailey lays siege to the Brokers' bastion', *Observer*, 26 February 1967.
5. J. Boswell, *The Life of Samuel Johnson*, 1791, Oxford University Press, vol.I, p.309.
6. cf. below, p. 176.
7. Central Office of Information, *Women in Britain*, London, 1960, H.M.S.O., p.1.
8. A.V. Dicey, 'Woman Suffrage', *Quarterly Review*, 210, 1909, p.277.

9. Letter to Gladstone, 6 May 1870; quoted in P. Guedalla, *The Queen and Mr Gladstone*, London, 1933, vol.I, p.227.
   The apprehensions of anti-suffragists are adequately summarised by Pethick-Lawrence (who himself fought for woman's enfranchisement).
   'The anti-suffragists said that it [enfranchisement of women] would drag women out from their natural sphere of the home into the arena of political strife, and impose on them obligations which the vast majority of them were unwilling to assume. They foretold that it would create dissension between husbands and wives. They did not believe that it would improve women's wages and conditions, because these depended on the economic law of supply and demand. They feared that women, when they formed the majority of the electorate would outvote men on matters of home and foreign policy and that men would have to bear the brunt of these decisions taken contrary to their more experienced judgement. To these gloomy prophecies, some of the men among them added the whisper that a regimen of women would impose on them impossibly strict standards of sex morality.' F.W. Pethick-Lawrence, *Fate Has Been Kind*, London, 1942, p.105.
10. cf. D. Easton, *A Framework for Political Analysis*, Englewood Cliffs, N.J., 1965.
11. Such a phenomenon is not, of course, peculiar to this country. In Russia, for example, women were active in the Populist Movement. (For an interesting brief account, see H. Kamen, 'Women and Revolution under Alexander II', *History Today*, 15 June 1965. In France, women were active in revolutionary clubs, and in pre-Independence India, in Gandhi's Civil Disobedience campaigns.
12. e.g. J. Kamm, *Rapiers and Battleaxes*, London, 1966; E. Flexner, *Century of Struggle*, Cambridge, Mass., 1959; R. Fulford, *Votes for Women*, London, 1957; C. Rover, *Women's suffrage and party politics in Britain, 1866–1914*, London, 1967; A. Sinclair, *The Better Half; the emancipation of American women*, London, 1966; A. Raeburn, *The Militant Suffragettes*, London, 1973; W.L. O'Neill, *Feminism in the United States and England*, London, 1969.
13. i.e. Women's restriction to, and specialisation in, certain subjects only, e.g. 'Welfare', health, children. He contrasts women's monovalence with the polyvalence attributed to men. M. Duverger, *The Political Role of Women*, Paris, 1955, p.126.
14. L. Namier, *The Structure of Politics at the Accession of George III*, London, 1928. The list would certainly include: H.J. Laski, *The British Cabinet*, London, 1928; H.R.G. Greaves, 'Personal Origins and Inter-relations of the Houses of Parliament since 1832', *Economica*, X, 1929; J. Bonnor, *The Four Labour Cabinets*, *Sociological Review*, 6, 1, July 1955; J.F.S. Ross, *Elections and Electors*, London, 1955, and his *Parliamentary Representation*, London, 1943; W.L. Guttsman, *The British Political Elite*, London, 1963; and the Nuffield series on General Elections which began

with the 1945 Election.

15. G.B., Ministry of Housing and Local Government, Committee on the Management of Local Government, volume 2, The Local Government Councillor, London, H.M.S.O., 1967.
16. e.g. work by L.J. Sharpe such as 'Elected representatives in Local Government', *British Journal of Sociology*, 13, 3, September 1962; J.M. Lee, *Social Leaders and Public Persons*, Oxford, 1963. A study which includes attitudes and opinions is that of Barking Council: A.M. Rees and T. Smith, *Town Councillors*, London, 1965.
17. e.g. J.F.S. Ross, 'Women and Parliamentary Elections', *British Journal of Sociology*, 4, 1953; Lady Gertrude Williams, 'The political role of women', unpublished ms. Fawcett Library, 1952; P. Brookes, *Women at Westminster*, London, 1967.
    Outside Britain, women's political role has been covered by M. Duverger, op.cit., in his study of women's political participation in France, the German Federal Republic, Norway and Yugoslavia. Norman Mackenzie, in his *Women in Australia*, (London, 1963) treated women's political role within a large-scale study of the place of women in Australian society.
18. On the question of the number of political activists it is difficult to be precise. Probably Rose's estimate is as nearly accurate as possible. 'The number of people who are regularly involved in politics either as part of their job or as what is erroneously known as leisure time activity, is of the order of about two per cent of the adult population.' R. Rose, *People in Politics*, London, 1970, p.81.
19. Hobhouse's Act (1831) gave women ratepayers the local franchise, and this principle continued. Interestingly, in 1918 the franchise was given to the wives of men ratepayers: ten years later husbands of women ratepayers were enfranchised. The 1870 Education Act permitted the election of School Boards by ratepayers of either sex, and no sex qualification barred women candidates.
20. E. Shinwell, *The Labour Story*, London, 1963, p.83 ff.
21. cf. L. Reid, *Charles James Fox*, London, 1969, pp.202–4.
22. The first full-length biography of Kathleen Glasier and her husband was published in 1971: L. Thompson, *The Enthusiasts*, London.
23. In the 1896 tour, starting from Chester and covering six counties, 14 of the 32 vanners were women. cf. *The Labour Annual*, 1898.
24. Calculated from 'The Directory of Social Reformers', *The Labour Annual*, 1900, pp.35–61.
25. Reported in 'Coming of Age Conference of the Independent Labour Party', Bradford, April 11, 12, 13, 14, 1914, *Report*, p.2.
26. Her publications included three novels, and such works as *Women and Socialism*, 1910 and *Women as Factory Inspectors and Certifying Surgeons*, 1895.
27. cf. A. Prentice, *History of the Anti-Corn Law League*, London, 1968.
28. Various examples may be suggested. The 'Grand National' had female lodges. Eleanor Marx Aveling helped organise the Gas Workers' Union, and was secretary to their first conference. For

details of numbers of women by trade cf. Trade Union Congress, *Women in the Trade Union Movement*, 1955, p.52 ff. In the 1890s the rise of general non-craft unions led to the inclusion of more women.

29. One of the most notable members was Lord Grey of Reform Bill fame.
30. Founded as the Democratic Federation in 1880 led by Hyndman, and one of the more extreme of the left wing groupings. The S.D.F., categorised here as a pressure group, in fact put up candidates at elections. At its peak in the early 1900s, membership was said to be of the order of eight to nine thousand. For Lady Warwick's activities on behalf of the S.D.F. cf. M. Blunden, *The Countess of Warwick*, London, 1967, p.189. Lady Warwick stood as Labour candidate for Warwick and Leamington in 1923.
31. Lord Snell, *Men, Movements and Myself*, London, 1936, p.112 ff.
32. Details of the Socialist League's early composition may be found in *Commonweal*, vol.I, 1885; cf. also P. Henderson, *William Morris, his Life Work and Friends*, London, 1967.
33. Percentages calculated from figures published in the relevant *Annual Reports*. Strictly comparable figures for each year are not available.
34. This group has been excluded from consideration here because of its sex-segregated character.
35. It is ironical to consider the work of such Fabians as, say, Annie Besant, or Beatrice Webb, at a time when it was widely considered unthinkable that, as women, they could be competent to vote. Yet as Margaret Cole has pointed out (*The Story of Fabian Socialism*, London, 1961, p.127), the Fabians, unlike the I.L.P., had only a lukewarm attitude to the women question. Beatrice Webb, to her later regret, once signed a manifesto against votes for women. It was not until 1906 that the Basis was amended to include the aim of equal citizenship between men and women. Interestingly, it was after this date that the Fabian Women's Group was founded.
36. The figure is the more interesting in view of the limited opportunities for women, discussed in Chapter 18, of J. Kamm's *Hope Deferred*, London, 1965.
37. Recorded in discussion with the late Dr Morley.
38. Miss Morten edited the *Letters of Abelard*, and wrote, in addition, on welfare and health topics.
39. F.M.L. Thompson, *English Landed Society in the Nineteenth Century*, London, 1963, p.18.
40. D. Cecil, *The Young Melbourne*, London, 1939, *passim*.
41. Countess of Oxford and Asquith, *More Memories*, London, 1933, p.147 (emphasis added).
42. 'In the autumn of 1896 Lady Warwick began to plan the meeting of the two men most important in her life at this time, the Prince of Wales and W.T. Stead . . . Whatever the precise origin of the meeting, it revealed Lady Warwick in a role she relished, as the

reconciler in private of two men whose influence and importance she perhaps exaggerated. There was no part Lady Warwick's histrionic personality liked more than that of "the power behind the throne". This was perhaps natural in view of the circumscribed opportunities for a woman at this time. As she later wrote to Stead: "Being a woman and thus cut off from public life which is open to men – worse luck – one's power is only in personal influence". M. Blunden, *The Countess of Warwick*, London, 1967, p.107. For the socialist period, cf. J. Paton, *Left Turn*, London, 1936, p.276 ff; C. Cross, *Philip Snowden*, London, 1966, p.225.

43. Lady Crewe was the daughter of Lord Rosebery. Her husband had held offices such as Secretary of State for the Colonies and Secretary of State for India.
44. cf. *The Times*, 10 January 1964.
45. Duff Cooper, *Old Men Forget*, London, 1953, p.98 ff. From the point of view of supportive as opposed to manipulative activities, it is interesting to note here that Duff Cooper's wife, an actress, went to America to star in a play in order to finance her husband's incursion into politics. He was thus enabled to resign his Foreign Office appointment.
46. *The Prime Minister's Daughter*, London, 1964; *The Minister*, London, 1961.
47. London, 1964, especially Chapter 6.
48. 'Vetting' of the wives of Tory candidates has been the subject of correspondence in the national press.
49. Personal communication.
50. E. Summerskill, *A Woman's World*, London, 1967, p.139.
51. J. Barrie, *What Every Woman Knows*, (1908); Hodder and Stoughton, London 1918, p.159).
52. cf. G. Smith, *When the Cheering Stopped*, New York, 1964.
53. For an excellent brief account cf. R.C.K. Ensor, *England 1870–1914*, Oxford, 1937, Appendix B.
54. cf. R. Jenkins, *Sir Charles Dilke*, London, 1958; B. Askwith, *Lady Dilke*, London, 1969.

Chapter 2 The Late-Comers

One of the major hazards in a study of this kind is that a focus on women's political activism in isolation from their male counterparts is apt to be, at best, lacking in balance, and at worst misleading. Yet with so small a number of women MPs and candidates any attempt at a sophisticated level of comparative analysis is equally dubious. What this chapter attempts, then, is to place women's participation in the political elite into some form of comparative framework, in an admittedly simplistic fashion. Trends and indicators only are in the main included here, and tabulations are kept to a minimum.

1. *Women as Elected Representatives*

The story of the widening of the franchise in this country was reaching its final chapter with the inclusion (in 1867) of many urban working-class men,[1] followed in 1884 by the agricultural labourers. Finally in 1918[2] began the belated admission of women, a process which was completed a decade later, when women were granted the franchise on the same terms as men. Reduction in the qualifying age for voting to eighteen years for both sexes, in time for the General Election of 1970, came as something of an epilogue. Both working-class men and women of whatever class are, therefore, late entrants to the political arena, not only in terms of achieving the vote, but more significantly as elected representatives, the second stage of their inclusion into the formal political sector.

Certainly there are substantial differences in the historical background to the entry of these two groups, notably that women entered after a four year war of a total kind never previously experienced. Even so, the situation for working-class men before enfranchisement, it may be suggested, was somewhat analogous to that of women. The activity of unenfranchised working class men in Trade Unionism, Chartism, Suffrage Societies[3] was such that they (no less than women) could not accurately be described as 'non-political' previous to the formal granting of the vote.

It seems, therefore, that there may be a useful comparison to be made not so much solely in male-female terms, but rather between the two latest groups to be assimilated into the political sector. This comparison may then be used to order a presentation of the details of women's political participation over time. The comparison between the late-comers has been made possible as a result of the work of Professor Richard Rose,[4] in which he traces the assimilation of working-class men into political leadership. There are, however, problems inherent in such a comparison. The criteria for identifying the two groups do not exactly coincide: working-class males, on the one hand, compared with all women irrespective of class, on the other. For the first group, while the identifying class characteristic may be modified by upward social mobility engendered by the phenomenon under consideration (i.e. assimilation into the political elite), working-class origins remain an absolute criterion. An additional limitation is that while the male group is considered solely in relation to the Labour Party, on the grounds that the latter's development was rooted in the implementation of the desire to achieve working-class representation, for women there is no such straightforward party link.

Professor Rose's study, then, is of the significance of class for what he isolates as 'the three main functions of a political party, namely the recruiting of political leaders, mobilising voters, and influencing policies on the allocation of resources and values'.[5] To do this, his analysis traces the assimilation of working-class men into political leadership beginning with the period from 1867–1906 when no party for Labour existed in the House of Commons, but working men were leaders in their own class – specific organisations such as Trade Unions and Co-operative Societies. Rose goes on to show how the return of a working-class bloc of MPs in 1906 was followed by a period up until 1922 when the P.L.P. remained almost exclusively a working class party. After 1922, the composition of the P.L.P. included a substantial, though still minor, element of non-working-class members. Finally, in the years after 1945, the middle class predominated among the Labour MPs, with only a substantial minority of working-class members.

How does the experience of women compare with that of working-class men, in the earliest period, in terms of Rose's findings on these indices? As Rose points out, while working class men were usually rebuffed in their efforts to obtain candidatures in the Liberal Party, they were nevertheless in leadership positions in class-specific organisations. The need to obtain working-class representation in Parliament, (much more than programmatic or ideal goals), Rose argues, led to the formation of the Labour Party. Certainly the parallel for women is not exact here. In the decades before their enfranchisement, women's participation in sex-specific organisations, and in party political organisations (as mentioned earlier) was considerable. In the event, no

Table 1 Women and Parliament, 1918–1970

	Conservative[3]			Labour			All Parties[1]		
	Men's[2] Success Rate	Women's Success Rate	Women's Handicap Factor	Men's Success Rate	Women's Success Rate	Women's Handicap Factor	Women Candidates as % of all Candidates	Women MPs as % of all MPs	Women's Handicap Factor
1918	86.0	0.0	0.0	16.0	0.0	0.0	1.0	0.1[4]	7.5
1922	71.8	20.0	0.0	35.1	0.0	3.59	2.3	0.3	7.2
1923	47.8	42.9	2.12	45.5	21.4	1.12	2.4	1.3	1.8
1924	75.7	25.0	6.71	30.5	4.5	3.03	2.9	0.7	4.5
1929	44.3	30.0	1.72	51.6	30.0	1.48	4.0	2.3	1.8
1931	89.9	81.3	0.0	11.4	0.0	1.12	4.8	2.4	2.0
1935	67.1	31.6	10.62	30.4	2.9	2.13	5.0	1.5	3.5
1945	32.1	7.1	1.43	66.9	46.7	4.50	5.2	3.8	1.4
1950	49.3	21.4	1.57	52.3	33.3	2.30	6.8	3.4	2.1
1951	53.2	24.0	1.84	49.3	26.8	2.22	5.6	2.7	2.1
1955	56.7	31.3	1.40	45.6	32.6	1.81	6.5	3.8	1.8
1959	59.0	44.4	1.09	41.7	38.2	1.33	5.1	3.9	1.3

1964	48.4	47.8	0.92	50.3	54.5	1.01	5.0	4.6	1.1
1966	40.5	33.3	0.92	58.4	63.3	1.21	4.7	4.0	1.1
1970	52.2	60.0	1.35	46.6	34.5	0.87	5.3	4.0	1.2

1. Including Independents and Liberals, Communists, Nationalists, etc.
2. Success Rate: Number of MPs expressed as a perçentage of number of candidates.
3. Women's handicap factor $\frac{\text{women candidates x men members}}{\text{women members x men candidates}}$ cf. Ross, *op. cit.* p.16.
4. Countess Markievicz was elected, but as a Sinn Feiner, did not take her seat.

woman's Party has emerged in Parliament,[6] and women have served in all three parties.

Next, how do women compare in terms of membership of the House of Commons? Table 1 attempts to answer this question.

The first point to be made is that in more than half a century, women have never even reached the proportion of five per cent of the MPs elected at any General Election. In 1964, the peak figure of 4.6 per cent was reached. With fluctuations, the pattern is of a very gradually increasing rate of success.

Women's very small contribution to elected representatives is paralleled in the proportion of candidates who are women. The pattern of women's contribution to total candidates at general elections tends to be of the order of two percentage points higher than for elected members, but it has still remained overall below seven per cent (6.8 per cent was achieved in 1950 when the figure was inflated by the large number of women candidates fielded by the Liberals).

On the whole, then, the trend over time has been upwards. But there are grounds to believe that there is a levelling off, that the rate of increase is slowing down, as is clear from Figure I. Women are not scaling the peaks; they are still very much in the foothills, as it were.

Taking all candidatures (including Independents) in the General Elections since 1918, just over one thousand women have sought election to Parliament, compared with around twenty two and a half thousand men. Thus it is clear that the electorate is given very little opportunity of considering a woman as a possible parliamentary representative, though there has been since 1918 rather more chance of considering a Labour woman than her Conservative counterpart (444 compared with 269 respectively). Looked at from another perspective, in the 1970 General Election, in only around fourteen per cent of all the constituencies was there the possibility of voting for a woman. Interestingly, in one constituency there were three women candidates, and in eight constituencies two women stood.

By party distribution of elected women members, the Labour Party has had one hundred and thirty four women candidates successful at General Elections in the period under consideration, compared with ninety seven women elected in the Conservative candidatures. These have been successful *candidatures*. In terms of the individual women who have at any time sat in the Commons (including those entering in by-elections), the figures are, for Labour, forty-nine, and for the Conservatives, thirty-eight. The range of length of service which these figures conceal, varies from a matter of months, to Dame Irene Ward's record service amounting to around thirty-seven years.

Women's success rate overall (the number of women elected expressed as a percentage of the number of women candidates) is increasing, but very slowly. Detailed comparison of men and women's success rates *between* the parties in less valuable, since women as much as men, tend to enter and leave Parliament on 'landslides'. Within each party, a comparison between the success rates of men and women on this relatively crude percentage index may be slightly more meaningful, but the small numbers of women involved is a major constraint. Given this reservation, it seems possible to conclude tentatively that in the past decade women's chance of success has been nearly approaching that of men. In 1966 (the year of Labour victory) Labour women's chances on average exceeded that of Labour men, and in the next General Election (the 1970 Conservative success) Conservative women's chance of success was on average greater than that of their male colleagues.

It is useful to apply a somewhat more sophisticated index of relative success, that of the women's handicap factor, formulated by J.F.S. Ross in 1953.[7] This factor attempts to serve as a measure of the average woman candidate's prospect of defeat, by comparison with that of the average male candidate.[8] It may be seen that the handicap for women of any party has gradually decreased over time, so that the woman's chances have gradually improved such that they approximated those of men from 1959 onwards.

Use of this index, within the Labour Party and the Conservative Party respectively, reveals the same general trend of improving chances of success for women. From 1945 to 1966, it seems clear that on average, Labour women were more likely to succeed than the average Conservative woman, though the differential is much too small to be validated statistically. In contrast, in 1970 Labour women's chances worsened, whereas the Conservative women, on the whole, had a very slightly better chance of success than their counterparts in the other party.

In summary, then, it can be shown that comparatively few women stand for Parliament, though once selected for a constituency, the chance of the 'average' woman candidate has, over the past decade, come to equal or even exceed that of the 'average' male candidate. There is not much real difference between the two major parties, except that in the past two General Elections, women have, on average, had slightly more chance of success than men, *when their party wins the election*.

Here again there are distortions operative, distortions associated with factors more easily identified than quantified. One form of inflation of the index occurs because of the length of service of some women, 'sitting members' who have established themselves securely. Then a major factor, perhaps more realistically the major imponderable, is that of the selection process for Parliamentary candidates. It is now almost a commonplace that the majority of MPs is selected not elected, since the majority of MPs sits for 'safe seats'.[9] Despite the increasing interest reflected in the literature on the subject,[10] selection remains an arcane and very sensitive area to investigate, and one which sometimes appears resistant to research in depth. Here it is sufficient to point out that to attempt to explain the paucity of women candidates in simple terms of sex-discrimination is much too facile.

Ross attributed the low rate of success of women compared with men to the fact of women having had more often to contest the worst seats,[11] and over time there is sufficient evidence for the assertion. In the 1935 General Election, out of a total of sixty-seven women candidates, nine were successful. Of those who lost, thirty-seven stood for seats which since 1918 had never been held by a member of their own party.[12] As Dr Edith Summerskill pointed out, it was not until 1955 that two women contested seats with a certainty of success.[13] Relevant also is a cluster of factors which may be grouped under the heading of 'seriousness of intention'.[14] A candidate in a 'hopeless seat', a constituency with a tradition of overwhelming majorities against that candidate's party, enters the contest secure in the knowledge that it is impossible to win. There is an important difference, it may be suggested, between a woman standing at an election merely in order to 'show the flag', and act as a focus of party activity, with no chance of success, and standing in order to gain experience, to become noticed, in order to be selected for a 'better' seat at the next election, i.e. as part of calculated programme to achieve election ultimately. In the first instance, where there is no serious intention of achieving a political career, a housewife may find the few weeks required for campaigning much easier to arrange than would a male candidate with a full-time job. This kind of factor is one which tends to invalidate, in part at least, any easy comparison between the sexes in terms of forfeiture of deposits.[15]

2. *Women in Office*

The next stage of comparison in terms of the assimilation of working men, and of women into the political elite, is that of the Cabinet and the Ministry. As Rose shows, in the period after the Second World War, the Parliamentary Labour Party has become and continues to be a body of predominantly middle-class politicians with a substantial minority of working-class members.[16] The inclusion of working-class men into the Cabinet follows a broadly similar pattern: no Labour Cabinet has ever been exclusively working-class. Although rather more than half of the members of the MacDonald Cabinet in the 1920s and of the Attlee Cabinet in 1945 were of working-class origin, the percentage of those of working-class background was much lower in the administration of Harold Wilson.

Table 2 Men and Women in Office, 1920–1970

	Cabinet		**Ministers not in Cabinet**		**Under Secretaries**		**Parliamentary Secretaries**	
	Women	Men	Women	Men	Women	Men	Women	Men
1920	0	20	0	9	0	9	0	14
1925	0	21	0	4	0	6	1[1]	11
1930	1[2]	18	0	6	0	7	1[3]	8
1935	0	20	0	5	0	8	0	8
1940	0	9	0	20	0	9	1[4]	13
1945	0	8	0	34	0	10	2[5]	21
1950	0	17	1[6]	15	1[7]	7	0	17
1955	0	18	0	16	0	11	1[8]	16
1960	0	19	0	20	0	11	2[9]	13
1968	1[10]	23	2[11]	31	2[12]	15	1[13]	19
1970	1[14]	18	1[15]	24	0	14	0	9

1. Education
2. Labour
3. Health
4. Health
5. (i) Health (ii) Home Affairs
6. National Insurance
7. Scotland
8. (i) Health
9. (i) Health (ii) Pensions
10. Overseas Development
11. (i) Home Office
    (ii) National Insurance
12. (i) Colonies (ii) Scotland
13. Public Works
14. Education
15. Scotland

Certainly the trend of women's recruitment to the Cabinet has never approached that of men of working-class origins. So few women have ever reached the Cabinet as to make proportions and percentages meaningless. At the time of writing, one woman only holds Cabinet rank (for Science and Education). The only other women Cabinet members formerly have been Miss Margaret Bondfield, Minister of Labour under MacDonald, Miss Ellen Wilkinson and Miss Horsburgh, Minister of Education 1945–7 and 1951–4 respectively, and Mrs. Barbara Castle, as Minister for Overseas Development and subsequently Minister of Transport in Harold Wilson's administration.

Differences by party begin to emerge when the field is widened to include the Ministry. Excluded from this analysis are those holding the unpaid position of Parliamentary Private Secretary, as they do not form part of the Ministry,[17] though this appointment may be the beginning of the route to office. Overall, of the women elected to the two major parties, twenty-eight per cent have held office at a level above that of Parliamentary Private Secretary. Since it has been established that the number of posts available in an Administration is sufficient to accommodate around twenty to twenty-eight per cent of the government supporters, if the government has a bare plurality only,[18] women have clearly been treated with something approaching generosity.

By party, a distinct contrast emerges. The Labour Party, with a slightly higher total of women elected over time, also shows a higher percentage of office holding, thirty-one per cent, compared with twenty-four per cent. In the 1964 Wilson administration, for example, there were seven women; a Cabinet Minister, two Ministers outside the Cabinet, and one Under Secretary, two Parliamentary Secretaries, and a Government Whip.

Several interacting factors are involved in building an administration. Choice of personnel is neither simple nor straightforward. Reconciliation of conflicting aims and interests, rewarding past services, safeguarding future loyalty, maintaining a balance between varying sectional interests in the party composition, and containing competitors, are all enmeshed in the intricate process of producing a viable Ministry.

Such factors apply equally, of course, to men and women, with one major difference. When there are few women in Parliament, inclusion of a woman in an administration may be a matter of deferring to sectional interests, on an additional dimension, quite other than, for example, including a member of the extreme left or right, in order to placate dissentients. The small proportion of women MPs may be construed as either offering little breadth of choice to a Prime Minister, or as allowing a woman of any ability more chance of being noticed.

Here there is a clear parallel between the assimilation of working-class men into political leadership and that of women. Richard Rose has written of working-class men in terms of the symbolic importance of persons who represent their electors in a social as well as an electoral sense. Rose suggests that the biographies of the early Labour leaders reveal the importance to them of symbolic representation. Certainly some of the few biographies of women MPs reflect an awareness of this kind of representation.[19] This evidence, however, needs to be balanced against other factors. It seems clear that women MPs are approached for help on questions relating to housing, the family, the problems of widows, etc.

In terms of the notion of the statutory women, who sat of right on various committees, the classic instance of tokenism, the wheel appears to have come full circle. In the early years, the arrangement was seen as an advance for women, even though some women MPs consider the situation amusing,[20] but by the time that the composition of the Race Relations Board was under discussion in the Lords, the inclusion of a woman or women *qua* woman was not acceptable.[21]

Symbolic representation of the male working class is shown by Rose to be of declining importance after 1945, since the proportion among Labour MPs has been declining, and they are less significant in Labour Cabinets. As has already been shown, in this sense, women's symbolic representation may not be in decline parallel to that of working-class men. Another dimension, however, may be added to this discussion. One useful criterion may be the allocation (or relegation) of women to areas which have been subsumed under the term 'feminine ideology'. The notion of feminine ideology relates to certain subjects being regarded as specially suitable to women's abilities and specialist knowledge – health, education, motherhood, family welfare, housing etc. – that is, all problems which are considered to be of special interest to women.[22] Yet the classification of certain ministerial portfolios as of the 'feminine ideology' type presents problems. Education, pensions, health, food, may be categorised as 'women's field' subjects; the Foreign Office, Commonwealth Relations, Defence, as part of a wider, more masculine-oriented field. But responsibility at national level in an advanced industrial society for the work of ministries classified as falling within the feminine ideology grouping is hardly a 'soft option' by any standards.

Are women who achieve office given responsibility only in the 'feminine ideology' sector? It has recently been suggested, in the Labour Party document on Discrimination, that those women who have succeeded in entering Parliament have shown that the contribution of women is not limited to the so-called women's subjects, but covers the whole political spectrum.[23] Generally this judgement may be true, particularly for the women of the Labour Party, but some qualification is necessary. There remains the question of relative emphasis between the narrower and the wider focus. On the whole it has tended to be the Labour administrations in which posts have been allocated to women very much outside the traditional format. Examples include Mrs. Castle's responsibilities for Overseas Development, Labour, and Transport, which she held in Wilson's administrations. On the other hand, Mrs. Thatcher is the third woman to become Minister of Education, and the responsibilities for Pensions, National Insurance etc. tend to be associated with women. There has as yet only been one woman at the Board of Trade, one at the Foreign Office, and there has yet to be a woman heading the Ministry of Defence.

An interesting sidelight on the issue of the inclusion of women in an administration came from the late Mrs. Jean Mann, MP. Mrs. Mann suggested that some women had been assigned to posts liable to render their holders unpopular. Examples cited were those of Margaret Bondfield, Minister of Labour in the 'disastrous' 1931 upheaval; Ellen Wilkinson as Minister of Education facing the 'onslaught of opposition from her own party members of Parliament'; Edith Summerskill, 'Food Minister when there was no food', 'Pensions Minister when there was no money because of external influences'.[24] Such instances, from one party over a limited period, might be extended to include Mrs. Barbara Castle walking the tightrope as Secretary of State for Employment and Productivity, or Mrs. Thatcher with responsibilities for Education when that sector is a subject of heated controversy.

3. *Women in Other Areas of Public Life*

There remain two other areas to consider, both of which are relevant to women's participation in the political elite. Both are non-elective. The innovation of Life Peerages in 1958 has meant an additional opportunity for women to participate in the political elite. As the practice of creating hereditary peerages appears to have been dropped by both major parties, the institution of the life peer becomes more significant. The complex intervening variables which modify the appointment of Life Peers once more bedevil statistical presentation.

Life peerages may be bestowed for political services, for provision for retirement from active competitive politics for the party stalwart, to ensure a spread of specialist knowledge and experience in the upper debating chamber.

Certainly men of working-class origins have become peers. The list would include Lord Shinwell, or Lord George-Brown. Of the women who have been created life peers, three main groupings are immediately apparent. The first two are categories shared equally by men and by women.

First are the ex-MPs. Among this group are to be found the former Dr Edith Summerskill, Miss Alice Bacon, Mrs. Eirene White, Miss Jennie Lee and Viscountess Davidson. Others have served on local authorities.

Secondly there are those who have had or are pursuing outstanding careers outside the strictly political, a successful editor, Baroness Birk, a former Permanent Secretary (Baroness Sharp), a University Professor (Baroness Seear).

Thirdly, there are those in whose appointment may be discerned the element of 'male equivalence'. This is a concept to be explored more fully in chapter Nine. Here the term is applied in the sense of the woman being honoured as a means of posthumous tribute to her husband. Baroness Macleod, widow of the late Iain Macleod, Baroness Philips, widow of the former General Secretary of the Labour Party, and Lady Spencer-Churchill are included in this grouping. Lady Sharples, the widow of the murdered Governor of Bermuda was made a Life Peer in 1973.

The three groups are not necessarily mutually exclusive. The members of the male-equivalent group have been active in voluntary work and in para-political work; one at least of those having a successful career had also sought election as a parliamentary candidate. The inter-connections are many.

By the way of something of an addendum to the political sector, it must be pointed out that women are under-represented in the areas which are designated by the term 'public life', at national level. Without attempting exhaustive coverage, a few examples from several fields may be adduced as illustration.

Over the years, women have been very much in the minority on Royal Commissions and Government instigated enquiries, even when women were much concerned in the subjects under consideration.[25] There is some evidence of change in this trend, however, as the Latey Committee on the age of majority consisted of five women and six men.

What evidence there is shows a considerable disparity between men's and women's membership on Rent Assessment Panels, on Mental Health[26] Review Tribunals, and on Regional Hospital Boards. Examples in public life may be proliferated, since women are very much in a minority on all governmental boards and agencies. No woman is a full or part-time member of either the Electricity Council, the Gas Council, the British Rail Board, British Airports Authority, UK Atomic Energy Authority, the National Coal Board, or the Post Office Board. Of the total full-time membership of 425 on 'Public Boards of a Commercial Character' as at January 1971, there were five women.[27]

4. *Women's Influence?*

It is difficult to relate the assimilation of women into the political elite to Rose's criterion of the allocation of resources and values, i.e. in terms of material and symbolic policies. Women, unlike working-class men, are not associated with one specific party. Since women are in a majority in the electorate, parties seeking women voters need to pay attention, or the cynical may suggest, lip service to what are considered to be the particular needs of women. Thus equal pay and the proposed anti-discrimination legislation do not divide the parties.

The period from the nineteenth century to the present has seen a complex of development of legislation which Marshall has traced,[28] showing the path from the granting to the individual of basic civil rights, through rights of citizenship, to the point where the twentieth century has added social and economic privileges, and a guaranteed standard of life.

It would be easy to ascribe some at least of this social legislation to the influence of women in Parliament and in the electorate, as some women would claim, on a *post hoc propter hoc* basis. But this seems not to be a tenable position, and, moreover, is one which is impossible to validate empirically. The Liberal administration's reforms of 1906–11, which laid the basis for a comprehensive insurance system, were in the period before women's emancipation. Even earlier were the first groping provisions of the early Factory Acts, moving slowly towards the concept of state responsibility for the individual. Mackenzie, discussing claims made in Australia about women's influence as a factor in such legislation as penal reform, health laws etc., brings forward interesting material to show that 'progressive' legislation was similar in states which were slower to give women the vote.[29] Moreover, Switzerland, where women were not granted the vote until the 1970s, is not substantially behind other countries in the field of social legislation.

Yet the fact remains that a considerable body of legislation favourable to women's situation has been enacted. This includes the changes in the legal status of women mentioned below,[30] their rights *vis-à-vis* their children, passport rights, their own earnings, their right to a share of the marital home, and in deciding its location, and welfare provisions such as payment of family allowances to the mother.

Women's record in the field of Private Members' Bills seems to afford some support for the notion of feminine ideology, though this is linked somewhat more clearly to early years after enfranchisement. In the first decade after enfranchisement there was a bill forbidding the sale of intoxicants to those under eighteen, and one on the registration of nursing homes. In the next period, up to and including the Second World War, in addition to bills on the Poor Law, the sale of methylated spirits, several bills fell into the 'feminine ideology' category, such subjects including bastardy, sentence of death on expectant mothers, adoption and hire purchase.

In the period after the war, Mrs. Castle has promoted a Criminal Law Amendment Bill, Miss Pike the Drainage Rates Bill, Mrs. Thatcher the Public Bodies (Admission to Meetings) Bill, and a British Nationality Bill was introduced by Mrs. Jeger. Other Bills, with a 'feminine ideology' orientation include Bills regulating the rights of entry of meter readers to private houses, protection of birds and animals, the removal of turnstiles in ladies' public lavatories, and bills to benefit nurses and young people. A caveat which runs through this study like a refrain, however, still applies. When women are credited with humanitarian motives and kindness to animals as revealed in Private Member legislation, this is not to arrogate to their sex the monopoly of such qualities to the exclusion of the male humanitarian or animal lover.

Women's contribution to the Statute Book by means of Private Members' Bills is, then, by no means a perfect criterion for evaluating either the achievement of women in the political sector, or the symbolic or material policies associated with women. Such a criterion presents problems. Excluded from a list of Private Members' Bills are those statutes originating in this manner which are subsequently taken over by the Government. Miss Vickers' Bill for the attachment of husband's earnings for a wife's maintenance after divorce ended as a piece of Government legislation. Certain Private Members' Bills initiate other action, such as the Government's establishment of a Royal Commission on divorce, consequent on the withdrawal of Mrs. Eirene White's Matrimonial Causes Bill. In addition, any piece of Private

Member legislation has to be seen against the fact that the vast majority of legislation is that of the Government programme, and that chance plays a double part both in obtaining a high place in the ballot, and in getting sufficient time for the bill on the floor of the House.

Once in the Commons women MPs have not tended to function as a group, with common aims and interests and only extremely rarely is there any evidence of some combining on a specific issue. Christabel Pankhurst in 1918 stood as a Women's Party candidate, the 'Party' which derived from the Women's Social and Political Union in the vanguard of the suffragette movement. Ironically, those women who eventually succeeded in election to Parliament were not the leaders of the fight to enter the House. The Women's Party in Parliament simply did not materialise. Interestingly enough, it was from Lady Astor, the first woman to take her seat, certainly no former suffragette, that the suggestion for a Women's Party came, and came to nothing.

As Mrs. M.A. Hamilton wrote of her Parliamentary experience after her election in 1929,

> The newspapers, of course, talked of the women MPs as though they were some kind of peculiar animal but . . . the House of Commons accepted no sex distinction, there, if nowhere else, one was treated simply as a member . . . we certainly were in 1929 a mixed lot, resistant to feminist grouping.[31]

From time to time there have been efforts by determined groups of women to obtain representation specifically by and for women. The notion of a woman's party is, then, a persistent one, and one which seems more usually to originate outside the elected assembly. The promotion of a woman's party is usually non-partisan, with the aim of promoting a specific feminine perspective and to put women into an elected assembly *qua* women. In the Second World War, the Women for Westminster campaign began, but no women's party resulted.[32] In the 1970s there occurs a new attempt again initially from outside Parliament, in the form of *Woman Power*, a movement aiming to achieve equal representation by women, to help women obtain nomination for the safe seats, and encourage women to enter both local and national politics, and to arouse women voters to the power of their vote.[33]

The 1960s and 1970s have seen a major revival of interest among political scientists in the subject of representation, so that Burke's contribution, though seminal, no longer seems sufficient. Two distinct concepts – the symbolic aspect of representation and the microcosmic – the representative by his personal characteristics, shared by others in the community, is held to form with his fellows a scaled-down facsimile of the universe they severally represent – tend to become blurred when considering women's representation.

Another area of political life which illustrates this merging, is that of the political party organisation, where women's sections of political parties persist, ancillary but not autonomous. A quotation from an analysis of the structure of the Labour Party helps illustrate this point.

> The backbone of the constituency party is the formal structure from the ward up to the Executive Committee. But there are also special sections of the party – Women's Sections and Youth Sections (Young Socialists), whose members meet separately. There are special Women's Annual Conferences and Young Socialist Annual Conferences where aspects of policy may be discussed . . . [34]

That there are segregated, women-only associations alongside the major party organisation implies the institutionalisation of inequality, and their lack of executive function or autonomy underlines this. Such associations, intended to safeguard women's interests, and perhaps provide a 'sheltered environment' for women's contributions, implies that women accept an inferior position, paternalism, direction. The 'flowered hat'[35] reports of annual conferences of women's political associations often, rather unkindly, stress this point. Certainly the feminine 'ghettos' whether of the kind just described or of seats reserved for women on the Labour Party Executive, or the TUC General Council, indicate a minority grouping, explicable in historical terms. This characterisation of women as a minority group is discussed below, in Chapter Nine. After the discussion of the entry of the late-comers into the political elite, one major aspect of women's political role may be properly considered in this chapter, that is, the voting behaviour of women.

5. *Voting Behaviour*

Is there such a phenomenon as the 'petticoat poll'? Any attempt at assessing women's political role must include a consideration of whether women as a sex differ from men in respect of voting behaviour and if so, in what ways and for what reasons. Though the problem may be simply stated it is not amenable to a simple solution.

Evidence on voting behaviour by sex is scanty in Britain since there is no means of finding how votes are cast or not cast by men and by women separately.[36] Since 1935 there have been no published statistics of the number of male and female qualified voters in each constituency. Discussion, therefore, cannot be founded on official national data, but must lean heavily on such studies as have been made. And these studies tend not to be directly concerned with women's political behaviour, but merely to touch on the topic incidentally. Material adduced here is consequently both fragmented rather than comprehensive, and based on reported data. Respondents state their voting intention, or retrospectively report whether they had or had not voted, and for what party.

That women, on the whole, are rather more likely than men to abstain from voting is now something of a commonplace. Empirical evidence for Britain is relatively plentiful, including Almond and Verba's findings, the work of Blondel, and other studies.[37]

The phenomenon is not unique to Britain, and has persisted over time. The pioneering work of Herbert Tingsten, using data drawn from the inter-war period from Sweden, Austria, Germany and Norway, makes clear that women did not use their votes to the same extent as men.[38] Duverger concludes from the four societies he studied (France, West Germany, Norway and Yugoslavia) that on the whole more women abstain proportionately than men, though the differential varies, and age is an important factor.[39] It would seem that the gap between men's and women's non-voting is decreasing over time. Yet the distinction is persistent. For example in the October 1962 French referendum, twenty-seven per cent of women were non-voters compared with seventeen per cent of men. At the legislative elections in the following month the comparable figures were thirty per cent and eighteen per cent respectively.[40]

Robert Lane summarises data for the United States showing that at every social level women vote less than men, though in Presidential elections the differential narrows.[41] Other studies show that the voting rate among women runs at a level consistently around ten per cent below that of men.[42] Evidence from Sweden reveals that there the differential is decreasing over time since by 1960 female turnout virtually approximates the male turnout.[43] In 1921 the difference in voting turnout was of the order of fifteen per cent, by 1940 the figure was just under four per cent, until finally in 1960 the differential was trivial at two per cent.

Women's tendency to abstain from voting rather more than do men is amply documented. Before attempts at explanation, it is necessary to put the issue in true perspective for Britain. The table which follows, shows voting turnout for both sexes together, over a period which covers the two-stage influx of women voters.

Table 3 Voting Turnout: General Elections 1910–1935[44]

Date	Turnout %
1910 (Dec.)	81.1
1918	58.9
1924	80.6
1929	79.5
1931	79.8
1935	74.4

The drop in turnout in 1918 is striking. In 1918, the male electorate of nearly thirteen million was expanded by the addition of around eight and a half million women. But the decline in turnout cannot be attributed to women's non-voting. The fragmentation of parties at this election and the coincidence of the ending of the World War may well be the major factors rather than women's enfranchisement; there is no means of determining which factors were most significant. In 1929 there was a male electorate of about thirteen and a half million, plus a female electorate of just over fifteen million. Thereafter, women were in a majority in many constituencies, yet the percentage of total votes cast shows very little difference after 1929, certainly nothing that can be confidently regarded as significant. The point of women's greater reluctance to vote, should not, therefore, be overemphasised.

The phenomenon of women's tendency to abstain from exercising the vote is comparatively easy to explain at some levels, but any hypotheses advanced can only be tentative. More difficult is any attempt to rank explanatory factors in order of significance. In this section some indication of explanatory approaches is provided. The larger issues of the relevance of political socialisation and the characterisation of women as a minority group are discussed in more detail elsewhere.

One cluster of reasons relates to women as the home-making and childbearing sex, with problems of caring for small children, caring for sick relatives preventing some women reaching the polling booth. Such reasons are increasingly less persuasive. Another cluster of factors is concerned with women's proved longer life expectancy. Old age may bring illness, disability, limited mobility, all of which may help account for a certain proportion of abstentions. The proportion may well rise with an ageing population. Lipset offers the cross-pressure hypothesis[45] to explain the tendency to abstention in women of the working class. The cross-pressures he cites are the push from the left from their class position and the values their husbands bring home from the factory, and from the right, the fact that women are the carriers of the dominant cultural and status values. Concern with status means largely concern with the values and practices of the social class above one's own, a class which is likely to have more conservative values than one's own.[46]

That voting turnout and the number of years of completed education increase together is a well-researched proposition.[47] And women, over time, have tended on the whole to have reached lower educational standards than men, though the differential has narrowed considerably latterly.[48] Additionally, level of education modifies other factors operative in an analysis of sex differences in political participation. Education is for example positively associated with degree of political efficacy (to be discussed below).

Similarly, the association between higher social economic status and higher rates of political participation is firmly established.[49] And education is one of the major indices grouped together in the motion of socio-economic status. It may be suggested that allocation of women to a socio-economic grouping is more difficult than that of men. The mass of women working tend to hold jobs which demand the lower levels of skill and qualifications.[50] But as the majority of women marries, there is always the possibility of upward social mobility which modifies any simplistic explanation of women's voting behaviour.

A further concept which links or elaborates some of the factors already mentioned is that of status inconsistency (or status incongruence, dissonance, as it is variously termed). It will be used here in its simplest form, as referring to a lack of congruence between an individual's status on stratification indices such as income, education and occupation. Essentially the relevance of this concept here lies in the fields of individual psychology and motivation. The individual whose ranking on various status indices are not congruent, is subjected to pressures and reacts to these psychological pressures. These reactions have been found to be very varied. Relationships have been discerned between status inconsistency and such diverse phenomena as liberalism, attempts to change the social order, and political extremism.[51]

Women, it may be suggested, are on the whole more likely than men to be status inconsistent, though this is a subject to the multiplicity of qualifications with which such sweeping generalisations have to be hedged. Women's educational qualifications may not jibe with the occupations they pursue. For example, whereas a boy with 'x' number of 'O' levels may go via a technical apprenticeship to the managerial level, a woman with a similar 'O' level qualification may become his secretary or clerical assistant. Then, women's own occupational status may not be consonant with the social status and income they derive from their husband. The dissonance generated on such grounds may, it is hypothesised, indirectly influence a woman towards retreat from making a voting decision. In the absence of completed empirical research, such an explanatory approach, though highly persuasive, remains speculative.

An interesting approach to the explanation of women's non-voting tendency may be particularly relevant to women's situation. Lancelot's interpretation rests on the idea of integration into society, that members of minorities, the less-integrated, tend to abstain rather more than the dominant groups.

> Les femmes, les jeunes, les pauvres, les minoritaires de toutes sortes s'abstiennent davantage que ceux qui, peu ou prou, contrôlent collectivement leurs destinées: hommes, adultes, patrons tous ceux qui, sans participer toujours à l'orientation directe de la société, beneficient au moins de la structure générale de la constrainte sociale.[52]

The general question of characterisation of a numerical majority (women) in terms of a minority group is discussed later.[53]

A further factor, in the women's non-voting syndrome, linked in part at least to the 'minority' approach, is that of political efficacy. This concept may be defined as 'the feeling that individual political action does have, or can have, an impact upon the political process, i.e. that it is worthwhile to perform one's civic duties. It is the feeling that political and social change is possible, and that the individual citizen can play a part in bringing about this change.[54] There is a duality here: the individual's image that he holds of himself, and the image which he holds of the political system of the society in which he lives.

That women tend to have a lower sense of political efficacy than men is well established.[55] Another aspect of duality arises here. Research has shown that the more highly educated are likely to feel more politically competent than the less educated: the higher income groups more than the lower paid groups the higher occupational and status groups more than lower occupational and status groupings.[56] On these individual criteria women score less than men, on the whole.

The non-voting proclivity of women is reflected in research findings of women's lower interest and information on political topics.[57] Generally, women tend not to see the sphere of politics as part of their role. Cultural *mores* are persistent and influential. A pioneering study of the early twenties, reported that the most frequent single cause of not voting in their sample was disbelief in women's voting, and a substantial number thought that women were not competent in the political field.[58] It is, then, in the field of political socialisation that may be found the roots of those explanations which stress association between withdrawal from voting and ideas of women's role in society. Once again this is a point to be taken up in more detail later.[59]

Establishing in what direction women vote cannot be documented comprehensively, again because of a deficiency of official statistical material of votes cast by sex. That there is a tendency of women to vote conservatively is clear, both for Britain[60] and in other countries. Evidence from surveys which have been made, though usually small-scale, all points in the same direction. Benney and his associates,[61] in a study of electoral behaviour in Greenwich, found that women appeared to be more conservative but that the degree varied by class and age. In the middle class it was very strong only among the younger voters; in the working classes women at every age were more likely to be conservative than men. Interesting material comes also from a study of working-class Conservatives, a study which provides a significant refinement to class-voting theory. Of this sample, it is shown that only among the elderly are women very much more likely to vote Conservative than men, slightly more in the forty to sixty-four group, whereas the proportions are equal among the twenty-three to thirty-four age group. They suggest, speculatively, that a tendency for women in the past to be more often Conservative than men may be decreasing.[62]

That the conservatism of women is not a phenomenon unique to this country is relatively easy to substantiate. In France, Duverger's evidence is that the women's vote is generally more to the centre, right-centre, and to the Christian parties than the men's vote.[63]

These findings are echoed in later work when Charzat points out that under the 5th Republic, 'Si l'on continue de distinguer deux groupes de partis: d'une part, ceux de gauche, socialisants et laiques; d'autre part, ceux modérés, gaullistes ou non, plus attachés à la réligion, on remarque que la première catégorie est toujours défavorisée par l'électorat feminin au bénéfice de la seconde.' Charzat goes on to conclude that it is clear that while men constitute the majority of the electorate of the left-parties, and women are in the majority of the conservative parties, the difference is a marginal one, (around ten to twelve points) but often a decisive one.[64] Additionally, Charzat stresses the stability of the feminine vote.

In Germany, women's support has been held to be responsible in 1919 for the considerable support for Hindenberg; for having swelled the National Socialist vote, and rather more recently for producing a majority for Adenauer's Christian Democrats.[65] Mackenzie reports similar tendencies in Australia, and this is corroborated by the Australian National University study in the Parkes electorate in 1955.[66] Data from Finland is in the same direction. In Italy, it has been established that more than two-thirds of those voting for the Communist and Socialist parties are men, whereas in contrast around two thirds of those voting Christian Democrat are women.[67]

Various explanatory approaches may be made in an attempt to understand women's conservatism. The problem is complex, and any tentative explanation cannot be pushed beyond broad outlines. First, social factors may be relevant. Isolation at home, and the lack of daily association with working colleagues, it may be suggested, make women feel insecure about their political judgements which lack reinforcement by others. This is an argument that could be extended to the point that insecurity is likely to involve reliance on the more conservative type of ideology. Yet isolation, relegation to a solitary life at home caring for children, is becoming very much less usual as more married women enter the work force.

As indicated elsewhere, whereas the proportion of women in the total working force remains fairly constant, the proportion of married women in the female labour force has risen and is rising. In other words, the social isolation of women in the sense of being outside the occupational sector is today less usual and of much shorter duration. The tendency seems to be for a career interrupted, not terminated by marriage and child care. The social isolation explanation loses cogency as time goes on. Even so, the fact that women tend to be much less unionised than men, means that married women's increased particip-ation in the occupational sector may not modify the conservative attitude to any great extent. Then the occupations in which women tend to predominate, such as clerical or secretarial work, are unlikely to become the preserve of militant unionism. 'Social isolation' is not then a totally satisfying explanation. Further complications and modific-ations need to be considered in conjunction with the social isolation factor.

Benney suggests that the relationship between sex and vote is not so marked as between age and vote. He argues that the Labour vote is a social novelty which the old adopt less readily than the young. Then women, being more socially isolated than men form their own ideas on patterns given by their family. Therefore, Benney argues that it might be expected that single women, more often following the lead of the older generation, would be more conservative than married women with husbands of their own age. His table[68] shows that the differences are in the expected direction. Despite this piece of evidence, it would seem that another contrasting hypothesis could be advanced. For granting that social isolation is one of the determining factors (that social isolation inherent in what Laski once called 'a dangerous instrument of reaction – the home'),[69] a single woman would surely be in a position more analogous to that of men, likely to be less conservative.

That husband and wife, in the majority of cases, tend to vote in the same way[70] is a further factor complicating attempts at explanation of women's voting behaviour. Even so, the crucial groups remain the single women, and widows, who have already been the subject of discussion.

If social isolation is a key variable, many tendencies at present seem to be moving towards breaking that isolation. The trends range from women's place in the occupational sector, the moves to provide further educational courses geared to the timetable of the married women, the associations which are springing up to meet the need for intellectual stimulus and companionship, quite apart from the more purposeful groups that may be termed part of the women's liberation movement. Whether over time these conscious efforts to break the isolation will result in discernible differences in women's abstention patterns is impossible to predict.

In Lipset's words 'All surveys of voting choice report major differences in the political allegiances of different age groups within specific strata, educational, religious or ethnic groups'.[71] Conservatism tends to be associated with age, and women's life expectancy exceeds that of men. This factor, of course, leads to and reinforces the greater social isolation of women in old age, when in Western industrialised societies around three times as many women as men live alone. It would be understandable for widows, at an advanced age, to cling to a party alignment which did not stress change, novelty, and re-constitution of social bases.

Butler and Stokes tend to question easy assumptions linking Conservatism to chronological age, which are based on the empirical material that Conservative strength is greater among older than among younger electors. From the evidence they present, they argue that the pattern to be observed is more consistent with an alternative concept, that it is the conservatism of established tendencies rather than Conservatism as such that increases with age.[72] The question of Conservatism versus the elements of conservatism is one which bedevils much of the discussion of women's voting behaviour. This type of argument reflects to an extent the Lynds' characterisation of women as the carriers of the dominant cultural and status values.[73]

A great deal of empirical work on voting behaviour has been concerned with groups biologically-age linked. The concept of political generations on the other hand is one which has come increasingly into prominence as an explanatory factor in recent years.[74] The link between political generations is that of shared experience – not only of spectacular events such as war or revolution. Having lived one's formative years in a time of depression, or a time when a particular party was making rapid headway, may also weld people into a political generation. In this way 'political age' may be more important in explanation than a biological age differential. The 'political generation' concept may, in fact, be regarded as one facet of the political socialisation process. Then, the notion of political generations, in terms of having shared a social collective experience, might, it could be argued, tend to the erosion or at least the reduction of differences in political orientations between the sexes.

Other factors need to be considered here. Veblen, writing at the end of the nineteenth century, stated: (Women)

> live under a regime of status handed down from an earlier stage of industrial development and thereby they preserve a frame of mind, and habits of thought, which incline them to an archaic view of things generally. At the same time, they stand in no such direct organic relation to the industrial process at large as would tend strongly to break down those habits of thought which for the modern industrial purpose, are obsolete. That is to say, the peculiar devoutness of women is a particular expression of that conservatism which the women of civilised communities owe in great measure to their economic position.[75]

Veblen's comments in relating 'devoutness' to economic position lead on to a consideration of the role of religious factors in contributing to, or reinforcing, women's orientation to right-centre voting. In continental societies there is an obvious link between the fact of women being more devout than men in religious observance, and their support of the Christian parties. Such an explanation for this country is less clear cut. There remains, however, some link, however tenuous between the fact that women tend to provide a majority of regular church-goers and Macaulay's description of the Church of England as 'the Tory party at prayer'.

Reference had already been made to the proposition that women's chances of becoming socially mobile may be greater than men's. This propensity may be another contributing factor towards understanding women's conservatism. In the US and Great Britain, both upward and downward mobility tend to be associated with the development of more conservative social attitudes and voting. 'The first relationship is generally explained by reference to social pressures to conform to a new milieu or by anticipatory socialisation. The second is explained as compensating for loss by a strong identification with a symbol of the lost status.'[76]

Women's tendency towards conservatism is then far better established than any theory attempting explanation of this tendency. Before leaving the subject an interesting paradox, still further complicating explanation, must be mentioned. Women, then, tend to vote to the right, yet are more associated, in elite terms, with parties of the left.[77] Paradoxically female emancipation has proved a disadvantage to parties of the left who were more instrumental in achieving enfranchisement.

Reasons underlying the apparently greater willingness on the part of the Labour Party to accept women into power wielding positions are more easy to suggest than to validate, and remain speculative. Historically, the Labour movement has always been more overtly sympathetic to equality for women. Keir Hardie was an early protagonist of votes for women. Taking into account the amount of work which women did in calling the Labour party into existence, in preaching socialism, working for women's Trade Unions, etc., before they had the vote, the position becomes less surprising. Material collected in the course of this study suggests that Labour party adherents believe that it is more easy for women to succeed in their own party. A further interesting, but as yet unsubstantiated point, is that if women tend to vote Conservative, and yet more women are in elite positions in the Labour party, this implies that men of the Labour side must be more prepared to support women in a position of responsibility.

In complete contrast, in relation to America and Norway, an interesting proposition has been put forward by Rokkan and Campbell, who suggest that since women are more status-sensitive than men in western societies, women are more likely to stand for office in higher-status rather than lower-status parties.[78] Satisfactory reasons for this total contradiction with the situation in Britain are difficult to find.

Other sex differences in orientation to political objects may be summarised here. The tendency of women be somewhat more intolerant, to have more of a moralistic orientation than men to be more in favour of controlling drinking, gambling, is fairly well established.[79] Women have also been found to be less ready than men to support policies which they interpret as aggressive.[80] Similarly, women, it has been found, are apt to be more pacifist on questions of war, on revolution, and more mild on questions of harsh punishment for crimes.[81] There is also support from empirical research for the proposition that women tend to be more candidate than issue-oriented.[82] In fact, women's preference for charismatic leadership may be illustrated by the landslide victory for Eisenhower in 1950.[83]

Women's attitude towards candidates of their own sex is interesting. Available public opinion evidence for this country shows relatively little difference between men and women's attitudes to a woman candidate. In 1959, a poll revealed that sixty-nine per cent of men and sixty-three per cent of the women interviewed reported that a woman candidate of the party of their choice would make no difference to their voting intention. Eighteen per cent of the women interviewed stated that they would be more inclined to vote for their party, and only ten per cent felt they would be less inclined to vote for the woman candidate.[84] Moreover, there is evidence that the proportion of women willing to vote for a well-qualified woman of their own party has increased. In 1965, a survey showed that seventy-six per cent of men would be prepared to vote for a woman compared with eighty-one per cent of women in the sample.[85] There seems support here for the well-known dictum that no candidate is worth more than five hundred votes.

Notes

1. Anomalies in the position of some male lodgers and adult males living in the parental home remained to be rectified in 1918.
2. At this date women became eligible for the first time to sit in the House of Commons. Women were, however, adopted as Parliamentary candidates several months before the necessary legislation was passed (for example, the Trade Unionist Miss Mary Macarthur as Labour candidate for Stourbridge, the first woman to be adopted).

3. There is a large literature on these subjects, and many biographies of these early activists, e.g. G.J. Holyoake's autobiography, *Sixty Years of an Agitator's Life,* (London, 1906), which touches on many areas and personalities of working-class agitation. For a general historical approach, cf. G.D.H. Cole, *British Working Class Politics, 1832–1914*, London, 1941.
4. R. Rose, 'Class and Party Divisions: Britain as a test case', *Sociology*, 2, 1968, 129–162. I am indebted to Professor Rose for suggesting the use of this article, on which this section of the study leans heavily.
5. op.cit., p.129.
6. cf. below, p. 36.
7. cf. J.F.S. Ross, 'Women and Parliamentary Elections', *British Journal of Sociology*, 4, 1953, p.17.
8. A woman's handicap factor of 2, for example, means that the average woman candidate's chance of success is half as good as the average male candidate's chance.
9. cf. D.E. Butler and A. King, *The British General Election of 1959*, London, 1960, p.230.
10. e.g. A. Ranney, *Pathways to Parliament*, London, 1965; M. Rush, *The Selection of Parliamentary Candidates*, London, 1969. This topic is discussed generally below, p.93.
11. Ross, op.cit., p.23.
12. E. Rathbone, in R. Strachey (ed.), *Our Freedom and its Results*, London, 1936, p.29, ff.
13. *Daily Herald,* 29 April 1955.
14. cf. below, p.105. This point emerged in empirical work on prospective candidates.
15. At the 1970 General Election eleven Conservative candidates out of a total of 628 candidates lost their deposit, and six out of 625 Labour candidates also forfeited their deposit. One out of twenty-five women Conservatives lost her deposit, as did eleven out of the twenty-two women Liberals.
16. op.cit.
17. On the other hand, five Parliamentary Private Secretaries were dismissed because of their revolt on the Ireland Bill, 1949, and seven were removed in 1967, because of their abstention in a division on application for membership of the E.E.C. Both cases occurred in Labour Administrations, cf. R.J. Jackson, *Rebels and Whips*, London, 1968, p.73 and p.218 n.
18. The percentage is, of course, reduced as the size of the majority increases. cf. P.G. Richards, *The Backbenchers*, London, 1972, p.206.
19. cf. M. Bondfield, *A Life's Work*, London, 1948, p.253. This kind of awareness was evident also in material gathered in interviews and by questionnaire of some of the women MPs in the inter-war period, but this woman label is much less evident, or even explicitly rejected by MPs, in the most recent periods.
20. Personal communication from the late Baroness Horsburgh.

21. cf. House of Lords, *Parliamentary Debates*, volume 296, 30 July 1968, p.175.
22. M. Duverger, op.cit., p.126.
23. The Labour Party, *Discrimination against Women*, London, 1972, p.35.
24. J. Mann, *Woman in Parliament*, London, 1962, p.39–40.
25. In the Royal Commission on Marriage and Divorce, there were seven women out of a total membership of twenty-six.
26. Women constituted sixteen per cent of the Review Tribunal and fourteen per cent of the Rent Assessment Panel which were investigated. (W.E. Cavenagh and D. Newton, 'The membership of two Administrative Tribunals', *Public Administration*, 48, 1970, p.454); a study of four Regional Hospital Boards, showed nineteen per cent of women in their membership, (M. Stewart, *Unpaid Public Servants*, Fabian Occasional Paper, 3, 1964, p.16).
27. Source: List of Members of Public Boards of a Commercial Character, as at 1 January 1971, *Cmnd.* 4611, London, 1971.
28. cf. T.H. Marshall, *Citizenship and Social Class*, Cambridge, 1950, p.10 ff.
29. N. MacKenzie, *Women in Australia*, London, 1963, p.57.
30. cf. below, p. 173 ff.
31. M.A. Hamilton, *Remembering my good friends*, London, 1944, p.180 ff.
32. There are examples of other moves towards the formation of a woman's party. An attempt was made to form such a party in America (cf. W.H. Chafe, *The American Woman*, London, 1972, p.37). The Australian 'Women for Canberra' Movement in 1942 was a movement parallel to the Women for Westminster campaign (cf. N. MacKenzie, op.cit., p.265 and pp.272–3). In Belgium, in 1972, the Partie Feministe Unifie was founded by a few women. It is too early to assess its possible impact on national politics (cf. *Woman's Report*, 1, (3), 1973.
33. Material kindly supplied by Mrs. Betty Dunmore, founder and secretary.
34. 'Our Penny Farthing Machine', special supplement, *Socialist Commentary*, October 1965, p.viii.
35. e.g. 'It did require an effort to see beyond the limitless millinery ingenuity of provincial England.' *Observer*, 23 May 1963. This is one example of the kind of approach which is still usual.
36. The provision of such data (by the use of coloured voting papers, for example), would be simple, inexpensive, and would not violate the secrecy of the ballot.
37. G. Almond and S. Verba, *The Civic Culture*, Boston, 1965, p.324–5; J. Blondel, *Voters Parties and Leaders*, Harmondsworth, 1963, p.55. Blondel's tabulations, drawn from material compiled in 1959, show that whereas men provide only forty-two per cent of the non-voters, women provided fifty-three per cent of the whole sample and yet fifty-eight per cent of the non-voters. Other supportive evidence comes from R.S. Milne and H.C. Mackenzie,

Marginal Seat, London, 1958, p.69; M. Benney et al., *How People Vote*, London, 1956, p.222; F. Bealey et al., *Constituency Politics*, London, 1965, p.230.

38. H. Tingsten, *Political Behaviour*, London, 1937, *passim*.
39. M. Duverger, op.cit., p.15 ff.
40. G. Charzat, *Les françaises sont-elles des citoyennes?*, Paris, 1972, p.13. There is a further qualification to be added to the issue of abstention in France. A higher proportion of women than men do not complete the formalities for inclusion on the electoral lists. The demands of military service affect and inflate the figures for men.
41. R.E. Lane, *Political Life*, Glencoe, Illinois, 1959, p.209 and Table 15, 1., p.210.
42. A. Campbell et al., *The American Voter*, New York, 1960, p.484.
43. Sources: 1921–48, *Historical Statistics of Sweden*, 1960, Table 27, p.269; 1960, *Statistical Abstract of Sweden*, 1964, Tables 436 and 438, pp.378 and 379. Figures for 1970, kindly supplied by the Royal Swedish Institute, Stockholm.
44. cf. the discussion on this point in G. Williams, 'The political role of women in England', unpublished ms., 1952, Fawcett Library, London.
45. S.M. Lipset, *Political Man*, London, 1960, p.208.
46. loc.cit.
47. op.cit., p.182.
48. cf. below, p.142.
49. cf. R. Dowse and J. Hughes, *Political Sociology*, London, 1972, p.293 ff. for a summary of the social correlates of political participation.
50. cf. below, p.151.
51. e.g. G.E. Lenski, 'Status crystallisation, a non-vertical dimension of social status', *American Sociological Review*, 19, 1954; G. Rush, 'Status Consistency and right-wing extremism, loc.cit. 32, 1967; J.A. Geshwender, 'Continuities in theories of status consistency and cognitive dissonance', *Social Forces*, 42, 2 December 1967; D. Eitzer, 'Status consistency and consistency of political beliefs', *Public Opinion Quarterly*, Winter, 72–3.
52. A. Lancelot, *L'Abstentionnisme en France*, Paris, 1969, p.216, quoted in Charzat, op.cit., p.23.
53. cf. below, p. 176
54. A. Campbell et al., 'Sense of political efficacy and political participation' in H. Eulau et al., (eds.), *Political Behaviour*, Glencoe, Illinois, 1956, p.172.
55. R.E. Lane, op.cit., p.214.
56. Reported in R. Dowse and J. Hughes, loc.cit.
57. G. Almond and S. Verba, *The Civic Culture*, Boston, 1965, p.393.
58. C.E. Merriam and H.F. Gosnell, *Non-Voting*, Chicago, 1924, p.113.
59. cf. below, p.43.
60. cf. F. Bealey et al., op.cit., p.171; F. Bealey et al., *Constituency Politics*, London, 1965, p.171; R.S. Milne and H.C. MacKenzie, op.cit., and *How People Vote*, 1956, p.107; P. Campbell et al.,

'Voting Behaviour in Droylsden in October 1951', *Manchester School*, 20, 1 January 1952; A.H. Birch and P. Campbell, 'Voting Behaviour in a Lancashire Constituency', *British Journal of Sociology*, 1950, 197–8.

61. M. Benney et al., op.cit., p.106.
62. R.T. McKenzie and A. Silver *Angels in Marble*, London, 1968, p.86 ff.
63. M. Duverger, op.cit., p.50; M. Dogan and J. Narbonne, *Les francaises face à la politique*, Paris, 1955, cf. Chapter 6.
64. Charzat, op.cit., p.25 ff.
65. For details of women's support of the right-centre parties in the West German Federal Republic elections of 1953 and 1957, cf. V.W. Kitzinger, *German Electoral Politics*, Oxford, 1960, p.289 ff. This bears out the work of Tingsten, op.cit., p.46, and of Duverger, op.cit., p.50. cf. also Chapter VIII below, p.
66. N. MacKenzie, op.cit., p.284.
67. cf. E. Allardt and P. Personen, 'Cleavages in Finnish Politics', in S. Lipset and S. Rokkan, *Party Systems and Voter Alignment*, New York, 1967, p.346.
68. Benney, op.cit., p.108.
69. *Daily Herald*, 20 May 1935.
70. M. Duverger, op.cit., p.46 ff.
71. S. Lipset, op.cit., p.264.
72. D. Butler and D. Stokes, *Political Change in Britain*, Harmondsworth, 1971, p.83.
73. R. Lynd and H.M. Lynd, *Middletown in Transition*, London, 1937, p.423 n.
74. D. Butler and D. Stokes, op.cit., p.322 ff. and p.65.
75. T. Veblen, *Theory of the Leisure Class* (first published in 1899), Mentor books edition, p.211.
76. R. Dowse and J. Hughes, op.cit., p.295.
77. cf. above p. . Other evidence may be drawn from M. Duverger, op.cit., p.90; Charzat, op.cit., p.98.
78. 'In the typical middle class parties', the Conservatives in Norway and the Republicans and the US, the differences between men and women in the proportions of actives are clearly smaller than in the 'lower status' parties . . . It is only in the non-socialist and Republican parties that the higher status women reach near-equality with the men in the proportion of actives: In the Socialist and the Democratic parties, women at a higher educational or occupational level still differ markedly from men at the same level in the proportion of actives.' S. Rokkan and A. Campbell, 'Norway and the United States of America', *International Social Science Quarterly*, XII, 1, 1960, p.96.
79. cf. R. Lane, op.cit., p.213; F. Greenstein, *Children and Politics*, 1962, p.107; D. Reisman, 'Orbits of Tolerance, Interviews, and Elites', *Public Opinion Quarterly*, 20, 1956, 49–73.
80. F. Greenstein, op.cit., p.107.
81. loc.cit.

82. That women tend to evaluate political objects on a lower level of conceptualisation than do men, is also relevant here. A. Campbell et al., *The Voter Decides*, Evanston, 1954, p.152 ff.
83. N. Polsby, *Politics and Social Life*, p.244–5, cf. also 'If men only had voted, it is improbable that Dr. Adenauer would ever have become Federal Chancellor . . . or that General De Gaulle would have been re-elected to the Presidency of 1965.' P. Pulzer, *Political Representation and Elections in Britain*, London, 1967, p.107. As in most issues of voting behaviour, here, too, factors are not discrete but overlapping and inter-acting. Here women's tendency to conservatism and their propensity to vote on personalities rather than on issues are difficult to isolate in terms of relative importance.
84. Reported by J.F.S. Ross, *Elections and Electors*, London, p.468.
85. Data kindly supplied by Social Surveys (Gallup Poll) Ltd.

Chapter 3 Women in Parliament; 1918–1970

The consideration of women's representation nationally, to be outlined here, looks at the characteristics of women elected to the House of Commons within three time periods. For the purposes of this investigation, each woman member is assigned to the period within which she was first elected. In this way it is hoped, first, to construct a form of profile for each period, as a preliminary to a more detailed, deeper and subjective study of a sample of women MPs. It is the latter investigation which is chiefly concerned with attitudes, opinions and evaluations of the role of women in politics *by* women in politics. Secondly, it is intended in the present chapter to consider any developments (over half a century) which may have occurred in the recruitment, background and careers of women MPs, in order to see whether any trends emerge. Finally, an attempt is made (though rather less than systematically) to indicate differences between women MPs and all MPs or male MPs only, where such comparisons appear significant.

The years from the election of the first woman to Parliament to the 1970 General Election may be divided into three periods. Any such division by 'historical period', on any criteria, is inevitably arbitrary and somewhat artificial, but with this reservation, there appear to be sufficient reasons for the divisions. Period I, 1918–28, covers the first decade from the granting of the initial, restricted franchise to women. It was a decade in which the flood-tide of women's representation which had been anticipated, with such vociferous dread by the 'anti's', certainly did not reach the shore. In these years, only ten women were elected. The period ends in 1928, the year when women were first granted the Parliamentary vote on the same terms as men. The second period runs from 1929 (the first General Election in which men and women voted on the same qualifications) until the end of the Second World War. The assumption on which the limits of this period are based (derived primarily from the numbers involved) is that the War may be seen as a watershed in the history of women's representation. The third and final period, the 'modern' period begins with the first post-war General Election of 1945 and continues until 1970, including the General Election of that year.

Table 4 Women MPs by party and by the period of first election

Party	Period I	Period II	Period III	Total
Labour	4	12	32	48
Conservative	4	13	21	38
Liberal	3	1	0	4
Other[1]	0	1	2	3
Total	11	27	55	93

1. Independent; Independent Unity; Scottish Nationalist.

It may be seen that over half of all women elected in these years have stood in the Labour interest, an excess of around ten per cent over the Conservatives. Because of the paucity of women's representation in numerical terms, the characteristics of the women MPs, by party, are considered mainly on a descriptive basis. Those percentages which are presented must be treated with caution, because of the small size of any of the subgroups under discussion.

1. *1918–1928*

In this period only eleven women sat in the House of Commons. Countess Markiewicz, the first woman to be elected, was a Sinn Feiner, and as such did not take her seat. Of the eleven, four were Conservatives, four Labour and three Liberal.[1]

The data on which to base any study of these eleven pioneers are adequate, but variable both in detail and in quality. The material available includes completed questionnaires from two former members, two autobiographies, and a recently published biography.[2] The election of these pioneering women generated biographical material in a wide variety of publications.[3] Additionally, biographical entries in reference books may be supplemented and checked both by detailed information generously supplied by friends and relatives of those who had died, and by the numerous press reports on the subject of these 'first' women.

In considering this group of women it is necessary first to consider how adequately the term group may be applied at all. Certain qualities clearly must have been shared. Initiative, determination, a willingness to 'go it alone' in an unfamiliar situation may be mentioned. But the distinctiveness of the Labour members in comparison with those of the other two parties is clear. In marital status the difference is most marked. All the Liberals and Conservatives were married at election: all the Labour members were single. The only Labour MP who was to marry did so more than ten years after having left the House of Commons. The problem of caring for children, or of having the wife-mother role conflict with the political one did not, therefore, arise for the Labour members. On the Conservative side, three of the four are known to have had children, as had two of the Liberals. Sole responsibility for family care tends to be a reason frequently cited as explaining the low numbers of women elected representatives. Making assumptions from husband's status or occupation, it seems that the problem for the members under consideration here would not be a serious one, as a substitute might be provided.

Allocation into class groupings tends to be more complex in the case of women than of men. For both sexes, of course, classification by social origins may be modified by the effects of social mobility. For a man, the mobility is almost invariably via the occupational structure. For the majority of women, the mobility may be either via the occupational structure, or by marriage, or through both occupation and marriage. Upward mobility through occupation may be much less important for women than for men, since a woman may have a pre-marriage job rather than a career. For women, then, the allocation may be made by any of three indices, of which husband's occupation is probably the more usual, since a married woman's status is normally a derived one.

Even so, on several indices, the Labour MPs tend to differ from the members of the other two parties. All but one of the Conservatives and Liberals are known to have been of middle or upper-class origins. Three of the four Conservatives had connections with the hereditary aristocracy by birth, marriage, or in both ways. Of the Liberals, one was married to a second baronet, and the husband of another was created a Viscount. In contrast, on the Labour side, only two of four might be said to be of middle-class origins.[4] Of the remaining two, one of working-class birth became upwardly mobile by virtue of her University education and professional occupation. The other, born into the 'skilled working classes'[5] of parents described as 'cultivated and distinctive people'[6] had, as chief woman organiser of a National Union a middle-class occupation before her election to Parliament.

Occupationally, the division is fairly clear between the 'poles' of the Conservatives plus Liberals, on the one hand, and the Labour members on the other. On the Conservative side, only one had been gainfully employed before her election, the others had done voluntary work in the First World War. The interesting exception is that of Mrs. Hilton Philipson. Her career, after having been 'discovered' working in a theatre Box Office, was that of a highly successful actress, mainly in musical comedy. Of the Labour Members only one had not been employed, but stated that 'she had done much social work'. The remaining three were a teacher, Trade Union official, and teacher-journalist-trade union organiser, respectively. Two of the Liberals had been teachers.

Looking at all the indices together, it is clear that over-representation of the upper and middle classes is pronounced. Such over-representation is, of course, not confined to women MPs at this time. J.F.S. Ross, in his work on the composition of Parliament, shows that in the inter-war years the aristocratic element (defined as peers, baronets, their heirs and other descendants) accounted for less than five per cent of the Labour members, approximately one-fifth of the Liberals and more than one-third of the Conservative membership.[7] In terms of occupational class, for the same period, Ross points out that 'two-thirds of the House consists of members having professional or semi-professional occupations or not gainfully occupied'.[8]

Using educational criteria, the distinctiveness of the Labour members again is fairly clear. Three of the four in the Labour group were graduates, whereas none of the Conservatives and only one Liberal is known to have had a University education. This is, overall, a high proportion of graduates compared both with the general situation of higher education for women in this period,[9] and with that of male MPs at that period.

On the question of age at election, it is possible to make allocations only for the Conservative and Labour members, since accurate data are not available for two of the Liberals. Reticence over age is by no means unusual for women, date of birth is frequently omitted from reference books, or there may be discrepancies between entries. In so far as comparisons may be made, it may be seen that the Labour women entered Parliament slightly later than their Conservative colleagues. Here women members reflected a pattern which has held good over the years for all MPs of either sex.

With such a small sample, detailed analysis of occupations before election is not productive. An approach which may be more meaningful in looking at these occupations concerns the type of work done and the qualities demanded by the work. Certain occupations appear to be linked by what may be termed for the sake of brevity, a 'communication factor'. This factor may be seen as implicit in those occupations which involve interaction with people, the skills and techniques of speech and the written word, the formulation and exchange of ideas. Such occupations include all kinds of teaching, the legal profession, public relations, journalism. An occupation which conforms to the communication type is that of Member of Parliament. It is suggested that it is no coincidence that a substantial proportion of women MPs have always been drawn from occupations in which they have developed at least some of the skills and techniques which are of especial value in a political career. This is a point to be taken up in greater detail later.[10] Here it is sufficient to note that the only Conservative in paid employment was an actress, two of the three Liberals were teachers, and that of the three Labour members who had been employed, two had been trade union officials (one after a period of teaching and one following shop work) and the other had been a teacher.

What other aspects of pre-election experience are relevant to the recruitment of women MPs at this time? Lack of completely comprehensive data means that the recording of family influence and precedent towards participation and public activity is almost certainly underestimated. 'Family influence' in the sense used here, the knowledge that parents, uncles, grandparents had taken an active part in public life or in politics, may be traced in over sixty per cent of the whole group regardless of party, rather more on the Labour side than among the Conservatives and Liberals.

Following on from this general degree of family influence, it is interesting to consider a more intense, more specialist variant of family influence; that is, the notion of the 'politicised family'. Once again this is a notion to be discussed as it recurs throughout this study and to receive fuller treatment elsewhere.[11] Briefly, the notion of the politicised family refers to a family situation in which a high level of political interest and activism is accepted, in which children are, as it were, exposed to a 'hot-house' atmosphere of political participation, or more formally, are socialised into an activist political role. Nationally, there have always been many examples of families in which the tradition of high public service has been established.

The incidence of membership of the politicised family is much more obvious in the background of the Labour side than among the other two parties. From the evidence available, it seems that all the Labour members were brought up in a politicised family, one with a background of trade union and Labour party activism, another with a 'radical' inheritance. An interesting example of this 'activist background' occurs in the case of Miss Susan Lawrence, for whom the precedents to participation and involvement were not for the Labour Party which she ultimately represented in Parliament. Miss Lawrence originally entered local politics as a Conservative. One of the Liberals was the daughter of a former Member of Parliament, and some precedence to public life could be traced in three of the four Conservative cases.

Distinguishing the Labour group from the other women MPs of this period is the distribution of the 'male equivalence factor'. This factor is particularly important in the earlier years of women's enfranchisement. Reference is made to male equivalence at several points in this study, and a more detailed discussion is included in Chapter Nine. The term is used here to denote a situation in which a woman in a particular power-wielding position, or seeking to gain that position, acts primarily as a substitute for a man. In the context of the first decade of women's entry into Parliament, male equivalence may be seen in two aspects, succeeding and, more unusually preceding, a husband in a Parliamentary constituency, left vacant by the death of her husband, or on his elevation to the Peerage. The woman acts as a substitute for her husband, working along the same lines as him, and expected to continue his policy. It may be suggested that the male equivalence factor would be likely to be rather more important in the early years of women's enfranchisement, when the role of Member of Parliament is a novel one for a woman. This seems to be so from the figures: more important in Period I than in the succeeding years. The male equivalence factor, then, may be seen in detail in this period when two of the four Conservatives elected were successful for seats which their husbands vacated to sit in the Lords. Still on the Conservative side, but preceding rather than following her husband into Parliament, Mrs. Hilton Philipson entered Parliament to keep a place for her husband whose election had been declared void on a question of election expenses. The constituents are reported to have liked Mrs. Hilton Philipson so much that it was considered unwise to change candidates, and her husband remained outside Parliament.

Two of the three Liberal women elected may also be classified as 'male equivalents'. Mrs. (later Vicountess) Runciman sat for St Ives for the year 1928–29 when her husband (then sitting for Swansea) took her place. This was clearly a 'holding operation', and Viscountess Runciman did not seek to extend her parliamentary career. Mrs. Wintringham won the seat made vacant on the sudden death of her husband, and contested the seat within three weeks of being widowed.

This is an extreme example, as because of previous illness and the effects of the shock of her husband's death, she did virtually no canvassing and made few public speeches. No Labour member entered the Commons as a male equivalent.

That male equivalence eased the entry of women into Parliament at this time is reflected in the fact that the five women involved were elected for the first time and at their first attempt, in by-elections. Only one of the Labour group, in contrast, was successful at her first attempt. It should be emphasised that the term 'male equivalent' is not used to connote inferiority, but rather the degree of advantage derived from vicarious experience via the husband, her knowledge of the constituents and their knowledge of her.

Motivation is notoriously difficult to probe, in any meaningful sense, involving as it does, unconscious and unacknowledged factors. To attempt to consider the question by means of reference sources, biographies and a few completed questionnaires is hazardous. Yet from the material available, uneven and incomplete as it is, it seems possible to discern some difference of orientation, of depth of ideological orientation, between the Conservative and Liberal groups on the one hand, and the Labour group on the other hand. There seems to be some link here with the incidence of male equivalence: the more strong the male equivalence factor, the less strong may be the ideological motivation. On this hypothesis, Conservatives and Liberals appear to have rather less deep political motivation than the Labour Group.

Various small pieces of evidence point in this direction also. It is clear from Margaret Bondfield's autobiography that her life was one of dedication to the furtherance of the Labour movement. Miss Wilkinson devoted her life to the Labour cause, as did Miss Susan Lawrence. An amusing sidelight comes from Earl Attlee's comment on the devotion of Miss Lawrence to the House of Commons. 'I recall how exiled Susan Lawrence was when she lost her seat. "Westminster, my happy home, when shall I come to thee", she would sing to me.'[12]

This period displays certain paradoxical features. Even as, in retrospect, enfranchisement of women tends to be attributed rather more to the occurrence of World War I than to suffrage agitation, so it may be seen that those who first entered Parliament were not those who had led the fight for admission. Eleanor Rathbone was herself later to be one of the very few exceptions to her own recognition of the 'often remarked anomaly that scarcely any of those who helped to open the door of Parliament succeeded in walking in: very few even tried.'[13] The validity of this judgement may be shown in two ways in this period. First, of the women elected to Parliament in the first ten years from enfranchisement, very few had been involved in suffrage activity, and were certainly not among the more notorious, headline-making leaders. On the Labour side, Miss Margaret Bondfield was a former President of the Adult Suffrage Society aiming at enfranchisement without a property qualification, while Miss Ellen Wilkinson was a one-time organiser for the National Union of Women's Suffrage Societies.

The second illustration of the validity of Miss Rathbone's point may be adduced from a consideration of two of the women who were successful in entering Parliament. The 'spectacular event' of Lady Astor's election drew comment in the many obituary notices at her death.

> To the women's organisations whose members had worked for years to make such an event possible, the emergence in this role of Lady Astor was something of a shock. They had visualised their first woman MP as somebody very different: Eleanor Rathbone, maybe, Millicent Fawcett, Mary MacArthur – someone with a notable record of feminist activity or social service . . . soon it became apparent that Lady Astor was, in fact, the fiercest feminist of them all and not afraid to show it.[14]

For a second example, that of the Duchess of Atholl may be cited, as one who had at one time been an anti-suffragist. As she explained in her autobiography,[15] while not joining an anti-suffragist organisation, she was, however, in favour of women having more experience of taking part in local government before they received the parliamentary vote, and had spoken to this effect at an anti-suffrage meeting.

Those women who were elected in the decade following limited enfranchisement were not, then, what might have been expected. Having been elected, what service did these pioneer women MPs give to the House of Commons? Obviously party fortunes play a major part here. The Liberals had the least length of service: two only served in Parliament until the year following their election, and one sat for three years. On the Conservative side, length of service was considerably longer. Lady Astor's service extended for over twenty-five years, ending when she did not seek re-election in 1945. One other member served for just over fifteen years, another for about six years, and one for seven. On the Labour side, service was split in two of the four cases, totalling approximately six and seven years respectively. One Labour member served for only one year and was unsuccessful in further contests; but one, Miss Ellen Wilkinson, served from 1924 until 1931, and then from 1935 until her death in 1947.

Among the Conservatives, the Duchess of Atholl was the only one to attain office as Parliamentary Secretary to the Board of Education. Miss Bondfield, after having also held this office, was later to become Minister of Labour. Ellen Wilkinson became Education Minister. Miss Susan Lawrence held the position of Parliamentary Secretary to the Ministry of Health. With the interesting exception of Miss Bondfield's Labour ministry, all these appointments lie in the social welfare sector. Even so the proportion of office-holding is considerable for so small a number of women.

2. *1929–1944*

The period which begins in 1929 and extends to 1944 is clearly a transitional one, a period of gradual expansion and consolidation. It is the first period in which women have the vote on a basis exactly comparable with that of men. For the first time there is no discrimination against women by age, since the introduction of the so-called 'flapper-vote'. Within this period, twenty-seven women were elected to Parliament for the first time, while six women, first elected before 1929, continued to serve at some time between that date and 1944.

For the purpose of this analysis, only those are included who were elected for the first time in this period, either in the Labour or in the Conservative interest, twelve and thirteen members respectively. In addition, one Liberal and one Independent were elected, but are excluded from this analysis. The material available includes biographical works,[16] some interview material and completed questionnaires, personal communications from close relatives and friends of some members who have died, supplemented and checked by reference sources. The material is, therefore, heterogeneous and somewhat uneven. Once again, with a total of only twenty-five under consideration, detailed analysis is unrealistic, and this number must be remembered when interpreting the comparatively few percentages that are used.

In this period, unlike the earlier one, the Labour members are not set apart from the Conservatives in terms of marital status. Instead, the majority on both sides (75 per cent of the Labour side and 61 per cent of the Conservatives) were married, or had been married, at the time of election. Of this 'married majority' most had children, but ages varied from an adult family to children of school age.

Even on the incomplete data available for age at entry to Parliament (no accurate information was obtained for two Conservatives and one

Labour member) it is clear that the major entry on each side came at or before the age of fifty. At least one-third on each side entered at a relatively early age, between thirty-one and forty years. One Labour member entered at sixty-eight years, the only entrant on either side over sixty.

Using the index of educational standards, the differential between parties is considerably more marked. Among the Conservatives, two members are known to have been graduates compared with eight of the Labour members (12 per cent and 53 per cent respectively). Additionally, two Labour members had qualified at Teachers' Training College and one had completed her education at a College for Missionaries. Only two of the twenty-five (both on the Labour side), had completed their education at an elementary school. The remainder of both parties had completed their education at private or secondary schools.

By social origins (considered on the basis of father's occupation) there is an element of homogeneity about most of the members of both parties, since on this criterion, over two-thirds of both parties are known to have belonged to the middle or upper classes. Over-representation of these strata is, therefore, pronounced, as no Conservative and only three Labour members had fathers who belonged to the working classes. This over-representation among women reflected the general class outlines of the House of Commons in the inter-war period.[17]

A somewhat similar pattern is evident when the occupations followed by members themselves before election and by the husbands of those who were married, come under consideration. Just under one half of the women Conservatives and one Labour member had had no paid occupation before their election. On the Labour side, two-thirds had employment which could be classified as middle-class, e.g. teachers, journalists. Only two strictly working-class occupations were recorded, both on the Labour side.

The pattern of predominantly middle-class representation is consistent when applied also to the occupations of the husbands of the married women MPs. On both sides, all had husbands whose occupations were middle-class or above. For the Labour group, this categorisation reveals a degree of social mobility since the three women members who come from working-class backgrounds married men who themselves were or were to become MPs. In all, exactly half of the Labour group were married to husbands who served, at some time, as MPs. In contrast, only two of the Conservatives were married to MPs.

It is interesting that in looking at the occupations of the women MPs in detail, with one marginal Conservative exception (that of a professional historian) the communication type of occupation may be seen in this period only on the Labour side, where the careers followed included teaching, journalism, and trade union organiser.

We have looked at the occupations followed by some of the women MPs before their election, and have noted the incidence on the Labour side of the communication type of career. But this is not the complete picture. What other kinds of experience had these MPs before their election? There is an interesting difference between the parties here. On the Labour side, experience as councillors at the various levels of local authorities, and work on the organisational side of the Labour and Trade Union movements were of almost equal importance, around one half of the total had each type of experience, some combining both types of experience. On the Conservative side, the pattern is different. The single most important factor (for just over one half of the group) was voluntary work, followed by service as councillors (including the LCC) and party activity equally important at around one quarter of the group. Again some members combined two or all three types of pre-election experience.

In this period, for the first time, there are examples of male equivalence among the Labour women members. Of the twelve women elected, three stood as 'male substitutes'. One 'succeeded' on the death of her husband (a brother of the Labour leader Keir Hardie). Lady Noel Buxton was elected to the seat which her husband vacated to take his place in the House of Lords. The case of Mrs. Dalton was rather different, but here was a very clear example of a woman acting entirely as a substitute for her husband. Mrs. Dalton preceded her husband in a Parliamentary constituency. Dr Dalton had been chosen as prospective candidate for Bishop Auckland while he was still serving as MP for Peckham. In 1929, the death of the member for Bishop Auckland caused an unexpected by-election. As her husband could not take the candidature, Mrs. Dalton was invited to stand. 'They want to get people into the habit of voting Dalton.'[18] Mrs. Dalton sat only for a few months in Parliament until her husband was returned for Bishop Auckland at the next General Election. According to her husband, she stood solely to help him, and never wanted to be an MP, much preferring her work on the L.C.C.[19]

The proportion of 'male equivalence' is approximately the same on the Conservative side. Three of the Conservatives were elected to the seat which their husbands had held. Viscountess Davidson was asked by the constituency party to stand as their candidate when her husband went to the House of Lords. Viscountess Davidson was regarded as 'the obvious successor' and was adopted unanimously. Two members entered Parliament by-elections for the vacancies left after their husband had been killed in action in the Second World War. Mrs. Beatrice Rathbone,[20] an American by birth, took her seat in 1941. Lady Apsley entered Parliament two years later. Having been injured in a hunting accident, Lady Apsley carried on her parliamentary activities from a wheel-chair. One other member of Parliament in this period had at least some of the benefits of male equivalence, since she carried on the name of her husband's family '. . . the wife of Mr. Ronald Copeland of the famous Spode pottery factory at Stoke and her election as MP for Stoke is quite in keeping with the Copeland tradition as Mr. William Taylor Copeland, who about a hundred years ago purchased the works from the Spode Trustees, was also MP for Stoke'.[21]

Evidence revealing the background of the politicised family is more considerable on the Labour side than among the Conservatives. On the Labour side,family precedence to public or political activism is easy to trace. Just under sixty per cent (probably an under-estimate) are known to have had parents with experience in public life. This family precedence, however, is not always to the Labour Party. For example, one had a father active in the Conservative interest, another came from a family of leading Liberals in her home town, and a third member had a father who had been Foreign Secretary in a Conservative administration. On the other hand, Miss Jennie Lee provided perhaps a classic example of the product of the politicised family, the third generation of Labour pioneers, whose grandfather and father had been organisers in the Miners' Union and active in the early Labour movement. Her home was a socialist one, her upbringing was socialist. 'We were growing too fast to have time to look behind. Soon, now, we would revolutionise the world. Our socialist hymns seemed to me to give a pretty good idea of what it was all about.'[22] In her school days, Miss Lee was much involved in socialist affairs, spending Sunday mornings at Socialist Sunday School, Sunday evenings at public meetings, with two evenings of the week devoted to collecting ILP dues.

On the Conservative side, the politicised family background is not so significant. Only about one-third of the total can be traced as having this kind of influence in their childhood. Of these, one is certainly very strong. Viscountess Davidson was the fourth generation of her family to sit in the House of Commons. Her father, grandfather, and great-grandfather preceded her, though they were not all of the same party or constituency. It is interesting to note here that Lady Davidson's father, Lord Dickenson, had tried to introduce a Bill to admit women to the Lords: he had already moved a similar bill at an earlier stage while he was in the House of Commons, and in a maiden speech to the LCC (1889) had supported a move to attempt to allow women to sit on County Councils.

When looking at details of successful candidatures, certain reservations are necessary. Particularly relevant here is party fortunes. Women tend to enter Parliament on landslides.

Table 5 Year of first election to Parliament

Year of Entry	Labour	Conservative	Total
	%	%	%
1929	58	0	28
1930	8	0	4
1931	9	76	44
1937	8	8	8
1938	17	0	8
1941	0	8	4
1943	0	8	4
Total	(N=12) 100	(N=13) 100	(N=25) 100

There is clearly an association between entering Parliament on landslides and an increased probability of success at a first candidature. The incidence of 'male equivalence' is even more clearly linked with a woman's success in her first Parliamentary candidature. In this period, particularly striking is the high percentage of success at the first attempt. On the Conservative side, just over two-thirds were successful the first time they stood, compared with a little over forty per cent of the Labour group. The majority on both sides entered at their first or second attempt.

Women not only tend to enter Parliament on 'landslides', but to leave on landslides also. A sizeable proportion of those entering in the peak years (1929 for Labour, 1931 for the Conservatives) did not long survive. On the Labour side, of the seven women entering in 1929, one (a 'male equivalent' mentioned earlier) served only a matter of months, and five served only until the 1931 General Election. The remaining MP lost her seat in 1931 but returned in 1945 and ultimately achieved ministerial rank. Similarly, on the Conservative side, seven of those entering in 1931 served only until 1935, two served until 1945, and one, with a five-year gap, served until 1959. Details of length of service may be misleading when personal factors such as age or ill-health, and external factors like party fortunes, the re-drawing of constituency boundaries cannot adequately be taken into account. Even so, it is significant that four of the Conservatives achieved more than fourteen years' service each (two had more than twenty years to their credit), and on the Labour side, three had more than twenty years service.[23]

As in the first period, the office holding and achievement of those elected within this period were by no means negligible considering how few women were elected. Ministerial office was held by Miss Jennie Lee, Dr (later Baroness) Summerskill on the Labour side and by Miss Florence (later Baroness) Horsburgh on the Conservative side. The post of Parliamentary Secretary was held by Miss Cazalet Keir under a Conservative administration, and Mrs. Adamson under a Labour government.

3. *1945–1970*

The period from the end of the Second World War up to and including the 1970 General Election shows (within the limit of the paucity of women's representation) a considerable increase in the numbers of women elected for the first time to the House of Commons. In these post-war years, the imbalance in favour of Labour members is apparent, thirty-two of whom were returned, as opposed to twenty-one Conservative women MPs. This disparity reflects a situation fairly common to other Western political systems[24] as has already been indicated.

For the first time, the material on which this section is based is more comprehensive. For some members[25] biographies have been published reference sources are more complete, and the woman MP continues to be of enduring interest to journalists. In addition, a considerable proportion of members generously provided material.[26]

That women tend to enter Parliament on landslides is clearly demonstrated in this period, when the year 1945 stands out clearly for

Labour. At no other election, either before or since, were fourteen 'new' members elected.

Rather more on the Conservative side than on the Labour side were in the thirty-one to forty age group when they entered the Commons. The 1970 General Election, in particular, brought in a small group of younger members in the Conservative interest. The division between parties in age is more noticeable when the age of fifty is chosen as a dividing line. No less than eighty-one per cent of the Conservatives were fifty or under when they took their seats for the first time, compared with a little over sixty per cent of their Labour colleagues. One member of each party has entered in her sixties. That Labour MPs have tended to be, on average, rather older than their Conservative colleagues is well established. In 1945, for example, the average age of those elected for the first time (of both sexes) was forty years and six months for Labour.[27] In 1970 approximately one-fifth of both Labour and Conservative Parties were under forty, but rather more of the Conservatives than Labour were under fifty years (58 per cent as compared with 50 per cent respectively). Labour had more members in the over sixty grouping than the Conservatives (twenty-three per cent compared with twelve per cent).[28]

As in the preceding period and in marked contrast to Period I, the majority on both sides were or had been married at election. There is however, a difference of the order of twenty per cent between the parties (eighty per cent of Labour members compared with a little over sixty per cent of the Conservatives). Around ten per cent of both sides were widowed or divorced.

In this period, the differential between the parties in terms of University education persists, but has decreased. Of the Conservatives, around thirty-eight per cent were graduates, and one had trained at RADA, and another qualified as a teacher. With the exception of one member who had completed her full-time education at an elementary school, the education of the remainder was completed at Secondary, Grammar or Independent School. By comparison, the Labour group included forty-five per cent with a University degree, two with a graduate qualification in music, and another with a sociology diploma. Around thirteen per cent had teaching qualifications, and about the same proportion had ended their full-time education at elementary school.[29]

In attempting a consideration of the occupational background of women members, the usual problems of accurate job-description over a twenty-year period, and members having had more than one occupation, are qualifying factors. With such reservations, certain generalisations may be made. First, the representation of manual workers is very slight. No Conservative had followed a manual occupation of any kind, and only about twelve per cent of the Labour group had done this type of work. The figures for manual workers for all MPs elected in 1970 may be used to provide a comparison, when the percentage for Conservative and Labour were 0.23 and 13 per cent respectively. All the women Conservatives for whom accurate information could be classified, had middle-class, or no paid occupation. Nine-tenths of the women in the Labour group had had occupations which were middle-class.

In terms of class, on the index of occupation, then, there is a considerable degree of consistency between the parties. Yet in terms of what has been termed the 'communication factor' in type of occupation pursued, a party difference becomes clear. Of the eighteen Conservatives who had been in paid employment before their election to Parliament, exactly half had been in lecturing, journalism, teaching, welfare work, or had practised at the Bar. Of their Labour colleagues, over seventy per cent had followed this type of occupation. This is a pattern which follows that of the first two periods. The party differential for women tends to follow that for members of the House of Commons of both sexes, but the communication factor is much more important among women.

Table 6 Percentage of members having followed a 'communication-type' occupation before election

	Labour %	Conservative %
Women MPs in period III	70	50
All MPs 1966	55	34
All MPs 1970[30]	57	36

In purely occupational terms, then, it is possible to indicate the areas which are the more important for the recruitment of women to Parliament. But other areas of recruitment related to experience before election are equally, if not more significant. The table below shows the kind of experience in the party, voluntary work, trade unions or as elected representative on a local authority which the women member in this period has had. The percentages will not add up to one hundred since a member may be found to have experience in more than one category.

Table 7 Pre-election experience of women MPs

	Labour %	Conservative %
Local government	63	62
Party: office holding	66[1]	24
Trade Union: office holding	9	0
Voluntary work	9	19
	N = 32	N = 21

1. includes five examples of Cooperative Party activism.

Local government emerges as the most significant pre-election experience in both parties, with party activism (office holding) as very much more important in Labour than in Conservative experience. Voluntary work appears somewhat more frequently among the Conservatives. It seems possible that activity in voluntary associations is under-estimated because under-reported.

Local government as an avenue to election to Parliament is of course not confined to women. In 1970, for example, around one-third of the Labour members elected and about one-quarter of the Conservatives could be traced as having had experience as local authority councillors.[31] In 1945, the proportion had been even higher, fifty-six and twenty-five per cent for Labour and Conservative members respectively.[32] The small numbers of women make firm conclusions impossible, but it seems clear that local government experience is a highly important first stage of experience for women's participation in the national political elite.

Recruitment areas may, then, be shown to differ between the parties, but it is interesting that in the incidence of family precedents to political activism, there is remarkably little variation from one party to another. Just under half of the Labour members (47 per cent) and forty-three per cent of Conservatives could be traced as having, or having had members of their (extended) family active in politics locally or nationally. For a few of the Labour members, mainly those in the older age group, precedents tended to be Liberal Party, since the Labour Party entered the parliamentary arena late.

Data are not sufficiently detailed to state categorically the percentage of those brought up in politicised families. Sufficient material is available, however, to show that to a sizeable proportion of them the notion of a 'politicised' family background may be applied. Among the Labour members, notable examples would include that of Shirley Summerskill, daughter of a woman MP (subsequently a life peeress), and the childhood experience of the late Mrs. Bessie Braddock, in a family of local activists. 'It goes back all my life – before I was born. My mother did it before me. I was brought up in the way of it.'[33] Others on the Labour side include a daughter of an MP and the daughter of a one-time General Secretary of the Labour Party. On the Conservative side, examples include one member who was the daughter of an MP, and another was the fourth generation of her family to sit in the House of Commons.

By the post-war period, the incidence of male equivalence as a factor mediating women's entry into Parliament had considerably decreased. On the Labour side, one member was elected to the seat which her husband had held until his death. Of the Conservatives, one was elected to a seat formerly held by her husband, while another was returned unopposed, after her father had died suddenly in an accident.

The background to women's representation in Parliament at this period has been briefly indicated. How difficult was it for them to achieve success? For a roughly equal proportion on each side (38 per cent and 34 per cent for Conservative and Labour respectively) there was first time success. An equal proportion of the Labour side, but only about 19 per cent of the Conservatives were successful at their second attempt. Overall, then, more than three-quarters of both parties were elected at the first, second or third attempt.

Relatively to their numbers, women in this period again appear to be treated generously in holding office. The development and differentiation of ministries and subsequent amalgamation or reallocation of responsibilities which may be differently designated make exact comparisons difficult. What may be seen, however, is certainly not the operation of discrimination against women, quite possibly the reverse. Among the Conservatives, Mrs. Thatcher was allotted a key Cabinet post, and ministerial portfolios were numerious. On the Labour side, Mrs. Castle held Cabinet rank, and other ministerial responsibilities were held by Mrs. Eirene White at the Foreign Office (minister of state), Lady Tweedsmuir, Mrs. Hart, and Mrs. Shirley Williams, who was minister for Education and Science and at the Home Office. An interesting indication subsequently of women's place in the competition for office is the rapidity with which some women members have been recently singled out for junior positions,[34] as a first stage to ministerial careers.

Notes

1. The only other woman ever to be elected as a Liberal, Lady Megan Lloyd George, who entered Parliament in 1929, later joined the Labour Party and stood in its interest.
2. Duchess of Atholl, *Working Partnership*, London, 1958; M. Bondfield, *My Life's Work*, London, 1948; C. Sykes, *Nancy: The Life of Lady Astor*, London, 1972.
3. J. Johnston, *A Hundred Commoners*, London, 1931; E. Wilkinson, 'Marion' (Dr Marion Phillips, MP), *The Labour Magazine*, 10, 1932.
4. The daughter of a canon and of a solicitor respectively.
5. op.cit.
6. R.B. Lees Smith, *Encyclopaedia of the Labour Movement*, London, 1928, p.304.
7. J.F.S. Ross, *Parliamentary Representation*, London, 1948, p.79.
8. op.cit., p.63. The tendency for the over-representation of the middle and upper classes among political activists at every level as compared with the class of members generally has been well established. cf. W.L. Guttsman, op.cit., p.27. Similar findings are reported in A. Ranney, *Pathways to Parliament*, London, 1965, and J. Blondel, *Voters, Parties and Leaders*, London, 1963. The use of the terms 'middle class' and 'working class' in the empirical sections of this study needs explanation, since class allocations in empirical studies tend to be idiosyncratic such that comparisons become hazardous. In 1961, the socio-economic categories used by the Registrar General were changed to a more detailed 17 category classification (reduced for some purposes to 7), neither of which grouping could be compared exactly with the previous 13 category classification. For the purpose of this study, therefore, the Registrar General's broad social class allocations have been used. 'Middle class' is used as a shorthand expression for 'middle class or above', i.e. R.G. I and II. Similarly 'working class' refers to the manual workers of R.G. IV and V. Occupations in R.G. III have been allocated to either working or middle class on the arbitrary criterion of whether the work is manual or not.
9. On educational opportunities for women at this time, cf. J. Kamm, op.cit., passim.
10. cf. below, p. 68.
11. cf. below, p. 162.

    It is interesting that the notion of the 'politicised family' has been developed as a concept applicable to local politics also, D. Marvick (ed.), *Political Decision Makers*, Glencoe, Illinois, 1961, p.210. A study of women councillors serving on Birmingham Council in a roughly comparable period (1911–28) shows the incidence of the politicised family in the backgrounds of three of the thirteen women elected at this time, a proportion which is likely to be an underestimate. cf. M.E. Currell, *Women in Politics*, unpublished Ph.D. thesis, 1965, Chapter 7.

12. Earl Attlee, 'The Attitudes of MPs and Active Peers', *Political Quarterly*, 30, 1959, p.31.
13. E. Rathbone, 'Changes in public life' in R. Strachey (ed.), *Our Freedom and its Results*, London, 1936, p.32. Examples of 'the very few who tried' are Christabel Pankhurst who stood at Smethwick in 1918; Mrs. Despard stood at Battersea, Mrs. Pethwick-Lawrence at Rusholme, and Mrs. W.C. Anderson (Mary MacArthur) contested Stourbridge. None of these was successful and none made a further attempt. Mrs. Corbett.Ashley stood as a Liberal in 1918, and subsequently, but never with success.
14. M. Stokes, *Observer*, 3 May 1964.
15. Duchess of Atholl, op.cit., p.73.
16. J. Lee, *This Great Journey*, London, 1963 (first published 1941); M.A. Hamilton, *Remembering My Good Friends*, London, 1944; E. Picton Turbervill, *Life is Good*, London, 1939; E. Summerskill, *A Woman's World*, London, 1967.
17. cf. J.F.S. Ross, op.cit., p.63.
18. H. Dalton, *Call Back Yesterday*, London, 1953, p.206.
19. 'A few days later J.R.M. [Ramsay McDonald] invited her to tea. He said he hoped that though of course she would be relinquishing Bishop Auckland to me at the General Election she was sufficiently interested in Parliament to be willing to stand somewhere else. She said she found the LCC much more interesting than the House . . . She said she had never wanted to be an MP, and was only here now to help me out of a difficulty.' loc.cit.
20. Mrs. Rathbone's husband was the great-nephew of Miss Eleanor Rathbone, MP.
21. *Staffordshire Advertiser*, 31 October 1931.
22. J. Lee, op.cit., p.49 ff.
23. Total years of service even if discontinuous.
24. cf. M. Duverger, op.cit., p.147. Interesting deviations from this pattern are reported for Norway and the United States where 'within the middle-class parties women at the higher levels of education and economic position are markedly more likely to approach positions of leadership', S. Rokkan and A. Campbell, 'Norway and the United States', *International Social Science Journal*, 12, 1, 1960, p.96. For general discussion on this distribution, cf. p.46.
25. e.g. J. and E. Braddock, *The Braddocks*, London, 1963. M. Toole, *Mrs. Bessie Braddock, MP*, London, 1957; W. D'Eath, *Barbara Castle*, London, 1970; J. Mann, *Woman in Parliament*, London, 1962; M. McCarthy (Mrs. M. McKay, MP), *Generation in Revolt*, London, 1953; L. Manning, *Life in Education*, London, 1972.
26. Material communicated by interview or by questionnaire is, of course, used anonymously.

27. Ross, op.cit., p.244. That Labour members are older than Conservative MPs at first election was shown for the years 1918–51 in Ross, *Elections and Electors*, London, 1955, p.391.
28. Derived from D. Butler and M. Pinto-Duschinsky, *The British General Election of 1970*, London, 1971, pp.301–3.
29. In contrast, the educational qualifications of all MPs in 1970 included 63 per cent of the Conservatives and 53 per cent of the Labour members with a University degree. Twenty per cent of the Labour group had completed their education at elementary school. Butler and Pinto Duschinsky, loc.cit.
30. Calculated from biographical material in The Times, *Guide to the House of Commons*, 1970.
31. loc.cit.
32. Ross, *Parliamentary Representation*, p.275.
33. Personal communication from a Labour member, now deceased.
34. e.g. Mrs. Thatcher was already Under Secretary at the Ministry of Pensions and National Insurance within two years of her election. On the Labour side, Mrs. Shirley Williams, elected in 1964, was Parliamentary Secretary to the Ministry of Labour in 1966 and Minister of State, Department of Education and Science, the following year.

Chapter 4 The Woman MP

Thus far, the account which has been given of women Members of Parliament has been in terms of percentages and proportions, first in electoral statistics, success rates and handicap factors, and secondly in detailing by time period of objective characteristics such as level of educational qualifications or pre-election experience and occupation. In this chapter, though percentages and proportions inevitably persist, the emphasis is much more on the subjective rather than the objective. It is intended here to add another more 'real' dimension to the study, in terms of the woman MP's perceptions of her career, her motivations and her evaluation of women's political role, using, whenever possible, the words of the women MPs themselves.

This kind of dimension has not been explored in any depth in the literature, since only passing references are to be found in biographies and autobiographies, in news reports, interviews and profiles of women MPs.[1] Such a lacuna in the literature is not confined to women members. A few studies have been made on specific topics relating to the career of the MP,[2] studies which have included some treatment of opinions and attitudes. Relatively little has been done in the field of what is now termed 'ambition theory'.[3]

Despite the lack of comparative data for male MPs, it still seems worthwhile to pursue the limited objective, the probing of the perceptions of women members. Justification for such a course lies in part in the potential use of this work as a pilot study for the further wider study which is necessary, and in part, because as has been suggested earlier, to some extent at least, certain problems of men and women in the political elite may differ in kind.

1. *The Focus of the Enquiry*

Details of the study may be found in Appendix I. Two limitations, both temporal, must be stressed in interpreting the data presented here. The material on which this study is based has been collected over a period of some years and relates to an extended time period. The earliest date of election of a respondent was 1923. At whatever date a survey of this kind is undertaken, however, it is bound to involve evaluation of events which took place many years in the past for some members, and for others much more recently. Similarly at any one date some members will be summarising in their answers a career nearing completion, while others will be at the beginning of their Parliamentary service. Because of the small numbers involved, the periods defined previously are not followed in this analysis. The material is, therefore, presented as a whole, not by individual time period, to avoid the danger of inflating the small numbers in percentage terms. As the assignment to time period was determined by the date of first election to Parliament, and as so many Parliamentary careers span a number of years, this lack of detail is not so serious.

A further reservation in the general interpretation of data lies in the disparity in numbers between Labour and Conservative respondents. The number of Labour respondents in the survey, as in the total number ever to have been elected to Parliament, is in excess of those elected in the Conservative interest. As already indicated, the distribution of respondents is not completely representative over time. Some members had died, others for reasons of age or illness were unable to participate. In addition, it is unfortunate that some women MPs were unwilling to take part. It becomes clear from the correspondence involved that Members of Parliament are the target of much research activity – from pressure groups, commercial organisations etc. – such that some degree of research resistance is developed.[4]

Finally, in order to implement the assurance of anonymity which was given to respondents quotations are not attributed to their authors. Regrettably, some liveliness and colour has been lost to the study by the sacrifice of any material which might give an indication of the identity of the individual concerned.

2. *Background and Recruitment*

The work of the Member of Parliament clearly demands a certain level of ability and skills regardless of sex. The development of these qualities into the expertise and 'professionalism' of the Parliamentarian may come in the course of a career as elected representative, and the 'socialisation' of the MP would be an important piece of work in itself. Some few indications of this process may emerge in the material in this chapter. Basically, however, this introductory section is concerned with the skills, background and experience acquired before election.

High on the list of the skills and qualities which are valuable is 'communication', which has already been considered as a characteristic in the analysis of the careers of women MPs over time,[5] with comparable figures for all members. It cannot be mere coincidence that the practice of law, for example, a 'communication' occupation, has been a fairly common precursor in the careers of many male politicians.[6] In seeking to trace recruitment patterns, women's service as local councillors, and their activity in voluntary associations and in party political organisations were considered in the previous chapter. In order to consider a little more deeply the relevance of the various areas of recruitment, respondents were asked to indicate what they had done before their election which they felt was of most use to them in their career in the Commons. An evaluation of their earlier experience was called for in this question.

As respondents often gave more than one kind of experience in their answers, the percentages quoted for each party will not total one hundred on each side. Work as councillors was the factor most frequently mentioned on both sides (by fifty-four per cent of the conservatives and forty-four per cent of the Labour group). Not only was this the most usual factor but it was one which was presented in more detail and with more emphasis than other points put forward. From a Labour member came the typical reply, 'Local authority work all the time: all the experience of committee work and speaking in public.' Equally explicit was a Conservative member, 'I was chairman of the Further Education Committee of the County Council. I know education. Few people know education from the grass roots. This committee also made me interested in industrial training and in industry.' In actual experience of local authority work, as opposed to perceptions of the usefulness of that experience, the distribution varies between the parties. Around two-thirds of the Labour respondents served in local government, with service for the Conservatives about fifteen per cent lower. On the Labour side, of almost equal importance with work as councillors was the career experience of members before election, with reference to teaching the most usual. In contrast, only one Conservative referred to her previous occupation.

Voluntary work was mentioned by rather more Conservative than Labour respondents, (nearly one-third compared to about one-tenth). Party activism, either national or local, was mentioned by only a little over ten per cent on either side. Interestingly, from the Labour group there were two references to service as directors of Cooperative Societies. Surprisingly, since at least one-third of the Labour group could be traced as having some background in Trade Union activity, only two mentioned this factor as useful preliminary experience. The remaining few references fall into no specific category. One reply from a Conservative who took her seat during the Second World War throws an interesting light on a survey which covers a considerable time span.

This answer concluded, 'Opening bazaars made me able to speak fairly well on almost any subject . . . travel to foreign countries gave me good ideas.' Then was added, 'Learning to fly and being a fairly good rider, fisherwoman, golfer and tennis player taught me how to talk of these things to others and prevented me becoming a bore on politics.' Incidentally, the 'fairly good rider' was Master of Foxhounds, and to be a woman pilot in the inter-war years was a considerable achievement.

What evidence is there of the politicised family as a background factor? Two questions were intended to illuminate this point. One asked whether the respondent was the first in her family to be active in political or public life, requesting details of precedents in these areas. The second question asked whether brothers or sisters (if any) became active in such fields. Answers given were sufficiently full to separate a politicised family background from a record of family interest in politics.

The incidence of the politicised family was almost identical for both parties, at around one-third of respondents, with no discernible differences by time period. Two Labour members were the daughters of MPs. A clear example of what is meant by a politicised family background may be quoted here. 'I grew up in a political home. All my life I've been involved in politics. I used to go to meetings with my mother and father when I was about six, and hear Annie Besant and Mary MacArthur. And I went canvassing with my parents.'

Family influence, then, may be seen as a factor in the recruitment of this sample of women members, but the survey reveals an important check on any facile over-emphasis on this association. While the members are small, it is clear that this form of socialisation is not one which is equally important for all the children in a family. There is no simple cause and effect association of family precedence to politics and the activism of the respondents. The siblings of respondents with this type of background, with one exception, were not themselves activists though some interest was reported. Other variables must, therefore intervene. Birth order may be relevant, but studies are still not very extensive in this area.[7] and the numbers in the present study too small to warrant conclusions.

Moving from the respondent's family background as a child to her current family situation, an attempt was made to consider the degree of political activity of the husbands of the named members of this sample. Approximately nine out of ten of the Labour Members were or had been married. Here political activity at some level seems to be a shared concern. Four Members were married to Members of Parliament, including one whose marriage took place after she had left the Commons, and a further member had a husband who was a Prospective Parliamentary Candidate. About one-third reported husband's party activism i.e. office holding, locally and about one-fifth reported that their husbands were local councillors, all of whom were also counted in the party activity category. Among the Conservatives excluding the single and those widowed before election, four of the nine members were married to MPs. There was very little activity on the part of husbands in the other instances. Respondents were asked whether their husbands had considered standing for Parliament, and from two Labour members came answers such as 'we can't both do it', with an indication that a husband's cooperation and support in running the home was valuable.

When the question of the practical problems of combining home life, and possibly a family, with a parliamentary career was raised the relatively high proportion in the sample of the single, the childless wife and the widowed was apparent. The problems of combining home and work did not loom so large as might have been expected. This is not to assume that the life of a woman Member is easy.[8] The enormous energy, stamina and industry required of her are obvious, but unquantifiable, elements in nearly every encounter with women parliamentarians. The material which resulted from this question cannot be tabulated meaningfully, since marriage, the ages of any children, location of the constituency, and private financial means all modify the significance of the replies given. A few relevant points which emerge from the answers may be raised here. First the provision of a 'domestic substitute for yourself' while acknowledged to be useful, may not be considered satisfactory if caring for children is involved. The help of a near relative may be much more acceptable. The answers seem to suggest that the perfect solution to the problems of married women and mothers as MPs looks unlikely to be one conceived in purely financial terms.

3. *The MP's Appraisal of Her Own Career*

Motivation is one of the most interesting and complex of the many questions associated with human behaviour, and one of the most difficult to evaluate. The discussion presented here makes no claim to be a study in motivation. Instead an analysis is made of the answers which respondents made when asked 'Looking back, what sort of reasons prompted you to seek election?' This question was supplemented by two others: (a) as to which individual or which factor most influenced the decision to stand for Parliament and (b) asking when respondents had first thought seriously of becoming an MP.

When reasons are sought for an initial decision which was made in some instances ten or fifteen years in the past (many more years in the exceptional case), the passage of time no doubt has some influence on the answers. Then there is the possibility of rationalisation *post hoc*, the desire to give the questioner what it is perceived is wanted, or the desire, conscious or unconscious to project a particular image, either personal or party. There may also be omissions or evasions, conscious or unconscious. Because of these considerations, it was decided not to make any attempt at a sophisticated approach, but rather to ask a cluster of simple straightforward questions, so that it was left to the respondent to choose at what level to answer.

A considerable variation in length of answers was interesting. To answer this question some respondents gave a brief account of their lives to show how the reasons developed, and the decision to stand for Parliament came about. Other answers were more laconic. As there are so few women compared with men in Parliament, and compared with the mass of women in the electorate, it might be expected that the forces impelling women to seek a Parliamentary career would be very powerful. It might seem reasonable to expect that most respondents would advance very distinctive reasons as accounting for their entry into politics, i.e. that they would be very highly motivated. It might also be expected that as the numbers are so few, at least a sizeable proportion of the reasons quoted could be expected to be common to both parties, united, as it were, in some form of common professionalism. The reasons cited over a wide range and shades of variation in approach. There seems to be some contrast between the parties to be seen in the answers. Percentages refer to the proportion of respondents who indicated each kind of response in their answer. As answers usually contained more than one focus, the total of percentages will not add up to one hundred. One type of answer, (36 per cent on the Labour side) easier to recognise than to define, consists of those in which there was the desire to effect ameliorative social change under the spur of existing conditions. One Conservative respondent mentioned social conditions as explaining her decision to stand. If to this group are added those answers which stress promotion of the ends of the Labour party, then the total (Labour) response in this field amounts to around sixty per cent of respondents. There seems to be no division to be remarked by time period. A member who had entered in 1945, over fifty years of age, said, 'I became interested in politics when I began work in the WEA . . . In the 1920s I saw a great deal of the miseries of the time, especially in the mining areas of South Wales . . . this was reinforced by the depression of the 1930s of which I also saw a great deal. A very similar answer came from a member elected almost twenty years later, and almost twenty years younger.

Also falling into this group are those answers revealing that personal experiences as a child helped to push in the direction of seeking a political solution in later life. One MP explained how she had come to join the ILP, which started the train of events leading to her being asked to stand for Parliament, but the basic reasons for so doing took her further back in her life story to explain, 'I'd always been interested. Mother was worried stiff about money. I was the only girl; I knew. It was a working-class home, but I visited relatives and saw the difference. Then at college I got together with people in the socialist society. Mother had always said "a fair day's wage for a fair day's work". It started then, I suppose, I knew the world of ordinary people . . . difficult circumstances, and I had intelligence to analyse the situation.'

Distinct from the family experience syndrome, rooted in reaction against conditions experienced, though often seen in association, is the factor of the positive and specific influence in the family towards politics, the 'politicised family' as a root of motivation. Such 'politicised family' influence was mentioned in the context of this question only on the Labour side.

Again only on the Labour side was there reported a desire to take part in Parliamentary action. Implicit in this is the need to reach the locus of power, 'to get things done'. Three of these replies came from those already involved in local government and voluntary work.

On the Conservative side only, just over one-quarter of the reasons mentioned related to male equivalence. No other reason for standing was given.

The exertion of pressure to stand by other people was mentioned by one-quarter of the Conservatives but by only about fifteen per cent of the Labour group. The pressure came in the form of an invitation to stand for a particular constituency. Answers to this question included 'it was being urged from sources and people who knew me'. Another said 'I was willing to help other folks come here (ie. House of Commons) but had no real ambition to be an MP myself . . . the man who got in . . . died suddenly. They said, "we're thinking about you to follow . . . you'll have to stand, you know" . . . but I've been reared in politics.' Another, Chairman of her local party organisation, stood when the adopted candidate suddenly withdrew. Two other respondents answered in terms of male 'equivalence'.

Interestingly enough such answers as being 'asked to stand', and the references to male equivalence, all come from the second time period, and the early part of the third period. It would be easy seriously to underestimate the force of the motivation of these *ad hoc* candidates. From other sections of the questionnaire, however, it appears clear that those asked to stand, or replacing their husbands, were to some degree and usually to a considerable degree, already involved in political activity. In some ways, the pressure of events, the need for an immediate decision, may be highly effective in crystallising the situation. The material seemed to show that confidence was drawn from the support expressed by others. All these factors may have tended to confirm what may have been a latent or perhaps unconscious willingness to serve if the opportunity arose.

A little under thirty per cent of the Conservatives, and a very slightly higher proportion of Labour respondents quoted 'interest in politics' as a reason for seeking election. The answers tended not to be further elaborated.

In order to develop some of these points further, the question of when respondents had first thought seriously of becoming an MP was raised.[9] The answers added little to previous information. Around one-quarter on each side reported some long term ambition. This group tended to have entered Parliament earlier, and in the 1960s, but numbers are again too small for detailed comparisons. No other pattern emerged in the answers. One reply, from a Labour member now deceased, detailed the process during which her ambition to become elected gradually developed. After seven hopeless seats, (both municipal and parliamentary, this respondent was becoming used to the 'propaganda fight' and the 'moral victory', as she termed her failures. Finally, for her eighth attempt, she was offered the nomination to a parliamentary seat, which it might be possible for her party to win.

These, then, are the reasons advanced by this group of women, varied in age, background, and Parliamentary experience, for wanting to enter Parliament. With the usual reservations on small numbers, and not attributing to women *qua* women some of the factors mentioned, plus the 'questionnaire resistance' which was becoming increasingly apparent over time, and may have tended towards producing the quick rather than complex answer, what tentative generalisations may be drawn from this data? There seems to be some tendency for women respondents from the Labour party to have strong reasons for wanting social change, and some are influenced by personal or family experience which has clearly made an emotional impact, and evoked response in terms of political beliefs and party identification. They are more likely to refer to their political family background as an additional reason. In contrast, Conservative respondents were somewhat more likely to perceive their decision to stand in terms of an *ad hoc* decision, or as an inevitable step, dictated by the sequence of events – 'interest in politics from age of sixteen – local council member'.

If there is some division (however inconclusive the data on which this is based) between the parties in terms of reasons for seeking to become a Member of Parliament, there is much more consensus on the perceptions of the positive and negative aspects of their life and work once elected. Once more, the time span is important, some are looking back on past careers, some are just beginning. In terms of satisfactions derived from the work, the parties were so near in the emphasis they placed on various factors that general discussion only is necessary. Enthusiasm tended to be a very marked common factor in the answers. Slightly more Conservatives than Labour respondents refused to specify particular parts of their work saying, emphatically, that they enjoyed it all. One respondent answered 'I love it all, I love being a backbencher. In the House, being a part of it, is like being a tiny part of history. I love meetings, the rowdier the better . . . ' The major satisfaction, mentioned by around one-third on both sides, was derived from 'helping people.' One member who gave this as a main satisfaction later revealed that she had answered over ten thousand letters in a five-year period.

There is here also the synthesis of wanting to help people and being in a position to do so effectively. In other words, the status and influence of a member of the legislature, to be used for the ends the woman MP herself determined was a source of gratification. The terms in which this satisfaction was phrased varied, and included in this category were 'the feeling that I was in a position to strive for better conditions in (her constituency); 'Giving departments a kick up the backside if they deserve it', 'getting things done as an MP.'

The extremely high degree of 'job satisfaction' as instanced in these answers by each party gave some indication of a group united at least in a common professionalism and well satisfied with their lot. The response to the question asking them what were the factors which gave them least satisfaction only reinforces this view. With one exception to be noted later, those who admitted to any negative aspects of their life (and around one in five of the whole sample did not) were admitting to the petty frustrations, the minor defects of an interesting career. All-night sittings, lack of adequate secretarial help, rushed weekends, travelling problems, were not, in the terms in which they were couched, perceived as serious frustrations. The sole exception was an answer 'having to obey the Whip' from a former Labour Member.

Answers to other questions intended to amplify these points reinforced the main feature already mentioned. Sitting Members were asked if they intended to stand for Parliament again, and while some objected to the question as stupid and/or redundant, others reiterated points of 'job satisfaction.'

Asked of what particular achievement in their career (without specification of parliamentary career) they were most proud, two of the whole group referred to an achievement before their election; of the rest, there was no clear pattern of replies. Most answers on either side (over half) referred to something in the 'getting things done' field. Around one-third of the Conservatives and one-fifth of the Labour respondents referred to a 'political achievement', in the sense of office-holding, piloting a Private Members' Bill, being the first or only woman on a particular committee.

Members were asked whether in their experience there were any disadvantages or advantages in their political career from the fact of being a woman. About one-third of the whole group claimed that they had experienced neither advantage nor disadvantage from their sex. Around one in five claimed that the only disadvantages were the ties of the home and family for a married woman. One member on each side gave an instance of illness at home, another that a woman member lacked the assistance of a wife. Advantages were claimed by nearly one-third of the Conservatives but only around one in ten of the Labour respondents. The advantages were those of being few in number and therefore more easily noticed. 'In the old days, a government had to put one woman in, now it's more. So a woman's chances are better than a man's.' An equal number on both sides (about ten per cent) reported both advantages and disadvantages, the former once in the House, the latter in seeking entry to Parliament. The disadvantage here was regarded as rooted in prejudice, specified as being *of* women *against* women in the selection process.

4. *The Political Role of Women: Perceptions*

The appraisal, in personal terms, of the satisfactions and dissatisfactions – the values – of the life of a woman MP needed to be supplemented in general terms by an assessment of the women MP's approach to the larger subject of women in the political elite. It is necessary to find where members of this political elite place the boundaries of the role, how they define the role, and where they apply constraints and restrictions. To this end, women MPs were asked a series of questions beginning with the somewhat obvious 'Do you think the numbers of women MPs should be increased?' Only one on each side stated categorically that they did not think that there should be more women in Parliament. Not surprisingly in this context, the majority (more than three-quarters in roughly equal proportions on each side) felt that there should be more women in Parliament. The answer of one Labour Member was 'We could do with more if only to spread the work round the rest of us. We're all overworked when they want a woman for this or that.' The remainder gave somewhat equivocal answers, or did not answer at all. The consensus of opinion that the numbers of women in Parliament should be increased, needs much more definition. In order to provide this definition, respondents were asked to suggest the optimum proportion of women to men in the House of Commons. The question proved to be unsatisfactory. Few were prepared to answer it, in the form in which it was asked. It is possible to see in one reply the suggestion that an optimum implies a limit, almost a quota. Only one ratio was suggested. One respondent maintained that 'to suggest a proportion would be pushing the feminist thing again'. Another refused to answer on the grounds that 'members are individuals and should be treated as such. Their sex should be irrelevant.' This comment may conceal the most truly feminist stance of all.

Those respondents who believed that the numbers of women should be increased were asked what means of effecting the increase they would suggest. Answers were again somewhat disappointing. There was no wealth of suggestions to increase the flow of women into politics, and also no discernible party variation. Encouragement was the main method suggested. A few on each side mentioned education. One felt that co-education would help the situation, one respondent suggested reversing, by education, the negative conditioning of women. In most of the answers there was a stress on the high calibre of woman required to be an MP.

This very selective group was asked what were the reasons, in their opinion, for there being so few women in Parliament. Most of the reasons advanced are familiar ones. It is the emphasis attributed to the various elements which is significant. Emphasis is indicated here by the percentage of members quoting each factor. The most usual answer given by both groups lay in the areas of women's sex role and the commitments and limitations associated with this role. Nearly two-thirds of the Labour group and almost exactly the same proportion of the Conservatives gave this kind of answer. Within this category there were different emphases. Some referred to the woman's home and family responsibilities as deterring women from seeking election. Others were more specific, arguing that married women with children would have to enter politics later than men. Some referred to the fact that the years between twenty-five and forty, when a man could build up a career by which his capacities could be judged, or his political reputation, were those devoted by a mother to her children. 'A lot of women, especially those with a family are restricted while children are young. All right if you live in London and can see them once a day. Otherwise women get in later after the family has grown up, and then there's a resistance to age.'

Not surprisingly, then, the traditional-geretic role of women was the prime factor here. Akin to the sex role cluster of reasons were two answers, both from the Labour side, from young MPs serving currently, that it was the conditioning of women to accept a traditional sex role, to feel that they should not seek to enter a man's world.

Next in order of importance, by the number of respondents referring to this group of factors, may be found answers suggesting that women are not treated equally with men, notably by selection committees. Over half of the Labour Members gave replies relating to prejudice against women (notably at selection level), as did nearly two-thirds of the Conservatives. Of these the majority, more or less undivided by party alignment, referred to elements of unfair treatment of those women who were eager to enter national politics. 'First there is resistance in selection conferences, resistance against women. They say, "the electorate won't stand it." It starts there. It's underlying resistance never or very rarely expressed, though I've heard it said.' One in five of the Labour group and nearly one in three of the Conservatives who answered in terms of prejudice, referred solely to the reluctance of women to support women. The replies included 'prejudice of other women', and 'Prejudice among women: felt they cannot cope so other women cannot.' If a woman has to fight prejudice and in so doing faces unfair odds, then the successful woman is seen as being 'better than a man'. This judgement was quoted by about one-fifth of the Labour members, but by just over ten per cent of the Conservatives. As one former MP replied unselfconsciously, 'women must be outstanding. There aren't many of us.'

Overall around four in ten of the Labour group and one in three of the Conservatives gave answers rooted in women's lacking some of the qualities necessary for success as an MP. Lack of driving ambition, determination to surmount obstacles were referred to here. In some few answers, however, the lack of push or ruthless ambition seemed to be perceived as a positive rather than a negative comment. Women's modesty and lack of confidence in their own ability were also mentioned.

Disadvantages associated with the work of the MP were mentioned by a few respondents, rather more on the Labour side. The 'ridiculous hours of Parliamentary sittings', and the precarious career prospects for the single woman were indicated as disincentive factors. 'One of the points which discourages single women from seeking a Parliamentary Career is the fact that there is a degree of uncertainty as we are all subject to the whims of the electors'. Another answer suggested 'being thrown out of a job at fifty'.

Opinions were asked on the role of women members of Parliament, whether women took an equal part with men in the work of the House of Commons. Nearly one hundred per cent on both sides were convinced, and in some cases vehement, that women took at least an equal part with men. The majority felt that women took a 'more than equal part'. There were only two answers which revealed reservations. From the Conservative side came the reply 'Yes, in Committee probably not in debate.'

Obviously this type of question is to some degree naive, in that it virtually invites a positive response. That such a response was by no means inevitable is proved in considering the next question. Comment was invited on a quotation to the effect that women have not shown, and do not show high qualities of leadership. This was the type of question which, in this context, virtually invites the disagreement i.e. the feminist-oriented answer. Yet the ultra-feminist approach was not universal, an indication of the honesty and thoughtfulness with which the questions were answered. The majority of replies on both sides stressed the small number of women who had been MPs, and said that they had little chance of showing their quality. About ten per cent, in almost equal numbers on each side, felt that while there had been a few outstanding women, the rest had been able but not brilliant. For example, on the Conservative side came the reply 'Yes, I see what she means. There have been very good women, but they have been lucky. Brilliant, but . . . ' In a sense, nearly all the answers sidetracked the question and answered more in terms of calibre and ability than leadership. The significance of this is difficult to evaluate.

An attempt was made to discover whether respondents saw women's contribution to national politics as a contribution oriented to women *qua* women, or in more general terms. In other words, those of Duverger, whether the contribution related to monovalence, a certain feminine specialisation, or to polyvalence.[11]

To within one percentage point equal numbers of both parties felt that a woman's contribution was the same as a man's. A further tiny group felt that women's contribution was the same as man's but that women had additional experience to use. As one Labour member phrased it, 'Apart from knowing more about housing, children, welfare, – naturally we know more – the same as men.' Two made the point that in addition to the general contribution, women can represent the views of over half the electorate. About one-third of each side accepted a limited view of women's political role, and specified a peculiarly feminine contribution to national level politics. There were two distinct facets to this 'womanly contribution' though some women mentioned both facets.

One group of answers focussed on distinctive qualities which they attributed to women – attention to detail, conscientiousness, bringing humanising qualities and common sense to their work, were the ones most often mentioned. These qualities were thought to colour the woman's approach to politics. From a young Labour member came the opinion, 'I always feel a woman is able to "put it over" to those who are less interested better than a man. She has the ability to seize on the essential details that matter . . . I think women are quicker on the uptake than men and they understand human problems. Perhaps they are less inhibited and can make better mixers than men and personal contacts.' Another of the same group believed that women's contribution lay in a '*feminine* concern in every field of politics', adding 'perhaps to retain our womanly qualities and to take them bang into the political whirlpool is the quality most required. It is fatal to ape men.' A second group of answers made reference to specific subjects, housewives' problems, widows' pensions, and all 'human problems', questions concerning child welfare, housing, etc., in which women had a particular knowledge and experience by virtue of their sex..

Asking the question on women's contribution based on what they *can* contribute was intended to allow opportunity for eliciting answers giving an 'ideal' or potential contribution; and a second, more factual question was asked, 'What are the subjects in which women tend to specialise?' with its own follow-up, asking why respondents thought this was so. On the topic of specialisation, approximately half on each side specified 'welfare subject' as those in which women found their specialism. Around fifteen percent of the Labour members and ten per cent of the Conservatives suggested the 'welfare' basis plus topics of individual choice. The Labour group was more likely to suggest a more general contribution, 'anything on which they have knowledge'. Around one-third of the Labour respondents made this type of point, compared with about thirteen per cent of Conservatives. From the Labour side came the answer, 'Prior to entering Parliament I would have said health, education. After observing my colleagues' activities in foreign affairs, Home Office activities etc. I am not so certain.'

Explanations chosen in support of the choice of specialism varies. Womanly qualities and sensitivity to human problems recur here, but there are other elements; one Labour member thought women specialised in welfare, but added 'they do so largely because it's expected of them. A Conservative member suggested, it is partly being jockeyed into it.' It is interesting that the opinions on specialisation and explanations propounded seem not to be associated with age grouping. It is not the case that the younger respondents more recently elected are more in favour of a general contribution. Opinions are associated neither with age group nor with date of entry.

Additional questions were asked, such as whether they considered there were women of the calibre for Cabinet rank, and whether they considered there were more of this calibre now than in the past. In the event these questions tended to probe a sensitive area, and response was not high. Over a long period comparisons tend to be unrealistic. With such problems the uneven and fairly randomly distributed answers could not be collated.

The attempt to draw up some outlines for a profile of the woman MP fortunately proved slightly more amenable to analysis. Asked what special qualities were needed for a successful MP, only one member on eah side answered that the qualities needed were the same ones which a male MP would need. One quarter of the Labour members, however, felt that no special qualities were needed.

Three main groups of answers can be isolated in the replies given by both sides. There appears to be no difference between the parties. Primarily, good health, stamina and energy were felt to be pre-requisite. The next group of answers suggested such qualities (applicable to either sex) as willingness to work hard, courage, perseverance and resilience. It is interesting that the 'womanly qualities' which run like a refrain through the other questions are only rarely mentioned here. Only one answer mentioned sympathy, and this was coupled with the additional 'and a hide like a rhinoceros'. The third major group of answers were related to some form of 'toughness' the 'ability to take knocks'. In context the answers suggested something much more than resilience.

In the sensitive area of the quality of toughness or suppression of femininity with which women in predominantly male preserves have sometimes been reproached, there was considerable consensus between the parties, though with differences in detail. Seventy per cent approximately of the total sample disagreed substantially with the proposition 'To get on in politics women have to be tough – unfeminine.' Only one on each side agreed with the judgement, reluctantly. The remainder declined to answer this question.

Answers disagreeing with the proposition tended to be emphatic, on the Conservative side two members castigated the proposition as ridiculously old fashioned. Within this general category of disagreement, there were answers which sought to interpret the question, by giving personal definitions. These were the respondents who felt that to be tough was not to be interpreted as unfeminine, but in terms of being firm, and decisive in a 'tough game'. In other words, 'tough' is completely dissociated from 'unfeminine'. For example, on the Labour side, came answers like 'intellectual toughness is necessary,' or 'not unfeminine, but politics is tough. Sometimes you have to be ruthless.' Another answer stated 'You have to be prepared to receive insults with dignity. There is no need to be unfeminine, though. You must fight with a sense of humour.'

Despite shortcomings of small numbers, the absence of sophisticated statistical techniques, and the fact of approaching those in the sample at a variety of stages in their political career and in their life cycle, one striking feature which may be claimed to emerge in this study is the degree of what may be called 'job satisfaction' which the respondents share. Respondents clearly enjoyed their work, the responsibilities, the status and the rewards. Enjoyment and satisfaction illuminated the response. And it is interesting that the degree of job satisfaction seems as relevant to those who said they were 'asked to stand' or 'had no ambition to be an MP', as to those who appear to have been more highly motivated. Two main components may be isolated in this complex of factors which make up the composite 'job satisfaction'. In part there is the human element, helping people, the enjoyment of being in demand, meeting interesting poeple. In part, the satisfaction appears to derive from the feeling of belonging to a high status decision-making body, expressed as 'you feel proud to be here'. Another part of the satisfaction appears to be related to being the occupant of a power-wielding position, being in a position to give effective help, affecting the drafting of legislation, making a department rectify a grievance. In a period when the powers of Parliament and in parlicular of the backbench Member are widely considered to have declined or be in decline, this power-oriented stance is the more interesting. At no point in any respondent's answers was there any reference to erosion of power.

The roots of human action are extensively explored by psychologists. Atkinson,[12] for example, writes, 'while not by any means exhausting the list of the springs of human action, hunger, achievement affiliation, power, sex, fear and aggression represents as comprehensive a list of the kinds of motivation studied by the same method as can be found anywhere in psychological literature.'

Affiliation (used here in the sense of the opposite of rejection and loneliness), and achievement, have already been shown to be relevant to the satisfaction felt by these women elected representatives. The power factor is also present, it may be argued, particularly if the definition and hypothesis of Veroff are applied to this material. Veroff's definition of the power motive[13] which 'is meant to include more than dominance' is relevant here. 'The power motive will be considered that disposition directing behaviour towards satisfactions contingent upon the control of the means of influencing other person(s). In the phenomenal sphere of the power-motivated individual he considers himself the 'gatekeeper' to certain decision-making of others.' Veroff's hypothesis seems to be amply supported in the material supplied by the MPs in relation to the enjoyment they derive from their work. 'Power motivation is positively related to the intensity of interests in the job satisfactions of being boss and being leader. These job satisfactions can be interpreted as positions in which the potentiality for controlling the means of influence is high.[14] It would seem then that of the human motivational forces which Atkinson listed, achievement, affiliation, power, and perhaps the context of some of the replies even justifies adding aggression, are all satisfied in the role of elected representative.

Lasswell has postulated a general hypothesis[15] that one of the main traits of the 'political personality' is the desire for power: the need to obtain deference and respect providing 'compensation' to the individual. 'Power', he says, 'is accentuated in personalities under certain conditions of motivation, skill and opportunity.'[16] While the material presented in this study cannot be used as evidence supporting this hypothesis, it does appear to be the case that the kind of power and power motivation to which Lasswell refers is one component of that satisfaction reported here by women respondents.

Enmeshed with the satisfactions experienced from their political role, is the absence of major dissatisfaction. MPs were asked what they found the least satisfying aspects of their work, and the vast majority or replies reported only the minor irritations.

Inherent in the satisfaction experienced from the work and position of an MP is an overt degree of self-confidence and self-satisfaction. This seems not to be associated with any one party. The sort of remark which was scattered throughout answers to questions or which occurred in general discussion, was illuminating. 'Those of us who survive are very good'; 'A woman has to be outstanding. There aren't many of us'; and the ubiquitous, 'A woman has to be twice as good as a man.'

Conclusions to this type of explanatory investigation are unlikely to be satisfactory except in so far as they point to further areas of research that need to be attempted. The last chapter of this study contains some indications of these areas, notably an analysis covering all elected representatives of either sex in a particular institution in order to determine whether women emerge as a coherent sub-group. Within such a large-scale investigation, one significant field to be investigated may be suggested from the material reported here, namely 'job satisfaction'.

Notes

1. e.g. 'Margaret Thatcher', *Observer*, 7 February 1971; 'Barbara Castle', *Observer* (Review), 28 September 1969.
2. S.E. Finer et al., *Backbench Opinion in the House of Commons*, 1955–59, London, 1961; H.B. Berrington, *Backbench Opinion in the House of Commons*, London, 1973; D. Leonard and V. Herman (eds.), *The Backbencher and Parliament*, London, 1972; R.J. Jackson, *Rebels and Whips*, London, 1968.
3. cf. L. Milbrath, 'Predispositions toward political contention', *Western Political Quarterly*, XII, March, 1960; J.D. Barber, *The Lawmakers*, New Haven, 1965.
4. On elite interviewing cf. R.M. Punnett, *Front Bench Opposition*, London, 1973, p.468ff.
5. cf. Chapter III.
6. Ross, analysing the occupations of MPs in the years from 1918–35 showed that 'pretty nearly one member in four is a lawyer by training if not in actual employment, and there are 200 times as many lawyers and 970 times as many barristers in the House as there are in the country, strength for strength'. In 1970, there were 23 Members whose main employment had been as lawyers, and ninety-three who had been practising as barristers (around one-fifth of the total members). This underestimates legal *qualifications*, however.
7. e.g. K. Kammeyer, 'Sibling position and the feminine role', *Journal*

of Marriage and the family, 29, 1967, 494–9.

8. Parliament sits from Monday to Thursday from 2.30 p.m. until (at least) 10.30 p.m., with a shorter timetable on Friday. In addition attendance at committees in the mornings, work in the constituency and in the party are time consuming. The Parliamentary recess, however, tends to coincide with school holidays. Parliament sits for about one hundred and fifty days per year.
9. An interesting investigation based on an extensive sample of state legislators and city council men in America attempted to probe how and when the legislators become interested in politics. The aim was to probe differences associated with pre-adult and adult socialisation. An interesting finding was that 'those politicised early recalled events and experiences that generally bespoke of personalised, dramatic, and diffuse socialisation experiences. Those socialised as adults were less personally involved. Pragmatism, specificity and casualness, accompanied their initial political introductions.' H. Eulau et al., 'Political socialisation and political roles', *Public Opinion Quarterly*, 30, 1966–7, pp.569–82.
10. Source, J. Mann (M.P. 1945–1959), *Woman in Parliament*, p.39. 'In the higher ranks of office, women MPs have not, in the past, shown high qualities of leadership. Nor do they today.'
11. M. Duverger, op.cit., p.126.
12. J.W. Atkinson, *Motives in Fantasy, Action and Society*, Princeton, 1958, p.45.
13. J. Veroff, in Atkinson, op.cit., p.106.
14. loc.cit., p.108.
15. cf. H.D. Lasswell, 'Power and Personality' in H. Eulau et al., (eds.), *Political Behaviour*, Glencoe, 1956, p.94.
16. op.cit., p.97.

Chapter 5 The Volunteers: Women as Prospective Parliamentary Candidates

Investigation of the activist political role of women is, of necessity, a study of only a minute fraction of the mass of the female population. Restricting the study to women MPs means that the investigation is limited to those women acceptable to the electorate: their final number is further modified by a complex of such factors as electoral swing, vagaries of the party machine, and luck. Such a limitation means also focussing on the established, on those who have acquired, or are in the process of acquiring, the identity and expertise of what is sometimes regarded as a proto-profession. One of the aims of this study as a whole is to assess the strength of this professionalism, and to find whether the demands made on women MPs, the image they must present, the type of work which they have in common, cut across the frontiers of party division.

The MP has survived two eliminating contests, that of the selection process and that by election: the prospective candidate has passed the first test only. As is clear in both Table I[1] and Figure 1, a basic reason for there being so few women in Parliament is that few women stand as candidates. To the extent of accepting nomination and facing a selection committee, prospective candidates are, in a sense, a self-selected group. Though there may be exceptions, this particular group has, in effect, identified with, and accepted a 'potential' role involving a degree of political activity far greater than that accepted by the vast majority of women.

1. *Selection Processes*

While, legally, there is nothing to prevent almost any adult, with one hundred and fifty pounds and with the support of ten like-minded friends, from standing for Parliament, in practice the situation is otherwise. Party endorsement is, in effect, the *sine qua non* of entry to Parliament. As Patterson has suggested, 'It would, therefore, seem that the paucity of women MPs is not attributable to the hostility of the electorate, whose deeply ingrained habit of voting for the party and not the person would probably not be radically altered by an increase in the number of women standing as candidates, but to the suspicions and reservations and prejudice of the selectorate.'[2] In an electoral system not based on any form of proportional representation, and in the

Figure 1 Women Candidates and Women Members of Parliament, 1918–1970 (absolute numbers)

absence of primary elections, it is the selection process, not the voter, which makes the choice between candidates of the same party. If, as can be established, roughly two-thirds of all parliamentary constituencies offer 'safe seats', then the majority of MPs is selected rather than elected, and moreover the selection process may be considered even more vital to the question of the representation of women in Parliament. Then the procedures of selection implemented by relatively few constituency activists are instrumental in determining the composition of the Parliamentary Party from which a Prime Minister selects his Cabinet.

In considering the selection process, essentially the focus here is on the two major parties only, and the Liberal Party and the two nationalist parties are excluded from this discussion. Penetrating the arcana of selection processes is clearly difficult. Indeed, it is only in the last few years that selection as such has received much scholarly attention.[3] Even so, it is still impossible to extract sufficient comparable quantifiable data to generalise on factors which contribute to one of the most crucial stages in the process, drawing up the short-list. Yet it is at this stage, it may be suspected, that any factors operative to the disadvantage fo women may be especially relevant. It is at this stage that a selection conference or committee may decide to interview no women, no men over fifty, etc.

These are not propositions amenable to empirical testing. There is, however, some supportive evidence to be adduced. Material collected in a local survey of councillors,[4] from talks with some local party officials at ward and constituency level, and from information gathered from the national survey gives some indication that women may tend to be more vulnerable than men at this level. Such indications, however, need to be evaluated with caution. The question of sex-discrimination, as indeed discrimination generally, lies in a highly sensitive area. Nevertheless, examples of attitudes supporting the contention of discrimination tend to persist over time. A few examples may be usefully cited here. In 1962, in an article headed 'Still a Man's World for Women Politicians', occurred the passage

> There is no doubt that in both the main parties . . . the most difficult hurdle for women is selection at constituency level. Nothing will ever remove from the thinking of party managers, high and low, the prejudice that any woman candidate starts with a vote discount against her; and all experience shows that usually active women workers in a constituency organisation share the prejudice and thereby give it most of its redoubted validity.[5]

Two years later, the writer of an article on women's political representation approached the two major parties to find 'why they had not adopted more women as candidates'. It was reported

> At the Conservative Central Office a spokesman deplored the fact and said that the reason lay with the constituency selection committees; women were finding it more difficult to be seen by them, let alone selected.
>
> Both the Central Office and the candidates themselves blame this on the older members of these committees. The younger ones are said to be far less biassed . . . The Labour Party, however, felt that there was little discrimination against their women. Their difficulty was, to find sufficient women to stand; they had virtually little reserve to call on, the reason being that many felt unable to offer themselves because of domestic or professional ties.[6]

Certainly the small number of women's candidatures is not due to lack of urging from the Central Party organisation. In 1963 the Selwyn Lloyd Report recommended that each Conservative Selection Committee should short-list one woman and one Trade Unionist. Two years later the Vice-Chairman of the same Party Organisation reiterated the appeal for more women MPs and candidates.[7] In November 1970, the National Agent of the Labour Party was reported as saying 'It would appear that women candidates have a stiffer fight to be selected than men', and was appealing to the rank and file of the party through constituency organisations to nominate more women and more factory workers as Parliamentary candidates. He was reported to be anxious to get more women nominated, and to have 'told the constituencies to give the women of the party greater opportunities, to encourage them in every possible way.'[8] Two years later, the National Labour Women's Advisory Committee set up a unit with the aim of bringing about the entry of more women into national and local politics. Its impact cannot be assessed as yet.

Detailed consideration of party selection procedures is out of place here.[9] A few comments, however, may usefully be made. The responsibility of choosing a parliamentary candidate is one of the most important functions of the constituency party. In both major parties, the selection of the candidate is the responsibility of a small number of constituency activists.[10] Essentially, constituency parties are autonomous with regard to the choice of candidate, and there is little difference between parties, except in so far as autonomy has tended to attract rather more emphasis on the Conservative side,and the Labour Party may have always tended to exert a little more central supervision.

Both parties accept more influence from the centre in by-elections.

The Conservative Central Office maintains a list of candidates, and there is a Vice-Chairman with special responsibility for candidates. Both parties retain a right of veto which is, however, invoked only very rarely. The Labour Party establishes two lists of candidates, one of Trade Union sponsored candidates, the other of those nominated but not financially sponsored. Trade Union sponsorship involves a substantial contribution to campaign expenses, thus relieving the constituency of what may be a serious financial burden. Women candidates tend to form only a very small percentage of the sponsored list,[11] which in practice tends to provide an introduction to the safer Labour seats. In the Conservative Party, since the Maxwell Fyfe reforms of 1948 the contribution that may be made to constituency funds by a candidate is limited to £25 per year, and by a member £50 per year. In this way, it has been suggested that women need not be at a financial disadvantage compared with men.

One factor which, it is suggested, is highly relevant to the recruitment of women candidates to the Labour interest may be indicated here. The Co-operative movement has provided an area of recruitment to which there seems no comparable counterpart for the Conservative Party. In part, this is related to the sponsorship of candidates by the Co-operative Party, for among these candidates is an admittedly small proportion of women. Of the women MPs elected in the Labour interest, fewer than one in ten have been sponsored by the Co-operative Party. But, it may be suggested the work of the Co-operative movement may be of equal if not greater importance in other levels of training and recruiting women political activists. The role of the Co-operative Women's Guild in providing educational courses, courses in public speaking, committee work, etc., and in promoting women's candidatures for local authorities, merits detailed investigation.

2. *Who are the Candidates?*

Who, then, are the women candidates, the potential recruits? Are there patterns to be found in the age, class, educational and occupational characteristics of women prospective candidates?

The type of material to be explored here in order to try to provide answers to these questions is related only to those women candidates who, at the time of the investigation, had never been previously elected. First, in terms of objective characteristics, a brief analysis is presented of those women candidates who have never sat in Parliament, at the General Elections of 1964, 1966 and 1970. The analysis is skeletal,

Table 8 Majorities Faced by Women Candidates, 1951–70[1]

Labour		Majorities Against				Majorities For					
		% <1000	% 1001–5000	% 5001–10,000	% >10,000	% <1,000	% 1001–5,000	% 5001–10,000	% >10,000	Total	N
1951	Members	5.9	5.9	5.9	0.0	11.8	17.6	35.3	17.6	100.0	(17)
	Others	13.0	13.0	39.2	34.8	0.0	0.0	0.0	0.0	100.0	(23)
	Total	10.0	10.0	25.0	20.0	5.0	7.5	5.0	7.5	100.0	(40)
1955[2]	Members	0.0	16.7	0.0	0.0	0.0	33.3	33.3	16.7	100.0	(6)
	Others	0.0	50.0	27.8	16.7	0.0	0.0	5.5	0.0	100.0	(18)
	Total	0.0	41.7	20.8	12.5	0.0	8.3	12.5	4.1	100.0	(24)
1959	Members	0.0	7.7	7.7	0.0	15.4	15.4	23.1	30.7	100.0	(13)
	Others	4.5	50.0	9.1	31.8	0.0	4.6	0.0	0.0	100.0	(22)
	Total	2.9	34.3	8.6	20.0	5.7	8.6	8.6	11.4	100.0	(35)
1964	Members	0.0	0.0	0.0	0.0	16.7	16.7	41.6	25.0	100.0	(12)
	Others	4.8	28.6	28.6	33.3	0.0	4.8	0.0	0.0	100.0	(21)
	Total	3.0	18.2	18.2	21.2	6.0	9.1	15.2	9.1	100.0	(33)
1966	Members	0.0	0.0	0.0	0.0	6.7	33.3	53.3	6.7	100.0	(15)
	Others	6.7	20.0	26.6	33.3	6.7	6.7	0.0	0.0	100.0	(15)
	Total	3.3	10.0	13.3	16.7	6.7	20.0	26.7	3.3	100.0	(30)
1970	Members	0.0	0.0	0.0	0.0	0.0	25.0	58.3	16.7	100.0	(12)
	Others	6.2	37.5	25.0	25.0	0.0	6.3	0.0	0.0	100.0	(16)
	Total	3.6	21.4	14.3	14.3	0.0	14.3	25.0	7.1	100.0	(28)

Conservative		Majorities Against				Majorities For					
		%	%	%	%	%	%	%	%	Total	N
		<1000	1001–5000	5001–10,000	>10,000	<1000	1001–5000	5000–10,000	>10,000		
1951	Members	0.0	0.0	14.3	0.0	14.3	0.0	71.4	0.0	100.0	(7)
	Others	0.0	5.6	33.3	61.1	0.0	0.0	0.0	0.0	100.0	(18)
	Total	0.0	4.0	28.0	44.0	4.0	0.0	20.0	0.0	100.0	(25)
1955[2]	Members	0.0	0.0	0.0	0.0	0.0	20.0	40.0	40.0	100.0	(5)
	Others	14.2	28.6	28.6	28.6	0.0	0.0	0.0	0.0	100.0	(14)
	Total	10.5	21.1	21.0	21.1	0.0	5.3	10.5	10.5	100.0	(19)
1959	Members	0.0	0.0	0.0	0.0	8.3	25.0	8.3	58.4	100.0	(12)
	Others	6.2	37.5	31.3	25.0	0.0	0.0	0.0	0.0	100.0	(16)
	Total	3.6	21.4	17.8	14.3	3.6	10.7	3.6	25.0	100.0	(28)
1964	Members	0.0	0.0	0.0	0.0	8.3	25.0	16.7	50.0	100.0	(12)
	Others	0.0	36.4	36.4	18.1	0.0	9.1	0.0	0.0	100.0	(11)
	Total	0.0	17.4	17.4	8.7	4.3	17.4	8.7	26.1	100.0	(23)
1966	Members	0.0	0.0	0.0	0.0	0.0	37.5	25.0	37.5	100.0	(8)
	Others	0.0	23.1	30.8	38.4	0.0	0.0	0.0	7.7	100.0	(13)
	Total	0.0	14.3	19.0	23.8	0.0	14.3	9.5	19.0	100.0	(21)
1970	Members	0.0	0.0	0.0	0.0	14.3	14.3	42.8	28.6	100.0	(7)
	Others	5.6	33.3	27.8	0.0	27.8	0.0	0.0	0.0	100.0	(18)
	Total	4.0	24.0	20.0	20.0	8.0	4.0	12.0	8.0	100.0	(25)

1. Sources: (i) 1951–66, Times, *House of Commons* for the relevant year, (ii) *Guide to the House of Commons,* 1970. 'Members' are those who have at any time sat in the House of Commons, and of these, the majority will be defending seats which they had held previous to the General Election. 'Others' are those who have never previously been elected. Majorities are those by which the seat was held at the previous General Election, or where applicable, a subsequent by-election.
2. Excluding candidates for constituencies subjected to major boundary revision.

without reference to opinions or attitudes. Secondly, in order to establish whether there have been any discernible changes (over approximately a decade), in the orientations of women candidates to the role of women in politics, an attempt was made in 1972–3 to replicate a survey of women candidates which was made in 1964.

The material to be used in the first part of this work is clearly not ideal, since the sources tend to be somewhat uneven in quality and degree of detail. In addition, the numbers involved are too small for sophisticated statistical analysis or the empirical validation of generalisations. Nevertheless, this part of the study provides some interesting indicators, which may be valuable in comparison with other data presented in the second part of this study of candidates, and provides a framework within which this second stage study may be interpreted.

Basic to any case for discrimination at selection level is the belief that women candidates are usually relegated to seats with a sizeable adverse majority, the 'hopeless seats'. Table 8 traces the situation which women have faced since 1951 as sitting members and as cadidates who have never been previously elected.

The initial distinction between these two groups of the elected and the 'potentials' is considerable. Clearly those who have achieved election and proved themselves have, for the most part, relatively safe seats. Time is obviously a factor here. From 1951 onwards an increasing percentage of Labour women sitting members have had safe seats, with a majority in excess of five thousand, and a substantial, though varying percentage in excess of ten thousand. Among the Conservatives, also, a growing percentage of sitting members have had majorities of over five thousand, and of over ten thousand.

Of Labour 'new' candidates only a very small proportion in the elections from 1955 onwards have had majorities in their favour. The proportion of those with 'hopeless seats' (arbitrarily defined as an adverse majority of ten thousand or more) has varied from around one-third, to a 'low' of a little under twenty per cent. Among the Conservatives, the solitary 'other' candidate with a majority of over ten thousand in her favour in the 1966 General Election followed a woman MP of her party who had held the seat for thirteen years until her sudden death. In 1970, unlike earlier elections, just over one-quarter of those never previously elected had a favourable majority, though of under one thousand. With fluctuations, there seems to be some evidence for a decline in the proportion of 'other' Conservative candidates who have to face adverse majorities in excess of five thousand. In 1951 nine out of ten 'other' candidates faced this situation. In 1966, the proportion was around two-thirds, and in 1970 the figure had decreased to a little under thirty per cent.

The majorities faced by women candidates over a period of around twenty years have been considered as a preliminary to a focus on the characteristics of women candidates in the last three General Elections.

Age structure for candidates at the three elections shows little stable patterning by pattern. The Labour Party has been slightly more likely to adopt a woman under thirty, but if the division is made at forty, then more Conservatives than Labour candidates have been adopted before the age of forty. It is now extremely unusual in either party for a candidate to be over sixty.

The question of age is likely to be linked, in part at least, to the number of contests that have been attempted. In 1964, just under 40 per cent of the Labour candidates and a little under one-third of the Conservatives were standing for the first time. In contrast two candidates on each side were making their fifth attempt. The oldest candidate on the Labour side, interestingly, had made her previous four attempts between 1923–9. The earliest attempt of a Conservative candidate was made in 1950. In the 1966 and 1970 elections the majority of candidatures were first, second or third attempts.

One change which is becoming clear over this period is the decline in the proportion of candidates who are or have been married. In 1964, the vast majority of candidates were married, a slightly higher proportion on the Labour side. In 1966 all but one of the Labour candidates had been married at the time of the campaign. In contrast roughly half of the Conservatives were single. This pattern of a higher proportion of married women, widows or divorcees among Labour candidates persisted, but in both parties the unmarried element has risen, so that in 1970, of the candidates who had never sat in Parliament, 59 per cent of the Conservatives and just under 40 per cent of the Labour side were unmarried.

The development is an interesting one, but not easily amenable to explanation, except that the trend is a reflection of the recruitment as candidates of young professional career women. Impressionistically, from the surveys of candidates it seems that the career of MPs *may* be beginning to be perceived as one proto-professional career among many, as a vehicle for individual abilities.

It is of course almost a sociological commonplace that the class composition of the elite of an organisation tends to be higher than that of the mass of the membership. This study of women candidates provides no contrary evidence. Using the criterion of the candidate's occupation this pattern becomes clear. Where a candidate has held several positions, an attempt is made to find the main career occupation of the candidate concerned. In 1966 of those whose main occupations could be accurately established, nearly eight in ten of the Labour side and about nine out of ten of the Conservatives had followed 'middle-class' occupations.[12] At the following General Election, all the Conservative candidates had held this type of occupation, while on the Labour side only one candidate had held a manual semi-skilled job before her marriage. For all the others for whom adequate information was available (all but two in either party) a middle-class occupation was recorded.

The middle-class occupational distribution is paralleled by the high educational qualifications of the candidates, which are unrepresentative in comparison with those of the general population.[13] In this the candidates resemble the women MPs whose level of education in general continues to be exceedingly high. There is in the candidates a decided tendency for there to be more graduates among the Labour group than the Conservative group, which holds good over time. The range for Labour was of the order of four in ten in 1964 but approximately six in ten in 1970. The latter proportion does not include one undergraduate and one candidate with a University diploma qualification. The comparable range for the Conservatives began in 1964 with a similar one in four proportion, but in 1970 the percentage of graduates was thirty-five per cent, a slight decrease from the previous General Election. The non-graduates appear to be fairly randomly distributed between various kinds of school, and types of training undertaken, such that no pattern emerges by party.

The significance of pre-Parliamentary experience in what has been termed the communication type of occupation has been shown in the case of women MPs, to be somewhat more important for Labour members than for Conservatives. Both the general importance and the party distribution hold good for candidates also. In 1964 half of the candidates had followed a communication-type occupation, with Conservatives at a level around ten per cent. A similar pattern holds good for 1966 and 1970. In the latter year, while Labour were again at the fifty per cent level, the figure for Conservatives was again around the fifteen per cent level.

Pre-adoption experience in other than occupational fields reveals no very clear division by party. Experience in local authority work of any level seemed exceptionally high in 1966 (when around two-thirds of both parties had served as councillors). In 1970, however, the figure was reduced to around one-third for Labour and about one-half for the Conservatives. Material available for voluntary activity and office holding within the party organisation is not sufficiently comprehensive to warrant firm conclusions. The evidence that is available, however, seems to point to some variation by party alignment, with voluntary work somewhat more prominent in the backgrounds of the Conservatives, and party activity rather more important among the Labour candidates.

3. *Women Parliamentary Candidates, 1964 and 1973*

Candidates, as has already been suggested, are identifying with and aspiring to a political role involving a degree of political activism unusual by the standards of their sex. It might be expected, then, that to an extent at least, the attitudes, opinions and evaluations of candidates would resemble those of the elected women representatives. It might be expected also that as women's role has been changing over time, so attitudes to women's political role might change also.

First, a reservation which runs through this work must be reiterated, namely that selecting a sample of women, asking them questions related to women and to themselves *as* women, must predetermine, at least to some degree, the orientation of their answers. That this direction appears to be minimal would seem to testify to the integrity with which the questionnaires were completed by the respondents.

The empirical work which attempts to test these hypotheses has as its base a study of women candidates (never previously elected) in 1964, with a similar study for comparative purposes in 1973. Because for each year the candidates were contacted well in advance of the General Election for which they were adopted, there is a discrepancy between the number of candidates ultimately adopted and the number of women candidates in the sample. This is a severe limitation on the material presented here, particularly since the Conservative group is very small in both 1964 and 1973. This imbalance need not be an insuperable limitation provided that the material is interpreted with this reservation. In effect, the Labour Party candidates in 1964 and 1973 are compared; with additional comparisons made with two small groups of Conservatives in the same years.

Details of the survey are in Appendix II. The questionnaire elicited both the objective characteristics of the candidates in addition to concentrating on the primary emphasis of perceptions, attitudes, and evaluations of the respondents. It is not claimed that the representativeness of the respondents to these two enquiries may be statistically proved. When, however, the characteristics of the 1964 sample of the respondents are compared with the characteristics of the total women candidates of that year, and the 1973 sample is compared with 1970 candidates, on all the indices such as education, class, occupation and pre-adoption experience, there are no major discrepancies between the samples and the total groups.

One of the interesting features of national level analysis of both men and women in the political elite over time is the evidence to be found of the incidence of political precedents and of the politicised family.[14] Political activity in this sense is defined at a fairly high level, including elected representatives, and excluding such answers as 'my parents were on committees' or 'always interested' though these activities might contribute to a child's political information and interest. In 1964, of the Labour group just under forty per cent reported a history of political or public work activity, including a respondent whose mother had been a Clarionist, and one whose grandfathers had been active respectively in the Fenian movement and in the Miners' Union. Other respondents mention a mother who was an MP,[15] and a mother active in the Co-operative Movement. The Conservatives reported an uncle who was an MP and a father a Parliamentary candidate, but the remaining references pointed to public work generally, rather than strictly party political activity. Of the 1973 candidates, family precedence to either public or public life may be traced in about half of the Labour and Conservative cases. But when the incidence of the 'politicised family' is sought, examples appear to be far fewer. One Conservative respondent was the daughter of a Commonwealth Minister of State. Among the Labour candidates, one was the daughter of a former Cabinet Minister, and four others reported a parental activity in party politics and in local government. Evidence of the politicised family may be therefore seen in nearly forty per cent of the Conservatives, and around one-third of the Labour respondents, in 1973.

Is there evidence of the politicised family in the families which these candidates are themselves founding? Of the respondents who were married in 1964, only around one-third of the Conservatives were married to a politically activist husband, whereas on the Labour side around four-fifths were married to men who were themselves involved in politics, three of whom were also prospective parliamentary candidates. In 1973, the party alignment had changed, so that only two Labour candidates of those who were married reported a politically active husband, in both cases candidates. The remaining Labour married respondents reported supportive activities and interest, rather than activism. On the Conservative side one husband was a parliamentary candidate, of the remaining married respondents, supportive activities, encouragement, etc., were reported.

In considering these aspirants to Parliament, this proto-elite, one of the more significant cluster of questions which demand answers lie in the area broadly termed 'motivation'. It is unrealistic to maintain that motivations may somehow be elicited by a relatively brief postal questionnaire. An adequate investigation of motivation requires sophisticated psychological techniques. What follows here is then, merely the examination of the answers to the simple question: 'Looking back, what sort of reasons prompted you to seek election to Parliament?' The answers may at least provide some indication of attitudes to and expectations of possible entry into the political elite. Similarly, the answers may provide some sidelights on the question of 'seriousness of intention'. This topic is clearly difficult to probe. A direct question on such a topic was not included on the questionnaire, since it seemed unlikely to provide adequate and acceptable data, when party loyalty might consciously or unconsciously induce respondents to be over-optimistic in assessing their chance of success.

It is interesting, however, that there are references relevant to this topic in replies to the question quoted above. In the sample of 1964, in the Labour group nearly seventy per cent of the candidates faced adverse majorities in excess of five thousand: in 1973 just under half faced such odds. The comparison cannot be made for the Conservatives over time, because several of the 1973 Conservative respondents returned their questionnaires anonymously. Even so, it remains clear that for a significant proportion of all respondents, questions using terms like 'entry into the political elite' are irrelevant, when in 1964 the adverse majorities included one of seventeen thousand and another of twenty-seven thousand, and in 1973 there were two of fourteen thousand and one of twenty-six thousand. In other words, there is in these figures the implicit question of how many of these women candidates are seriously expecting or wanting to begin a career in the Commons from the result of the forthcoming election. Before looking at this question, however, there must first be excluded a quite different category of candidates who will fight the election to gain experience and to become known,[16] intending to nurse the constituency to success or to obtain a constituency with more hope of success.

Two replies illustrate the distinction. In 1964 a Labour candidate began her answer 'For MP read candidate', and continued 'to put forward a socialist point of view in this rural constituency where there is no one else with the ability and freedom to do so.' In 1973 an answer from a Labour respondent again read concisely: 'Was asked. Had intended to wait until the next time around because of the children, but this constituency is not only unwinnable but one mile away. Good training for a more serious run next time, I hope.' Replies relevant to this point came in various forms from 'was asked to stand', to 'a flagging local party desperate for a young local candidate', and 'I didn't seek it at all. I was asked if I'd be willing . . . I had no reason to say no.' Certainly these answers seem to offer irrefutable testimony to the honesty with which these questionnaires were completed. With such a small proportion of respondents mentioning this kind of factor over time, any conclusions on differences by party is likely to be meaningless.

The question of how far candidates are seeking entry to Parliament, or how far they recognise the candidacy as an end in itself, 'showing the flag for the party' as one respondent put it, is a complex one. The report of a survey[17] conducted after the 1966 election pointed out that no theory of power-seeking can explain why hundreds of people fight elections as Liberals, when in about nineteen out of twenty cases they are bound to lose. Significantly, this report revealed the importance of campaigning as an end in itself. With these considerations in mind, the reasons respondents gave for seeking to enter Parliament may be examined.

In the Labour group, the most frequently quoted reason for seeking election (as qualified by the discussion above) was the desire to promote the interest of their own party (given by fifty per cent of Labour respondents in 1964 and by around ten per cent fewer in 1973). As each respondent could cite several or in some cases many reasons, the percentages quoted will not add up to one hundred for the total answers to this question.

It is interesting that in the 1964 group the majority in this category had reasons for wanting to promote a Labour viewpoint which were rooted in their own life experience, e.g. of difficult conditions during their childhood. By 1973, answers in this category were not of the personally-based type, but couched in much more general terms. Such replies included 'Strong wish that left-wing ideas should be better represented in Parliament.' 'I want to join with others in promoting socialism in the place where it matters.' The answers may be general in the sense of not relating directly to personal background, but they are sometimes specific in the sense of seeking a more representative Parliamentary Labour Party, as may be seen from the left-wing example already quoted and the other answers mentioning this kind of approach. A further small proportion of around ten per cent were giving answers akin to this category, when they mentioned the desire to be 'as close as possible to the decision-making institutions', again in the party interest.

Around one-third of the Labour respondents in 1964 but less than one-fifth in the later survey wrote of their interest in politics. A typical answer was 'with a serious interest in politics, elective office is the logical conclusion'. A much higher proportion (one-half) of Conservatives in 1973 than of Labour gave interest in politics as a reason for standing for Parliament, though in 1964 the proportion of both the Labour and Conservative groups had been exactly the same. Promotion of party interests and policy was at a much lower level in both years for Conservatives than for the Labour group.

In view of the whole tenor of the questionnaire, it is interesting that in the 1964 survey, no Labour or Conservative respondent mentioned as a reason for seeking election their belief that more women MPs were needed. In 1973, however, on the Labour side only, twenty-seven per cent of respondents gave as a reason for their candidature that 'the female voter is ill-represented', or referred to 'the minute members of women in Parliament and in particular, even smaller numbers who are married, have children'. Another wrote, 'I believe society and politics have no right to repress me and my sister Party members into being the tea-makers and not the policy makers of the Party.'

Another interesting development in the 1973 survey lies in the group of answers (given by just over one-fifth of the Labour respondents and five of the eight Conservatives), which refers to the respondent's personal qualities and abilities which she considers would be valuable in the national political arena. To some extent, then, these answers approach the boundaries of the category already indicated, that of personal involvement in decision-making in order to promote particular programmes. To an extent, also, they approach the boundaries of a category again only evident in 1973, that of dissatisfaction with the present performance of the decision-making process. Yet the 'personal abilities and contribution' category of answers is qualitatively and subtly different from these other orientations, in that they are explicit statements of a confidence in a high valuation of the respondents' own potential contribution. Typical of answers of this kind are 'a feeling that I have experience and ideas which could and should be used', 'My belief that Parliament was the best vehicle for my abilities', or 'My inherent talent'.

To continue to trace women candidates' path to the status of

Prospective Parliamentary Candidate, and at the same time gather information on the selection process, questions were asked about experience at the selection stage. The whole process of selection is, as has been pointed out, not easily amenable to quantitative analysis. Material that is available from participants, in any capacity, may be limited, partial, subject to the vagaries of memory, or unconsciously biased. In addition it is not possible to obtain comprehensive data on the work of selection bodies with which to balance or validate this survey material. With such reservations, the question was asked whether the candidates had encountered advantages or disadvantages during selection from the fact of being a woman.

Across the board of party and time, the most common perception of the selection process was of the process involving both disadvantages and advantages. This category was much larger for the Labour group in 1964 than nine years later (sixty-three per cent compared with around thirty per cent). For the Conservatives the percentage was stable at about forty per cent for both years. Essentially those giving this type of answer referred on the one hand to a woman being 'different', 'more easily remembered', 'the advantage of novelty', and on the other to 'hide-bound traditional selections', and 'decisions based on wifely duties and risks of pregnancy'.

It is interesting that the 1973 Labour respondents, considering they had experienced both advantages and disadvantages, tended to refer to the encouragement from the centre to produce more women as candidates. The distinction that was made by this group of respondents, distinguished between the various levels of selection. A lengthy answer of this kind reads,

> In the early stages it is a distinct disadvantage and difficult to get a nomination because women are thought of as not being strong enough candidates and trade union branches are discriminatory. After nomination and in the lobbying process a woman is disadvantaged because she cannot meet the majority of selection voters (men) on their own ground . . . It is at this early stage where women have the advantage of meeting the largest number of selection conference voters in a semi-social way and it is at this stage where votes are often committed to an individual candidate. A woman is at an advantage when it comes to shortlisting because most parties think they must be 'seen' to give opportunities to women and they must at least have a woman shortlisted. At a selection conference she has a great advantage because she is distinguished by being different. With any personality or speaking ability she immediately commands

interest: what she says is remembered . . .

A few respondents, on both sides and at both survey years reported that they had experienced neither disadvantage nor advantage. Disadvantages only were perceived by around one-quarter of both groups of Labour respondents, but by a decreasing proportion of Conservatives over time. The disadvantages were in similar terms to those mentioned in the rather ambivalent answers quoted above. Advantages only were only a tiny percentage in any year, the maximum being only around ten per cent.

In evaluating the answers which have been given, a few points may be made. If there is prejudice against women in some areas, the contrary may well be true in others. Women's organisations, for example, are unlikely to nominate a male candidate. Then the question of women's support for women is also relevant. Prejudice against women may not be solely the prerogative of the male sex. If more women become party officers, and more are included in selection conferences and committees, this need not necessarily mean an increase in the number of women selected.

Going back to the earliest stages of seeking candidature, it seems clear that the hurdle of becoming short-listed ina constituency is not the most difficult the intending candidate has to surmount. Around eighty per cent of the respondents in both parties and in both years were short-listed at their first attempt. This high percentage, has however to be considered in relation to the 'safeness' of the seats for which they were short-listed.

Respondents were asked what kind of support, if any, they had received from women's organisations. In the answers there is no pattern by party or by year. The range of replies is considerable, from 'nil', 'no support', or 'practically none' to those reporting enthusiastic support. The answers to a further question about support and assistance in candidatures were also apparently unrelated to any variable such as the year of the survey or the party of the candidate. An assertion of the late Mrs. Jean Mann MP was quoted to the effect that like most women in public life she owed all the positions she occupied to men – they pushed her into it from the start. The question was then asked whether this pattern would have been true in the respondent's case. The majority of respondents gave negative answers, though the answers were often qualified in some way, with a stress on the personal qualities and determination of the candidate herself.

A major section of this study was devoted to exploring the perceptions of these highly selective groups of women with regard to the political role of women. To this end candidates were asked what in their opinion were the reasons for there being so few women in Parliament. Once again many respondents gave several factors in their replies, so that the percentages which are referred to in discussion will not total one hundred for each party.

In 1964 as in 1973 the reason most frequently suggested by either party is part of the cluster of factors associated with home and family commitments. The proportions giving these answers varied by party such that this reason was mentioned more frequently by the Conservatives in both years (eighty-six per cent and sixty per cent compared with Labour's sixty-two and forty-five per cent for 1964 and 1973, respectively. Included in this category are answers indicating disadvantages for women 'the wife of a male candidate helps' . . . 'very difficult to combine parliamentary work with a family', 'mainly domestic problems', 'inconvenient Parliamentary hours'.

One shift in evaluation which is discernible over time in these answers on both sides is extremely interesting but not easily quantifiable. In 1964 the answers referred to women's traditional generic role as limiting her activities outside the home and, therefore, in the political elite. In some of this category of answer in 1973, respondents were indicating that women were *considered* to have limitations arising from their sex. One such answer reads: 'The fact that family care is *deemed* to be the woman's job, and few husbands participate in it sufficiently to make heavy political commitment practicable for a wife. (Mine did).' Another respondent suggests '*too many constraints both real and psychological*', and from a Labour candidate the answer was given 'they're too interested in cooking their husband's supper and bringing their children up – they need liberating from themselves.' From a young Labour candidate in 1973 came the answer 'the risk that those selecting often feel that they are taking with a woman.' A Conservative wrote, 'some women expect to suffer prejudice against them by selection committees.'

The latter quotation is linked with a factor which is mentioned by a proportion of women in both parties in 1973 only (around thirty per cent of the Labour group and twenty per cent of the Conservatives). The reference here is 'the social structure', or 'social conditions applicable to women's political role', and also 'general conditioning which is that men are the decision-makers, men are concerned with the outside world and women with the inside.'

Prejudice against women as a reason for the small element of representation of women in Parliament is seen as declining over time, from around two-thirds of both parties in 1964 to less than half of the Labour group in 1973, and around one-quarter of the Conservatives at this time. Terminology has changed also. The prejudice of 1964 has given way to the fashionable term discrimination in 1973.

Women's qualities and abilities no longer seem to be considered a negative factor. The only evidence of such negative evaluation is in comments that women tend to be reluctant to 'push themselves forward', but this is of minimal importance in the later survey.

In 1964 when the question was asked (somewhat superfluously within the context of this kind of questionnaire) whether respondents felt that there should be increased numbers of women in Parliament, overwhelmingly (a little under ninety per cent) both parties were in favour of a higher proportion of women. In 1973, as might be expected, this question evoked a qualitatively and quantitatively different response. Around half of the respondents of both parties agreed that the numbers of women should be increased and suggested, in the follow-up question, practical methods of achieving this, such as interesting women in local government, promoting educationally relevant courses, etc. The remaining respondents, however, answered the question either in terms of wanting no 'artificial' inflation of women's representation, but qualified members of either sex, or in radical terms looking towards changed social structure and social attitudes which would affect women's role generally. The latter group were specific in being against any form of discrimination in women's favour. In some of the latter answers there appeared to be echoes of the vocabulary of women's liberation.

In order to probe attitudes to women's political role more deeply, an additional question was inserted in the 1973 study which asked whether respondents thought that there was an optimum proportion of women in Parliament. Not unexpectedly the reaction elicited by this question was mixed, and the question was castigated by one respondent as chauvinist. Unfortunately the question appeared to be misunderstood by some respondents. Taking the usable answers, there were two main orientations roughly divided equally between the parties. One group (around forty per cent) maintained that Parliament should reflect in its membership the sex profile of the population at large. A slightly smaller proportion considered that ability not gender should be the criterion, and felt that over time a reasonable balance would be achieved between the sexes.

A further question was asked: what respondents considered women could contribute to political life nationally. The wording of the question suggested a 'specific' female contribution. It is then the more significant that in 1964 around one-half of the Labour respondents and one-third of the Conservatives rejected a sex-determined contribution for women. They expressed clearly (occasionally vehemently) the view that women's contribution to national level should be as human beings not as women. These answers were linked with rejection of a limited, feminine 'welfare' role for women. 'Women should regard politics as broadly as men and not feel obliged to limit themselves to welfare topics.'

In 1964 the proportion expressing the view that women should contribute as individuals were virtually identical in size and party distribution (at around sixty per cent). 'No more and no less than a man', 'sex is irrelevant', is typical of this type of answer. Yet this type of answer was modified by an interesting addendum from around one in four of the Labour respondents who primarily gave this 'general', 'equal' answer. This interesting small group proposed a women's contribution that is the same as men's, but with a different perspective, inherent in women, or arising from a different life experience. An example that illustrates this essentially ambivalent approach is 'Everything that men can contribute, plus tolerance, commonsense, efficiency, loyalty, sweetness of temper and voice' . . .

Women's qualities, the qualities inherent in the sex, were cited by around twenty-five per cent of the respondents of both parties in 1964. In 1973, women's qualities and 'special' experience were mentioned by most of the Conservatives but by only around one-fifth of the Labour group. This kind of orientation may be implicit in the reply 'Though I do not believe that there are purely "women's subjects", I think that the biological differences between men and women cause them to react in accord with their normal drives in fundamentally varied ways. The woman's contribution in politics is to balance the male influence and to add a harmonising voice to discussions on matters of vital importance to the whole of society.'

The surveys reported here have tended to raise further questions, rather than to provide conclusive answers. Some indications of change have been pointed out in the perceptions of these candidates of the role of women in the political elite. The main point that has to be stressed is that these are indications, pointers only, not empirically established trends. The main conclusion to this study, therefore, is that more empirical research in depth needs to be taken over time.

Notes

1. See above p.24.
2. P. Paterson, *The Selectorate*, London, 1967, p.45 ff.
3. cf. P. Paterson, op. cit.; A. Rannay, *Pathways to Parliament*, London, 1965; M. Rush, *The Selection of Parliamentary Candidates*, London, 1969.
4. cf. M.E. Currell, unpublished Ph D. thesis, University of Birmingham, 1965, Chapter 6.
5. *The Times*, 28 May 1962.
6. loc. cit., 12 September 1964.
7. Central Press Office Release, 9801, 10 December 1965.
8. *The Times*, 11 November 1970. Some indications of a change in attitudes towards women were reported in the 1973 study of women Labour candidates.
9. For a major study of selection processes, cf. M. Rush, op. cit.
10. In the Conservative Party the final choice of candidate is presented for what tends to be formal approval to the members' meeting in the constituency. On one occasion, at least, this has led to a rejection of the candidate, and his replacement. cf. Appendix Three.
11. cf. M. Rush, op. cit., p.222. In 1945 Trade Union members made up 30 per cent of Labour MPs. After the 1970 election the proportion was 39 per cent. Women MPs who have been sponsored by Trade Unions include Mrs. R. Short (TGWU).
12. For details of the method of class allocations used cf.above, p.71, n.8.
13. On the Labour side, more graduate candidates had attended the London School of Economics (either as undergraduates or postgraduates) than any other University.
14. The question was asked: 'Are you the first in your family to be active in politics or in public life, locally or nationally?' Details of the relationship to the respondent, the positions held, and approximate dates, were also requested.
15. Interestingly enough, reference sources revealed that one candidate was the daughter of a Labour Party leader at national level. In the completed questionnaire no mention was made of this background, but whether an accidental omission was made is not known.
16. cf. for example the career patterns of Mrs. Shirley Williams, successful in her fourth contest, or from the Conservative side, Mrs. Elaine Kellett, who entered Parliament at her sixth attempt.
17. D. Kavanagh, *Constituency Electioneering*, London, 1970.

Chapter 6 Women's Liberation

The tenor of this study as a whole probably makes the inclusion of a section on Women's Liberation seem a somewhat unexpected, indeed unlikely, addendum. The main question to be posed, then, is in what sense can this amorphous inchoate mass of disparate groups, currents of thought, and tendencies, popularly termed 'movement', come within the purview of a study focussed on the political role of women?

Can the activities of Women's Liberation adherents be construed as political activities? The answer hinges on the meaning attached to 'political' about which there is hardly consensus among commentators. Yet if certain criteria are adopted for defining the political, then Women's Liberation may be seen as a politically as well as socially oriented movement. The criterion, crudely expressed in the phrase that 'politics has to do with power'[1] certainly fits in with the notion that 'liberating' women implies more than change on a personal individual level (though this is included), but rather involves the reallocation and reconstitution of the elements of a society's power structure. Even within this 'power category' there are several variations in approach. At what may be termed the macro-level, there is the theme of world societies being based ultimately on the power and dominance of men and the subordination of women. In contrast, Kate Millett's thesis seems to draw together both macro- and micro-levels, when she views the relationship between the sexes as a continuing power struggle, with women at times idolised, patronised, but 'always with the basic element of their exploitation'.[2] David Easton's perspective of politics as involving the 'authoritative allocation of values in a society'[3] is highly relevant to categorising Women's Liberation. The reconstitution of social values is, as will be seen, a fundamental aim among a sizeable proportion of the adherents of the movement.

1. *The British Experience*

The genesis of the British form of Women's Liberation may be traced to the United States. Its ideas began to reach Britain in the late 1960s.[4] In considering origins, various foci may be isolated, ranging from the strike of women machinists at the Ford works at Dagenham, the Wives' Campaign (based on Hull) to achieve higher safety standards for trawlermen, the coalescence of various left-wing groups to found the publication *Socialist Woman*. As women's groups began to proliferate, some based on Universities, some smaller, linked to locality, terms such as 'rap group', 'consciousness-raising', 'male chauvinism' began to gain currency in the literature. The year 1970 saw a conference of some five hundred activists of the many disparate groups and quasi-organisations which were, in a very loose way, beginning to move in a somewhat similar direction. Despite the rather ironical reception from the press it is from this time in Britain that the movement as such dates.

Because of the diversity of the groups involved, it is somewhat unrealistic to discuss 'the aims of the Movement', as if there were uniformity and consistency of approach. What may be said is that the short-term objectives of the majority of the groups tend to include some or all of the following four points: equal pay, equal educational opportunity, free abortion and contraception on demand, and the availability of nursery and day-care provision for children.

The range of groups which may be considered as part of Women's Liberation runs from revolutionary-left organisations (of various complexions, semi-Trotskyist groups, Maoists) to groups, mainly of middle-class membership, whose immediate aim is obtaining entry for women into the higher levels of a specific occupational structure.[5] The contradictions and ambiguities of the Women's Liberation Movement are many, but the situation becomes slightly more clear if two themes are kept analytically distinct. At the one level, 'consciousness-raising' (to be engendered by such devices as the 'rap-group' with a deliberate avoidance of leadership positions) means that the committed individual is intended to acquire a changed perception of herself, her problems, and her place in society. In this way, it is suggested, the personal problem and the personal perspective becomes transmuted into a social and political issue. From this derives, therefore, the second theme, that the movement aims at a societal reconstruction.

The very diversity of the range of groups and their disappearance or coalescence with other groups, makes the total membership difficult to determine, however roughly. The difficulty is intensified since today, virtually every and any effort not only to change but even to comment on the status of women tends rapidly to acquire the 'Women's Lib' label. Size, therefore, remains speculative, and probably at any time would not exceed around four or five thousand adherents. For the women's suffrage movement at the beginning of this century the comparable figure was probably around two or three hundred thousand. Similarly, attempts at considering the class composition of the movement are hazardous. On the whole, though, it may be suggested that whereas there seems sufficient evidence of the substantially middle-class composition of the American movement, there may be a larger working-class element in its British counterpart. This may be seen in the setting up of the National Joint Action Committee for Women's Rights, a Trade Union inspired organisation, which was, however, short-lived.

2. *Conceptualisation of the Women's Liberation Movement*

How is the Women's Liberation orientation to be distinguished from the long line of organisations and associations which have, over time, sought to amend the status of women? There seems no easy solution.

It must be stressed that any discussion of the various conceptualisations that may be applied to Women's Liberation in Britain cannot be confined merely to the experience and literature of Britain. Much of the literature and theoretical discussion which has been influential in this country has originated in the American Movement.

Another major qualifying factor that has to be considered in all analysis on this subject is that it is perhaps too early to attempt a final classification of the agglomeration of associations, groups and workshops which have been in existence, often a fitful, flickering existence, for hardly a decade. Such conceptualisations as may be tested are by no means discrete, but rather may be seen as outlining the dimensions, often 'intersecting' dimensions. A second qualifying factor is that it is not all moves towards change in women's status that are channelled into Women's Liberation. Women's Liberation is, then, not the sole institutionalised expression of women's aspirations in the 1960s and '70s. It exists at the same time as many other sex-specific organisations and associations: the proliferation is considerable. For example, the women's groups which send representatives to the government-sponsored Woman's National Commission include those with educational aims, professional[6] and religious groups, but not those groups whose primary object is the extension of women's rights. Women's Liberation then is *one* expression of the response of women to their situation, whether societal, economic or occupational.

An immediately obvious conceptualisation is the classification of Women's Liberation as a lineal descendant of the suffragettes, as the latest manifestation in the long tradition of feminism. Yet the choice of a feminist classification for the movement raises as many problems as it solves. First, the concept of feminism is a protean one, and one which tends to be used frequently in confused and ambiguous ways. The word is used indifferently to mean both the teaching and ideologies developed concerning women's status *vis-à-vis* men, and in another sense, feminism is used to connote the organised efforts to implement such doctrines. A third, popular meaning, often with a somewhat pejorative connotation is that of intensely held views, the deep commitment to the 'rights of women' which are often sources of ridicule. Then the conceptualisation of neofeminism suffers because, until recently, with one notable exception,[7] first wave feminism (in the first two senses of the term) of the nineteenth and early twentieth century gained more attention from historians than from sociologists. Indeed it seems to be the focus of the literature on Women's Liberation which seems to be responsible for the intensification of interest in feminism and more specifically in the activity of the suffragettes.

Within the conceptualisation of Women's Liberation as neofeminist, there is room for much variety of approach. The first dichotomy which seems to run through much discussion on this point is that between reformist and revolutionary perspectives. Whereas the goals may be similar, the means employed to achieve them vary. On the reformist side the identifying feature is the belief that social equality of the sexes may be achieved within the framework of existing society. The radical feminists may then be those who see the achieving of their ends only by means of revolution, a total reconstruction of society. But the reformist-revolutionary distinction is not wholly satisfactory in identifying characteristics of Women's Liberation; it seems clear that the holistic approach to the question of women's status (whatever means are envisaged to achieve the ends) is a theme uniting the disparate groups. On this basis, the reformist, ameliorative stance falls outside the Women's Liberation Movement proper. An example of this is cited by Mitchell when she indicates that the National Organisation of Women, 'the largest of all American groups is reformist and is not now regarded as a part of Women's Liberation either by itself or by most other groups'.[8] Smelser's typology of 'collective behaviour' is useful here. Women's Liberation falls into his categorisation of the value-oriented movement, identified for Smelser by the collective attempt to restore, protect, modify or create values in the name of a generalised value-oriented belief.[9] Both the individual and the society are subject to a basic reconstruction, in this case the woman's 'consciousness-raising' and the attempt to reconstitute society on the basis of a new valuation of 'women's place'. The value-oriented movement involves also, on a lower level of generality, the redefinition of norms as well. A value-oriented movement is then in contrast to the many specific (norm-oriented) movements aiming at equality of opportunity in education, and economic and occupational opportunity.

Within the radical feminist grouping there are a variety of positions, but these positions may be reduced to two basic orientations on another dimension. Then the dichotomy is between those who start from the basic premise that it is the exploitation of women by men which is central, and from which may be derived all other forms of exploitation, and those who adhere to class analysis to explain women's situation in society, and look to a socialist revolution as the necessary precursor of a revalued status for women. In other words, the target for Women's Liberation may be seen either as male dominance, or as the capitalist system which contributes to that dominance.

Some commentators see Women's Liberation as a radical movement separate from leftist orientations, with a specific base that is not derived from Marxist analysis. Various attempts have been made to produce a philosophical basis for the Women's Liberation stance other than in class terms, or with a base which combines a sex analysis with class analysis, thus transcending the latter.

Thus the American Shulamith Firestone[10] analyses society as organised primarily around the power of the male sex over females. Attacking class analysis as limited, she attempts to develop a materialist view of history based on sex itself. Firestone's solution and the ultimate feminist position, is to look forward to a future when technology will remove from women the physical committment to being the child-bearing sex; in other words, technology will eliminate 'biological determinism'. A somewhat similar perspective is implicit in those of the Feminists, an American group aiming at the annihilation of sex roles, or of SCUM, the abbreviation for the bizarre title of the Society for Cutting Up Men, which includes in its programme the overthrow of government and the elimination of the money system, automation, and the destruction of the male sex. In this setting there is disgust and hatred of men regarded as the agents of oppression. A basic determinant of interpretations of the Movement, then, is whether the 'women's struggle' is conceptualised as completely discrete, and sex-based, or whether on a Marxist analysis, women's situation is seen as part of a wider revolutionary struggle, as one oppressed group among many. Women's work in a capitalist society is seen as marginal to the total economy, and women have a false consciousness of their status. Women's Liberation is thus construed as in an 'organic relationship with the other forms which the struggle has taken'.[11] An explicit example of this type of approach from British experience is that shown in the *Socialist Woman Manifesto*, 1972.

The only way to change this society for a better one is through a

> working-class revolution, and this must involve women and men. A socialist revolution would end the exploitation of men and women workers for the profit of the employing class, and would create the possibility of ending all oppression such as that experienced by women.
>
> We give priority to the struggles of working-class women both as the most oppressed and as those in potentially the strongest position to organise against the central economic basis of women's oppression in this society.[12]

The idea of 'Liberation for women being unattainable within a capitalist society' has been explored fairly fully in the literature. But the class analysis categorisation becomes blurred when much of this work is considered. The synthesis of feminist-socialist aimed at by Firestone has already been mentioned. Juliet Mitchell, for example, bases her thinking on class analysis, but explores and explains this basis by adding a feminist analysis of women's position.[13] Sheila Rowbotham has attempted to draw together Marxism and feminism with the theme that 'the liberation of women necessitates the liberation of all human beings',[14] and argues that the so-called women's question is a whole people question. This is somewhat reminiscent of Simone de Beauvoir's analysis[15] of man as transcendent, seeking to dominate woman, 'the other'. Her schema was placed in an essentially materialist framework.

A conceptualisation on a rather different level is to see Women's Liberation in terms of one set of its origins, namely simply as an element of the counter-culture. Women's Liberation then slots into the framework of an anti-authority stance, linked with a range of activism which includes Children's Liberation aimed at organised efforts to reduce authoritarianism in schools, the Gay Liberation Movement, the hippy movement, and the development of communes.

The link with the counter-culture is perhaps more strong in the American setting, which would give some aspects of Women's Liberation a parentage of the New Left, enmeshed with Civil Rights, groups opposing the Vietnam War, the politics of experience. A certain degree of identity of personnel is, no doubt, involved here. The 'pedigree' of the British movement it may be suggested is probably less complex.

Women's Liberation, it has been shown, is relevant to 'the political' and, as such, a factor germane to this study. The implications of the existence of this movement for the political role of women as the term is used in other sections of the study are far more difficult to evaluate.

The relationship between feminism and the movement for political rights, used by feminism as an agency, and coincident, in timing, at the beginning of this century, was equally resistant to analysis. For the Women's Liberation Movement, historical perspective, which is of decisive importance, is lacking at this stage. A few points may be made, however, though they must for the present remain speculative. The possible effect of the mobilisation of women, their interaction with other women, the breaking of the isolation of being at home caring for small children may be to reduce the proportion of women who abstain from voting, and increase the number of those seeking an activist role.

There may be indirect, 'chain-reaction' factors from the effects of Women's Liberation operative in the 'conventional' political sector. If women are motivated to seek 'self-realisation' to fulfil their potential, these ambitions may be displaced on to political ends. Perhaps, in the long term, that substantially more women visibly occupied the higher echelons in many professions would render women equally acceptable in a position of elected representative. It is possible to imagine the effects of women's interaction in Women's Lib. groups, as helping to erode the suggested 'minority' tendency for women not to support ambitious members of their own sex.

On the other hand, the possibility remains that sex-specific associations (and very few Women's Liberation groups accept male members) reinforces the 'special' 'different' view of women, and their specific contribution to society. Again on the negative, albeit cynical side, the possibility of Women's Liberation activity antagonising both men[16] and women in some of its more extreme manifestations cannot be totally excluded. On this viewpoint, the entry of women into the political elite would not benefit from the movement.

Notes

1. cf. R. Dahl, *Modern Political Analysis*, Englewood Cliffs, New Jersey, 1963, Chapter 5.
2. K. Millett, *Sexual Politics*, London, 1969, p.24 ff.
   This approach is somewhat similar to that of R.V. Sampson, in his *Equality and Power*, London, 1965, cf. especially Chapter 3.
3. D. Easton, *A Framework for Political Analysis*, Englewood Cliffs, 1965, p.50.
4. For details of the Movement in the USA cf. H. Dudar, 'Women's Lib: the War on "Sexism", in C. Epstein and W.J. Goode (eds.), *The Other Half*, Englewood Cliffs, 1971, pp.165–75. For a concise account of the British experience, cf. S. Rowbotham, 'The

beginnings of Women's Liberation in Britain', pp.91–102 in M. Wandor (ed.), *The Body Politic*, London, 1972. Women's Liberation is an international phenomenon, and this is the more interesting since it occurs in societies in which there is considerable variation in the status of women. The range of manifestations of the trend runs from the more bizarre activities of the Dolle Minas in Holland, through the M.L.F. in France, and the more 'political' Women's Electoral Lobby which came into prominence at the 1972 elections in Australia.

5. e.g. the Women and Media group.
6. e.g. the National Federation of University Women.
7. J.A. Banks and O. Banks, who make this point are themselves the exception, cf. 'Feminism and social change, a case study of a social movement', in G.K. Zollschan and W. Hirsch (eds)., *Explorations in Social Change*, London, 1964, pp.547–69. The work of these authors includes *Feminism and Family Planning in Victorian England*, Liverpool, 1964. The suffragette movement has recently received more scholarly attention, e.g. A. Raeburn, *The Militant Suffragettes*, London, 1973; S. Rowbotham, *Hidden from History*, London, 1973, especially Chapter 15. A. Carter, *Direct Action and Liberal Democracy*, London, 1973, pp.48–56; W. O'Neill, *The Woman Movement*, London, 1969.
8. cf. Juliet Mitchell, op. cit., p.11. It is ironical that to N.O.W., and to its founder, Betty Friedan, author of *The Feminine Mystique*, 1963, is generally attributed the genesis of 'Women's Liberation'.
9. N. Smelser, *Theory of Collective Behaviour*, London, 1962, p.313.
10. cf. *The Dialectic of Sex*, London, 1972.
11. Branka Magas, 'Sex politics: class politics', *New Left Review*, 66, 1971, p.69.
12. *Socialist Woman*, Summer, 1972.
13. op. cit.
14. *Women, Resistance and Revolution*, London, 1972, p.11.
15. S. de Beauvoir, *The Nature of the Second Sex*, (first published 1949), London, Four Square, 1963, p.13.
16. As an interesting response to so much literature on the status of women, has come literature, of varying degrees of seriousness on men and their 'enslaved' position. e.g. E. Vilar, *The Manipulated Man*, London, 1972, or S. Mead, *Free the Male Man*, London, 1973. In addition, the Women's Liberation analysis is beginning to evoke a critical response, e.g. A. Stassinopolous, *The Female Woman*, London, 1973.

Chapter 7 Political Women: Cross National Comparisons

With the primary emphasis of this study on the part played by women in British politics, thus far comparative material has been advanced at various stages only in so far as it illuminates a particular issue. Yet the British experience may be seen in a much more meaningful light if it is placed in a broader perspective. Then the minutiae of the analysis of women's contribution to Cabinets, to total elected representatives and to candidates may be seen as one manifestation of a more general phenomenon, the political role of women in the representative democratic systems associated with Western advanced technological societies. From this base, it is then possible to compare and contrast the ways in which women relate to politics in other kinds of political systems, notably those of the Communist Sector, or of the Third World.

Any consideration of the political role of women cross-nationally is beset with paradox, more easily indicated than explained. The low rates of women's participation common to most industrialised societies of the West may be contrasted with the existence of three women Prime Ministers in other, mainly less developed areas. In India, there is Mrs. Indira Gandhi, often described as 'the most powerful woman in the world', in Sri Lanka (formerly Ceylon), Mrs. Bandaranaike leads the Government, and in Israel Mrs. Golda Meir heads her country in a period of recurrent war. An internal inconsistency is evident also, since those states with a woman as chief executive are not those with a substantial proportion of women serving as elected representatives, as might be expected. A second kind of paradox derives from the discrepancy between prescription and practice relating to women's place in the Communist states. It is these contrasts which will be the focus of this chapter, as opposed to a presentation of anything that could be construed as a comprehensive coverage of women's political participation on a world basis.

The difficulties of adequately presenting comparative data between various societies are many. Briefly, the problems include the ways in which electoral statistics vary, and are not always readily available for specific dates. Exact comparison between different kinds of elected assemblies is not always rewarding. A straightforward comparison of women's representation in the House of Commons and in the Supreme Soviet is unrealistic, since the two bodies are not strictly comparable as 'legislatures' in anything other than nomenclature.

For these reasons, and in order to avoid the listing of a mass of detailed statistics hedged with qualifying footnotes, a basically descriptive-analytic approach has been adopted, with statistics reduced to a minimum.

1. *Western Political Systems*

A few examples are sufficient to show that Britain is by no means unique in the few women holding elite positions in its political system. First, two of Britain's fellow members in the EEC, both equally highly industrialised, are considered.

In France[1] the figure for women in the National Assembly seems to be stabilising at around two per cent. This represents a decrease since women were enfranchised after the Second World War. Of the 1946 Assembly, six per cent were women, by 1951 the figure stood at three and a half per cent, and by 1968 the current two per cent had been reached. This pattern of decline is followed by women's candidatures, i.e. from a high point of fourteen per cent in 1946, to eleven per cent in 1951. Five years later the figure plummeted to a little under four per cent, at around which level the figure has stabilised. In the Senate, the decline in women's representation is not so obvious, three per cent in 1946 giving way to two per cent from the late 'sixties onwards.

In the National Assembly the decline is interesting: nothing comparable to the 'high' of 1946 occurred in Britain either after the Second World War or after enfranchisement. For France there appear to be at least three major contributing and interacting factors in any attempt at explanation. First, the 1946 figure reflects an element of male equivalence. Here were the widows of heroes of the wartime Resistance movement, who tended not to remain in politics after the immediate post-war period. The second factor is related to relative party success. The 1946 figure included twenty-nine communists. The decline may be seen as related to the fairly long-term success of the right-centre in which, as has been suggested, women are the less likely to achieve elite positions.[2] Thirdly, voting method appears to be relevant. In the Fourth Republic, a system of proportional representation was used, based on the *département* as unit. In 1958, however, the system of voting reverted to a method which had been used for a long period in the Third Republic.[3] This method, *scrutin d'arrondissement*, was based on the single-member constituency, with the use of a second ballot. It is this system, it may be suggested, that is less advantageous for women's representation.[4] It is more difficult for women to achieve candidature, since women who are not well-known tend to be relegated to the hopeless seats. 'Le type de scrutin par investiture uninominale faisait adopter dans chaque parti une attitude prudente: si les candidates avaient déjà fait leurs preuves on pouvait les proposer; si elles étaient nouvelles venues, on pouvait les diriger vers les circonscriptions "purgatoires" ou même "suicides"[5]

Locally there is no comparable decline from a post-war high point. Instead the figure for women in municipal councils was three per cent in 1947 and just over four per cent in 1971.[6]

What contribution have women made at ministerial level? One woman has held the post of Minister of Health, and three others have been under-secretaries of state, but within the 'feminine ideology' category such as education and social affairs. This specialisation appears to be confined to ministerial responsibility. It has been shown that the contribution of women deputies appears to cover a much more comprehensive field.[7]

The history of the political experience of women in the West German Republic differs qualitatively from that of France, although the present rate of women's representation is somewhat more comparable. In Germany, women were enfranchised after the First World War. Women's representation in the inter-war period was relatively substantial, at just under ten per cent in the constituent Assembly of the Weimar Republic, dropping to around six to seven per cent in the Reichstags of the later 'twenties.

After the Second World War, in 1949 to 1953 women's representation in the Bundestag was steady at about nine per cent. Today, however, the proportion is lower, at a little under six per cent in the 1972 election to the Bundestag, a slight decrease on the 1965 figure.[8] Two points are relevant here. The tendency of women to be more successful among parties of the left persists, but the differential is marginal. In 1965, for example, of the total women elected, nineteen belonged to the Social Democratic Party, fifteen to the Christian Democratic Union/Christian Social Union, and two were of the Free Democratic Party.[9]

Method of voting in its application to women's representation is again relevant. By the second Electoral Law, half of the deputies to the Bundestag are elected in single member districts, the remaining half being derived from party lists.[10] Each voter is entitled to one vote for the individual candidate, and a second on a state-wide basis. As Sontheimer has pointed out, 'as a rule women are only elected by the

Land lists.'[11] In the 1972 election the majority (twenty-three) entered via the party lists. But party affiliations, when again women have more chance of election success with the Socialists rather than with the Christian Democrats, prevents firm conclusions on this point.

Women have made very little headway in office-holding. In 1961, the first woman federal minister was appointed interestingly enough in the C.D.U./C.S.U. administration. A few other women have held office in the Land Governments. But in 1972 Annemarie Renger took office as President of the West German Bundestag, the first woman ever to hold this position.

In broad terms, then, in the two European examples cited, women's participation in politics is at more or less the same level as in the British example. Certain other countries in Western Europe are not conspicuously different. A low rate of women's participation is common to Holland, Italy, Austria. In Switzerland women were not enfranchised at the federal level until the 'seventies. In Australia and New Zealand, to which the Westminster model was exported, women's participation has been slow to increase. Despite long-term opportunities (Australia was one of the first states to enfranchise women, in 1901) women have at no time formed a significant proportion of elected representatives either at state or Federal level. As Mackenzie has shown, by 1960 only thirty women had at any time been elected.[12] Nor does the current situation reveal much change in the level of women's representation. In 1960 there was no woman in the Federal Parliament and only seven sat in State Parliaments. After the 1972[13] election there were two women in the State Parliament (1.7 per cent approximately) and only thirteen in all the State Parliaments. In the (Federal) Senate, women in 1960 formed around eight per cent, but in the 1972 election no woman was returned, though two were returned in the next year. This decline is the more interesting since the elections to this body are by proportional representation, which is usually held to be more rather than less conducive to the representation of women.[14]

In New Zealand, a comparable situation obtains. In the House of Representatives, of the eighty-seven members in 1972, just under five per cent were women. One woman held a portfolio in the Executive Council as Minister of Tourism, and Associate Minister of Social Welfare.[15]

The position of women in the United States, where very few women hold or have held elite positions in politics may be quickly summarised. Only eighty-six women have sat in Congress of whom seventy-five have served in the House of Representatives, ten in the Senate, and one,

Margaret Chase Smith, has been elected in both Chambers. The operator of 'male equivalence' in the 'widow's succession' has mediated the entry of a proportion of these women to the House of Representatives.[16] To put the numbers into perspective, the fourteen women to be elected to the Ninety-Third Congress of 1971–72, represent the highest proportion since the Eighty-Seventh Congress ten years earlier. The maximum number of women Senators was reached in 1953–54 with three women. No woman has ever been a member of the Supreme Court, and very few have held major Cabinet posts. Frances Perkins was Secretary of Labour in the Roosevelt administration, 'the one occasion when a woman did succeed in gaining political influence occurred when Mrs. Roosevelt was an occupant of the White House and the President actively encouraged female participation in party affairs'.[17] Oveta Culp Hobby was Secretary of Health and Education to Eisenhower. At present, Mrs. Ann Armstrong is the only woman in the Nixon Cabinet. Her role is generalist, without the responsibility of a department.

The range of women's representation in state legislatures is wider than at Federal level, but clearly very limited, when an official handbook can state: 'In 1967 there was at least one woman in the lower house of every state and women held seats in the upper house of thirty states'.[18] The proportion of women in the lower house was as high as fifteen per cent in New Hampshire, and in Arizona, but in only four states was the proportion in excess of ten per cent. In Texas, Kansas, S. Carolina and Alabama, women formed less than one per cent of the members of the lower house. When these proportions are considered within the context of the figures for women's representation in Federal institutions (stabilising at about two per cent in the House of Representatives), then it is clear that the representation of women in American politics is at a lower level than in Britain.

Women's contribution to the political elite in the Western societies so far considered stands at a consistently low level. The Swedish experience, however, differs in certain respects, in that from a base of three per cent of the Riksdag in 1938, there has been a steady increase (seven per cent in 1948), until in 1969, the proportion of women reached fourteen per cent. Since 1970 the Riksdag has been unicameral, but the proportion of women has remained constant at around fourteen per cent.[19] This seems a relatively high level of participation, and it is probably not without significance that proportional representation is employed. 'Proportional fairness is not to be primarily achieved in each constituency, but in the whole country regarded as a single constituency. Hence in addition to three hundred and ten fixed constituency seats, forty seats are distributed "at large" so as to obtain a fair, nationally proportional result.'[20] Local government showed a proportion of women more akin to the level of women's representation in Britain. In the municipal councils, women formed fourteen per cent of membership in 1971,[21] and from 1966–70, women's contribution to the total of local government councillors had risen from twelve to fourteen per cent.[22] But even with such a relatively large proportion of women in the Riksdag, no woman was appointed as a Cabinet Minister until 1947. In 1972, of nineteen Cabinet Ministers, only two were women.[23]

There are other interesting anomalies and contrasts in Sweden, the country where the debate on sex roles is probably the most advanced of any society. Women in Sweden have rights to equal guardianship of children, individual taxation for wives, the entry to the priesthood, family support services for the working mother, and many other rights which are still 'aims' to feminist groups in other societies. Yet sex differentials persist. To take two examples, in proportion to their membership, women are seriously under-represented in the leadership of Trade Unions, and women tend to earn less than men despite the formal requirements of equal pay. Moreover, the level of women's representation, according to some women's groups, is too low to make women's voices effective. In an article translated as 'one woman alone has no power'[25] are reiterated the familiar arguments: a few brilliant women cannot effect change, more women are needed on policy-making committees, public opinion must be educated to bring more women into politics. Since 1938, there has been an organisation devoted to the 'Improved Representation of Women'.

2. *The Communist Sector*

In the Communist countries, the ethic of sex equality has been more overtly stressed over a much longer period than in most other societies. In 1917 the February Revolution ended formal limitations on women's rights. In the 1936 Constitution, equality is explicit in Article 122.

> Women in the USSR are accorded all equal rights on an equal footing with men in all spheres of economic, government, political and other social and cultural activity. The possibility of exercising these rights is ensured by women being accorded the same rights with men to work, payment for work, rest and leisure, social insurance and education and also by state protection of the interests of mother and child.[26]

Two world wars left women in a numerical majority in the population, such that even in 1970 the discrepancy was of the order of 130 million : 111 million. Measures have been introduced to provide communal facilities and services to counteract the demands of child-rearing in order to release women for productive work.

Women in the USSR are then accorded 'all equal rights with men in all spheres of political activity.' How does this technical equality work out in practice? In summary form the levels of women's representation may be rapidly charted. Around thirty per cent of the Supreme Soviet in 1970 were women.[27] In the Supreme Soviets of the Autonomous Republics (with regional variations) women's representation tends to run at around thirty to thirty-five per cent.[28] There is evidence also that the nearer to grass roots level, the higher the proportion of women. For example it has been established that women members of local soviets (whether of the municipality, village or settlement) formed around forty per cent of the total membership.

Throughout the Communist block the percentage of women deputies to national legislatures is relatively high, with the interesting 'low' for Yugoslavia.[29] Clearly if this index of women's political participation is used, then the Communist bloc is justified in its claims of a greater degree of equality for women. There are, however, factors modifying such claims which preclude accepting the formal situation at its face value.

First, as Lennon points out,[30] only approximately seven per cent of women members are bona fide party or State officials. The others are what are termed in Russia 'best daughters' 'honorific party picked, one-term deputies from various professions and production sectors, the arts, and other areas of Soviet life'.[31] Then the figure for representation in local soviets, though large, does not include any significant proportion of women as Chairmen. Their representation as office-holders is minimal.

It seems reasonable, therefore, to postulate that the nearer the locus of real power, the nearer to the pinnacle of the hierarchy of policy-making, the fewer the women. Women's position in the Supreme Soviet and in the local soviets merely underlines this proposition, since these legislatures are not law-making bodies (in the sense of initiating legislation) in anything but name. They are clearly subordinate to the organs of the party, tending to have the function of endorsing and applauding decisions already made elsewhere. In terms of power-wielding their activities are negligible.

In the more powerful body of the Council of Ministers, which numbers approximately one hundred, there is currently only one woman, Yekaterina Furtseva.[32] This woman minister, perhaps an example of 'symbolic representation', is also unique in having served during the Kruschev period as a member of the Presidium (later Politburo) of the party, the sole woman ever to have achieved this distinction.

As has been indicated, power inheres in the party rather than in the governmental structures. In the membership of the CPSU, only about twenty per cent are women. In the decision-making levels, even as local party secretaries, women are rare. At the higher levels of decision-making, the position is even more clear. With the exception already mentioned, no woman achieves the 'inner circle' of the Politburo. It has been shown that women formed just under four per cent of the Central Committee of the Congress of 1970,[33] and only around eight per cent of the *buro* of the Komsomol. The latter figure is the more surprising, since the Komsomol is the youth section of the party, and in this section women are in a majority.

In some significant respects, then, the similarities of women's political role in the USSR (notably their low level of representation in the elite positions of political decision-making) and in the West, are striking. 'Tokenism' persists in both societies, since Britain's 'statutory woman', for example, is paralleled in the one woman who has to be included in all regional delegations sent to Moscow to the Party Congresses.

Despite the emphasis on sexual equality reinforced by the educational system, open access to occupations and state services to release women for productive work, women do not take anything approaching an equal part with men in many fields including the political. The situation in the political sector is very much analogous to the way in which, in the occupational sector, women tend to be under-represented in the positions that require managerial decision-making and executive functions,[34] even when women are in a majority in a particular profession.[35] Under-representation of women in the occupational elite is of course a point of similarity with Western societies. There are other parallels. In 1956, Kruschev, addressing the Twentieth Party Congress, complained that 'very few women hold leading party and soviet positions'. He continued to point out that 'many party and soviet bodies exhibit timidity about putting women in executive posts'.[36] The tone and phrasing of this quotation seem very familiar.

3. *India, Israel and Sri Lanka*

Lastly some brief reference must be made to three of the countries which have women Prime Ministers. In India, Mrs. Gandhi has been

Prime Minister since 1966, and with a strong majority since 1970. Mrs. Gandhi has been no caretaker, interim choice and has survived despite massive problems including monsoon failure in 1966 and 1967, the language issue, and war with Pakistan. This Prime Minister has split her party and survived, and in her term of office has come the green revolution, giving some element of hope in the battle against starvation.

Indira Gandhi succeeded Shastri, after serving in his Cabinet in the relatively obscure post of Minister of Information and Broadcasting. It is perhaps significant that Mrs. Gandhi was the daughter of the first Prime Minister of India, Nehru, to whom she had acted as hostess and aide. Within two years of his death, she had herself become Prime Minister at the age of forty-nine. There is here, then, possibly some element of male equivalence, in the sense of a close family and working association with an elite political male. There is certainly here the important inference of the politicised family.

The paradox of the Indian situation is that the achievement of Mrs. Gandhi has to be seen against a background of a very low rate of participation by women in politics. Women's membership of the first Lok Sabha elected in 1952 amounted to just under four per cent. By 1957 the figure was just over five per cent,[37] and by 1967 about six per cent.[38] In 1967 only one other woman was a member of the administration with responsibilities in information and broadcasting. Women in the parties are also represented at a very low level. Kochanek found that women formed only around four per cent of the All-India Congress Committee of 1956.[39]

The situation is the more interesting since a woman holds the supreme power-wielding situation in a society in which the majority of women is not socially or economically on an equality with men, and where purdah still persists though to a limited and rapidly decreasing extent. The ambivalence and ambiguity of the situation seems impossible to explain adequately. Speculatively, and tentatively personal abilities, intellect, the elusive element of 'personality' seem important, so important as to override some of the other considerations. Secondly, with uneven development in a continent in a post-colonial situation, it may be possible for a certain elitist, highly educated sub-group (at the top of the political hierarchy) to accept an able successful woman in a power position. This acceptance may then be mediated from the elite downwards to the masses, in a way which does not, somehow, violate cultural norms.

The situation of a woman Prime Minister in Israel again tends to defy easy explanation. Mrs. Golda Meir, of Russian origin and American upbringing, had retired from political life after having reached the position of Foreign Minister. When Mrs. Meir became Prime Minister in 1969, the situation was seen initially as an interim stopgap measure on the sudden death of the previous Prime Minister. Mrs. Meir, however, rapidly asserted that control which has persisted through crisis-ridden years and two wars. The position of a woman as Prime Minister in a war situation is the more remarkable since Mrs. Meir became Prime Minister at around seventy years of age.

There appears to be no neat correspondence between the level of women in politics and in the elite positions of society and the woman Prime Minister. In Israel women's position may be dissimilar from that of women in other societies in that women are liable to serve in the armed forces, though for a shorter period, actively and on reserve, than men. Women work in the Kibbutzim on equal terms with men, but only a limited proportion of the population live in this way, and there is a wide variation in the way of life of the various forms of Kibbutz. In the total working population women are still under the level of one-third.[40] In the Knesset, there has never been more than ten per cent women.

What explanations that are convincing may be sought for the tremendous gap between the political role of *one* woman, and of the rest? How, within the religious background factors, is a woman regarded as acceptable? Any explanatory factors are more easy to indicate than to validate. The situation of a 'new' country, with frontiers to be defended by women as well as men in the army, the pioneering spirit engendered by this and by the melting pot of ethnic origins, may be relevant here to the novelty of the acceptance of a woman serving in the highest political office.

Personality and image may also be significant. In Mrs. Meir are blended the image of unpretentious homely grandmother, and the strength of character, determination and independence of the leader.

The list of the 'deviants', women in a power-wielding position of a magnitude unusual by the standards of their sex could be lengthened to include Mrs. Sirmavo Bandaranaike, Prime Minister of Sri Lanka. Again the social political and cultural factors are not favourable to women's complete equality with men. Initially, Mrs. Bandaranaike became Prime Minister as a male equivalent when her husband was assassinated in 1959. In the following year his wife with apparently no previous political ambitions in her background became the world's first woman Prime Minister. In 1965 she fell from power, but in 1970 came back to head a coalition government, which had to face armed insurrection. The male equivalent explanatory factor, while of primary importance perhaps in 1960, can hardly be considered in the same light as explaining the return to power ten years later. It seems that other explanations should be sought. Certainly no generalised explanation is sufficient to link these exceptional 'women in politics'. Explanation, to be meaningful, probably needs to be based in a complex of personality interactions, cultural factors, and the exigencies of history.

Notes

1. Sources for France include M. Duverger, op.cit., Chapter 2; J.H. Chaton, 'Les femmes françaises en 1972', Tendances, No.75, February 1972, p.23 ff.; G. Charzat, *Les Françaises sont-elles des citoyennes*? Paris, 1972, p.96 ff. A. Michel and G. Texier, *La condition de la française d'aujourd'hui*, Paris, 1964; R.E.M. Irving, *Christian Democracy in France*, London, 1973.
2. For the British experience, cf. above p.30. The paradox is the more obvious there when it is considered that the Conservatives (counting service in coalitions as well as Conservative administrations) in this century have been in office for nearly two-thirds of the time. The situation in France is discussed in Duverger, op.cit., p.90, and by Charzat, op.cit., Chapter 7.
3. P. Avril, *Politics in France*, Harmondsworth, 1969, Appendix 4.
4. e.g. G. Charzat, op.cit., p.100.
5. J. Chaton, op.cit., p.24.
6. G. Charzat, op.cit., p.103.
7. J. Chaton, loc.cit.
8. 'The 1972 Bundestag Election, A Historic Event?' *InterNationes*, 1972, p.31.
9. In absolute numbers, female membership by party (in 1965) shows the same pattern: C.D.U, 37, 119; S.P.D., 123, 565; F.D.P., 5,500. Proportionally, this distribution is not nearly so marked. Women constituted 13 per cent of C.D.U. membership; 5 per cent of C.S.U. and 17 per cent of S.P.D. (cited in *Germany Reports*, 'Women's Affairs', 1969, p.23).
10. For a concise explanation of the system, cf. S.H. Beer et al., *Patterns of Government*, New York, 1962, pp.518–9.
11. K. Sontheimer, *The Government and Politics of West Germany*, London, 1972, p.112.
12. op.cit., p.264. For details of the incidence of 'male equivalence', cf. p.266.
13. Material kindly supplied by Australia House, London.
14. MacKenzie, op.cit., p.276 ff., discusses why 'it is apparently easier for women to be nominated and elected to the Commonwealth Senate than to other parliamentary seats' in terms of method of voting.

15. Government of New Zealand, *Digest of Statistics*, Wellington, 1973, p. 266 ff.
16. cf. below, Chapter IX. For an example of a woman Governor of Texas in the 1920s, as a male equivalent, cf. W.H. Chafe, *The American Woman*, New York, 1972, p.38.
17. W. Chafe, op.cit., p.39.
18. US Department of Labour, *Handbook on Women Workers*, 1969, p.125.
19. Sources: The Joint Female Labour Council, *Woman in Sweden in the Light of Statistics*, Stockholm, 1973, p.94; *Historical Statistics of Sweden*, 1960, Table 27, p.269; *Hertha*, 5, 1969, and 3, 1973 (publication of the Frederika Bremer Association).
20. Government of Sweden, *Sweden*, Stockholm, 1972, p.
21. Joint Female Labour Council, op.cit., p.94 ff.
22. loc. cit.
23. On attempts to increase women's representation at all levels, cf. Y. Toijer-Nilsson, *Hertha*, 5, 1969, pp.14–16.
24. Joint Female Labour Council, op.cit., p.54 ff.
25. Ulla Lindstrom, a member of the Riksdag.
26. Constitution of the USSR, Moscow, Foreign Languages Publishing House, 1962, p.100.
27. L. Lennon, 'Women in the USSR', *Problems of Communism*, July–August, 1971.
28. D.R. Brown (ed.) *The Role and Status of Women in the Soviet Union*, New York, 1968, Table 16, p.41.
29. e.g. Hungary (1967) 30 per cent; Poland (1969) 13 per cent; Mongolia (1969) 22 per cent; Rumania (1969) 14 per cent. Source: *World Marxist Review*, Supplement to Vol.13, August 1970, p.17, quoted in R. Gripp, *The Political System of Communism*, London, 1973, p.144.

    It is interesting that in China, as in the Russian bloc, women have not penetrated into the higher echelons of the party. The only woman menber of the Politburo is the wife of Mao Tse Tung. For a quotation from the official *People's Daily*, urging women's increased political activism, cf. *Woman's Report* (Fawcett Society, London), 1,4,1973, p.8.
30. op. cit., p.50.
31. loc. cit.
32. As Minister of Culture.
33. Lennon, op.cit.; on the composition of party elites over time, cf. also V. Alexandrova, 'The Soviet Union', in R. Patai (ed.), *Women in the Modern World*, London, 1967, p.406; D. Brown, op. cit.
34. M. Field, in D. Brown, op.cit., p.14.
35. e.g. in medicine, where women now constitute about seventy per cent of all qualified practitioners, a decrease from nearer ninety per cent in the late 'fifties.
36. *Pravda*, 15 February 1956.
37. T.K. Unnithan, *Gandhi in Free India*, 1965, p.145.
38. Government of India, *Who's Who*, Lok Sabha (House of the

People), 1964, New Delhi, 1967.
39. S.A. Kochanek, *The Congress Party of India*, 1968, p.366.
40. State of Israel, Ministry of Labour, *Manpower in Israel*, 1966, p.37.

Chapter 8 The Changing Role of Women in Society

Having charted in varying degrees of detail the level of women's participation in the political sector, it now remains to adduce some of the factors which seem to be relevant to that participation. In this chapter, then, the changing feminine role, women's experience of the educational sector, and their participation in the occupational structure, are considered from the point of view of their possible relevance to the ways in which women relate to politics.

1. *The Feminine Role*

To consider women's political role in isolation from women's role generally would be a pointless exercise. Attitudes to the status of women, changes in women's role and the images and stereotypes generated by such attitudes and changes all impinge on the issue of how women relate to politics. Yet so much has been written on women latterly[1] as to render detailed statistics and discussion repetitive and redundant. It is, therefore, proposed rather to focus on such trends and general indicators as may be suggested are of significance for our main concern of women's political activism. Some factual, some descriptive, some basically explanatory factors will be taken up in turn. The approach may be eclectic: it is hoped, however, to show that between such varied elements as the educational structure, the occupational structure, sex roles and political roles, there is a complex interaction. It is only in this way that discrepancies may be thrown into prominence between the legal and political rights which exist and the customs habits of thought and tradition which may not be consonant with the formally enacted situation.

Central to any discussion of women's position and role in society at large are factors relative to the area which Parsons[2] has termed the root functions of women, or, in the terminology of Banks,[3] reproductive determinism. The whole complex of commitment to family and home is implicit in women's being the child-bearing sex, though over the centuries, various attempts, both philosophical and experimental, have been made to free women from the shackles of her biological environment. Such attempts have ranged from Plato's scheme for producing women Guardians, trained in exactly the same way as men, and free from the duty of caring for children, through the interesting

Hutterite communities[4] now to be seen in America, to the experiments of the various forms of Kibbutz.[5] Perhaps also should be added to the list the ways in which a country like Russia provides a supportive network of creches, extended school hours and communal provision of meals in order to leave women free for productive work.

The history of the family in Western society may be briefly indicated. In the pre-industrial period, kinship was emphasised as a fundamental social institution in the area of family life. At the same time, economic activity was home-centred. With industrial society came the break up of the intertwined familial and economic role of women, and economic activity became increasingly extra-familial. In industrial society there was an increasing emphasis on the nuclear rather than the extended kin-group, and on a sharp sex-role differentiation between men and women. This increasing isolation of the nuclear family has been interpreted as an adaptive response to the importance of increased mobility in industrialisation, and the increased differentiation of interests and involvement of members of a kin group. Finally, in post-industrial society, stress tends to be laid more and more on partnership in family life, equality between husband and wife, joint activities and sharing in financial responsibility for the home by means of economic activity outside it. It seems probable that in Western advanced technological society, the general pattern of the nuclear family, whether or not based on the institution of marriage as we now know it, is likely to survive into the immediate future.

If the nuclear family is a persistent pattern, then it could be argued that women's role as involving a primary, overriding commitment to child-bearing, child-rearing and home must persist also. That this is not necessarily so is the result of essentially demographic changes which over the past seventy or so years have affected the pattern of women's life-phases. In turn, not only women's role but also the stereotypes and images of that role (and incidentally of men's role) are modified.

It is the interaction of three demographic factors, in particular, that has changed not only the sequence of woman's life span but the relative length of those phases. Lowering of the average age at marriage,[6] decrease in family size[7] when with improved methods of contraception women obtained in Bernard Shaw's phrase their 'ultimate freedom', and increasing life expectancy are all crucial factors. For a female baby born between 1838–44 the life expectancy was 42 years. Born in the 1920s a girl had a life expectancy of nearly sixty years. By 1970, the figure had risen to 75.1 years.[8] It is this demographic revolution which makes all other changes conceivable. Until it is physically possible for a woman to take on commitments apart from her family for most of her adult life, formal political emancipation and legal equality of the sexes may, for some strata, mean little.

As Titmuss has pointed out, the average working-class mother in the industrial towns in 1900

> could expect if she survived to fifty-five, to live not much more than another twelve years by the time she reached the comparative ease, the reproductive grazing fields of the middle fifties. The situation today is remarkably different . . . by the time the typical mother of today has virtually completed the cycle of motherhood she still has half her total life expectancy to live.[9]

Whereas at the beginning of this century, the average woman could expect to spend one-third of her life producing and nursing children today the figure is around one-fifteenth. Associated with this is a different attitude to ageing, a pushing back of the frontiers of old age. Age and widowhood is no longer designated by style or colour of dress.

Overall, the situation may be summed up quite simply. More people are marrying, they are marrying earlier, but more marriages are ending in divorce. Divorce does not, however, appear to induce disillusionment with marriage: re-marriage is common. Early marriage does not mean significant increases in family size, neither does the reduction in infant mortality rates.

The timing of the demographic revolution is apposite. The new domestic situation for most women has been emerging when changes in educational provision for girls and in the range of jobs and careers available to women have provided additional incentives to take a much broader view of the feminine role. But too much must not be made of coincidence in timing. The fall of the birth rate in England coincided roughly with the rise of feminism so that a causal relationship between the two factors might be hypothesised. This association is, however, not found acceptable by the authors of a historical-sociological study who concluded that there was no evidence that 'emancipated' women in the feminist sense of the word, once married, had fewer children than those in the same social class who were 'unemancipated'. They point out that family planning became established in English middle-class families while feminism as an organised movement was still in the early stages of development.[10] It is only in the last few years, of course, that limitation in family size has been looked at from a perspective other than that of the nuclear family, the overburdened mother, and so on. Family allowances, family income supplements, have buttressed the larger family. Recently, however, with increasing awareness of world population projections, the revolutionary idea is beginning to be canvassed that a woman's right to produce children may not be forever inalienable. The distance from the right to abortion to the right to childbirth is a considerable one.

Nevertheless women's role cannot be divorced from the context of the family, though both her place in the family and the position of the family in society has changed and is changing, over the past hundred or so years. Leaving aside regional and sub-cultural variations, side by side with the 'demographic revolution' that has been described has come the gradual (legal) erosion of the man's dictatorial powers over wife and children, the emergence of 'economic woman' and the gradual diffusion through the classes of household technology. The demographic changes have been paralleled in virtually the same time span by the family's shedding of some of its former responsibilities, and their assumption by the State in terms of concessional and welfare provisions. A great deal of time-consuming effort has been removed from child-rearing, and the welfare state has removed some of the worst anxieties from parents. Parsons sees the evolution of the family as essentially involving differentiation and specialisation of function rather than decline, such that the family's basic functions become primary socialisation of children and stabilisation of adult personalities.[11]

Thus far, an outline has been traced of the ways in which the demographic revolution has modified the pattern of woman's life as dictated by her biology. But as C. Wright Mills has pointed out, 'the facts of biology themselves take on the values that we give them . . . and woman is an historical creation'.[12] Women may have thus far acquired the right to a level of technical equality, their status remains equivocal. It is not without significance, it may be added, that in many different societies one of the hallmarks of this technical equality, namely the franchise, has been achieved in the fluid conditions and psychological climate of war or its aftermath, or of a post-revolutionary period.[13]

The approach we have exemplified in Mills' terminology is one which is shared basically by such diverse writers as Margaret Mead in her seminal works[14] or Eva Figes in *Patriarchal Attitudes*, written in 1970. David Riesman's comments are in a somewhat similar vein. 'I think what I would ideally like to see in our society is that sex become an ascribed rather than an achieved status. That one is simply born a girl or a boy and that's it. And no worry about an activity's de-feminising or emasculating one.'[15] In other words, there has been, over time, an increasing questioning of acceptance of genetic differences as the sole determinants of sex-roles. More and more, sex roles are being seen as learned behaviour, as assigned roles acquired by social conditioning. In one sense, this may be seen as a reflection of the continuing nature-nurture debate, when the currently fashionable stress on the nurture (cultural) side of the dichotomy seems relatively unchallenged. An interesting exception to this is Lionel Tiger's contention that there is a genetic basis for male dominance in that male bonding is, he maintains, a biological pattern, and what he terms 'society's spinal column'.[16]

Generally it seems true that developments towards equality of the sexes have been paralleled by the increasing tendency to minimise the implications of the physical differences of sex. Yet changing conventions and the effects of socialisation cannot override completely the fact of a man's higher metabolic rate resulting in more concentrated use of energy, differences in physique, differences in age of physical maturity, etc.[17] Precisely how far any emotional or temperamental differences between the sexes are determined by physiological considerations, or dictated by socialisation patterns remains open to debate.

However much the feminine role has changed and is changing, one constant remains. The feminine and masculine roles are interdependent, and inextricably linked, so that women's role cannot be seen in isolation. However amorphous women's role may appear at any period, it is always defined by the complementary male role. Conflicting expectations of sex roles lead to stress and dissonance. The process of change in this context, then, may be seen as the functioning of two articulated roles: change may generate resistance, which in turn is followed by adaptive response. At points where the two roles do not exactly fit, friction is likely to be seen in, for example, the votes for women campaign. Understanding the discrepancies between the legal enactments of civic equality and the actual customs and norms of society, means considering vestigial sex roles, notably from the era when man was the family's sole agent in the political and occupational spheres.

In Sweden, the debate on sex roles has proceeded beyond the duality of woman's role (home and work) to a consideration of men's two-fold role. Myrdal believes the viability of a more equitable sharing of family responsibilities is stronger than ever.[18] The serious suggestion of 'maternity leave' for fathers, made in an American University and by the Head of the British Civil Service,[19] provides some indication of radical change in the social climate. In this connection, moves towards equal pay acquire an extra significance. Similarly, linked to equal pay in a Labour Party policy document, *Towards Equality*, published in 1969, are equal social security benefits, a similar retiring age for both sexes, and equal contributions. Such provisions, were they implemented, would spell the end of the Beveridge assumption of a wife as a dependant, almost an appendage of her husband for social security purposes. A somewhat similar development came in the early 1970s when it was made possible for a wife's earned income to be assessed for taxation separately from that of her husband.

It may not be going too far to relate David Riesman's schema to the current situation of a move towards the erosion of sex role differences. On this basis, it might be argued that the diminution of such differences is linked to an 'other-directed' society, a society in which 'contemporaries are the source of direction for the individual – either those known to him or those with whom he is indirectly acquainted, through friends and through the mass media.'[20]

There is an abundance of examples with which to illustrate the blurring of sex role differences, examples which might include both women as wrestlers or footballers, and the reduction of apparent sex differences in the androgynous life complete with unisex clothing. Mirra Komarovsky has emphasised competing frameworks for the feminine role, insights which Kammeyer[21] has developed in empirial research. Two alternatives, contradictory and exclusive, are suggested as facing American college girls. One is the feminine or 'traditional', the other, which interests us here, is the 'modern' stereotype which partly obliterates the differences between the sexes inthat it demands of women much the same virtues, behaviour and attitudes as are demanded of their male contemporaries.

In attempting to bring together, though in eclectic fashion, what may be of relevance ultimately to a consideration of women's political role, there is another factor, or rather a cultural dimension to be added, in Chombart de Lauwe's formulation,[22] that of the 'images of women in society'. Image is both perception and representation, and is the result of a complex elaboration made up from elements borrowed from perception, memories, and imagination, plus the addition of affective elements. Models in this sense are on a higher level of generality, and there is a complex interaction between normative models directing the elaboration of images, and the behaviour prompted by the images. More simply, images and models, according to Chombart de Lauwe, are important as they become the engines or the brakes in the transformation of family structures, relations between the sexes, and in the professions, etc. Images, then, guide both behaviour and attitudes. They generate myths, which themselves will transform the genesis of new myths. In the context of this approach, as of other approaches such as that of socialisation to a political role, education is highly significant.

2. *The Educational Sector*

While legally no distinction exists between educational opportunity for boys and girls, and at all levels there is virtual identity of curricula, yet the educational system tends to be an area in which formal legal equality of the sexes is not precisely implemented in the actual situation. In practice, there are sex-linked divergences in the use made of the educational facilities available. This sex differential (to be outlined later) is, it is suggested here, highly relevant to the central theme of how women relate to politics. First, and of most obvious relevance, is the association found by political sociologists between standards of educational attainment, and political information and cognition, voting and non-voting, and political efficacy.[23] Outside the family, agencies of education are among the most crucial factors in effecting both formal socialisation generally and political socialisation.[24] On the assumption that the education provided by a society reflects the felt needs of that society, then the education of girls must reflect society's impression of the role of women. Judging from the use which girls tend to make of the education currently provided for them, present-day society's attitude to the role of women seems blurred and ambivalent. Perhaps this is not so surprising in a chapter in women's history which is still fluid and transitional.

The need to consider women's educational experience is essential, in addition, because of the relationship to the occupational structure. Level of education, to a considerable extent, determines the level and type of occupation followed. It is to be suggested later that women's location in the occupational sector has an important relevance to the way in which women participate in the political sector.

As has already been stated, there are differences between the sexes in the demands they make on the educational system, differences both in terms of the length of full-time education, and in the courses and subjects chosen. Enough has been written and is readily available on this topic to make details unnecessary here, and only the outlines are indicated where they are important to the main theme.

In primary and secondary schools there is normally a similar basic curriculum, with additions (usually alternatives)[25] of woodwork or domestic science, football or hockey. Usually it is those girls who are in the 'B' and 'C' streams of selective schools who tend to give more time to housecraft, cookery, etc., and boys in similar streams who specialise in metalwork and woodwork. Taken to extremes, it is possible to argue that there is a differential here in preparing these children for traditional sex-typed roles, as opposed to 'A' streams, whose academic sights are set on 'A' levels and University entrance.

In practice, there is considerable divergence in the ways in which girls as compared with boys make use of the opportunities available to them. The numbers of boys and girls in the early stages of secondary education are roughly the same, but fewer girls than boys reach 'A' levels. As the Robbins Report pointed out,[26] there is a progressive widening of the difference in school experience between boys and girls; girls with five or more 'O' levels tend to leave school earlier than boys; for every ten of those boys who stay on to eighteen or over, only eight girls do so. Similarly, on leaving school there is a considerable discrepancy between boys and girls undertaking Day-Release courses. In 1970, for boys 38.8 per cent of those eligible were involved, whereas the corresponding percentage for girls was only 10.1 per cent.[27]

Overall, a higher proportion of qualified boys than girls seek University entrance, such that the Robbins Report concluded that 'the reserve of untapped ability is greater among girls than among boys'.[28] This factor appears to be one of the major reasons in Robbins coming down against replacing grants by loans, though the committee did not use the term 'negative dowry' which has been suggested if loans applied to women. The report stated

> On balance we do not recommend immediate recourse to a system of financing students by loans. At a time when many parents are only just beginning to acquire the habit of contemplating higher education for such of their children, *especially girls*, as are capable of benefitting by it, we think it probable that it would have undesirable disincentive effects.[29]

The proportion of women to men students in higher education is by no means equal, though the female-quota system is operative only in selection to Medical Schools. For University students, generally, over a ten-year period, the following table illustrates the disproportion in the number of graduates and diploma-holders.

Traditionally, this disproportion has been most marked in the Oxbridge colleges. The opening of additional women's colleges and, in 1972, some men's colleges allowing entrance to a token intake of women have made only a marginal difference.

An important factor in the higher education sector is the diversion

Table 9 Degrees and Diplomas Awarded, 1958–68[30]

Year	Men	Women	Women as % of total	(N)
1958	12,851	4,323	25.2	17,174
1961–2	15,209	4,728	23.7	19,937
1964–5	17,232	6,746	28.1	23,978
1968–9	27,092	11,118	29.1	38,210

of able girls into training for teaching at Colleges of Education. Here women heavily outnumber men. In 1961–62 there were around five thousand men taking these courses compared with about twelve thousand women. This disparity between the sexes has remained fairly constant over the past decade, so that by 1970 the relative figures were of the order of eleven thousand and twenty-eight thousand respectively.[31] It will be interesting to see whether the proportion of men will rise once the B.Ed. becomes established and prestigious, and whether the hold of women in primary education will be challenged. Certainly for the present, Jackson and Marsden's comments[32] on the peculiarly in-breeding nature of education (which they likened to a machine that manufactures its own spare parts) seem, ten years later, still particularly true of women's education, despite the gradual movement away from single sex schools.

Turning from the type and length of educational courses followed by boys and girls to the variations of options within the courses, the marked difference in the subjects which boys and girls tend to take is very clear. Without detailed analysis, it may be stated that whereas generally boys tend to take mathematics, science, Greek, English language, more girls opt for biology, English literature, religious knowledge, art and music.[33] Something akin to sex-typing of subjects may be seen from subjects at A level.

The differential in subjects studied at school not surprisingly persists at University level. Science, applied science, and technology are predominantly male preserves,[35] while for Arts subjects the reverse is generally true. In the Social Sciences, the distribution between the sexes is somewhat less uneven.[36] The paradox of the contrast between virtual identity of curricula offered, on the one hand, and the

Table 10 Leavers with two or more A levels,[34] by subject specialism, 1969–70

	Percentage of total	
	Boys	Girls
Science	46	19
Social Science	3	1
Arts	17	46
Science-social science	7	5
Science-Arts	4	6
Social Science-Arts	20	20
Science-Social Science-Arts	2	2

differential use which each sex makes of them demands some comment in elaboration. The reasons for the identity of curricula in boys' and girls' schools are clearly historical. The early feminists, in seeking equality with men in the field of education sought to obtain for girls a replica of that already in existence for boys. It is easy today to criticise this confusion of equality with identity, a confusion with an undertone of masculine protest. In the perspective of a period when difference could and frequently did connote inferiority, this ultra-feminist approach is more understandable. Men, by reason of their superior education and access to high status occupations could be, in many fields of activity, superior to women. It is interesting that there have been very few suggestions made over the years for a specifically feminine-oriented education for girls, though some elements in the Women's Liberation Movement may provide exceptions to this generalisation.[37]

The major contribution to the literature on education specifically related to women comes from Newsom in the post-war period. In brief, at school level, Newsom recommends for girls a stress on English language, physical education (backed by elementary biology, physiology and chemistry) the structure of modern society, with more time allowed for the creative arts, domestic science and leisure activities. At University, Newsom suggests the establishment of additional degree courses to include, for example, the visual and auditory arts, or public health, housing, education and town planning, in a historical, theoretical and practical approach, which, while appealing also to men, would be primarily designed for women.[38] In this connection it is interesting to note that the proposal to found an entirely new University solely for women, mooted in the 1890s, did not find acceptance,[39] and instead in the 1960s and '70s there has been a move away from single-sex colleges.

Any suggestion of educational courses specifically designed for women is inevitably based on two factors at least. The first is a clear notion of the sex role, to fulfilment of which this education is directed. The second factor is a particular notion of the configuration of women's particular abilities and aptitudes. The question of differing abilities between the sexes remains an emotive and sensitive issue, but with an increasingly scientific and objective approach, data is accumulating on this point. There is some evidence that girls' capacities and abilities develop somewhat differently from those of boys.[40] And whereas there is no difference by sex in the average IQ, among men, more scores cluster at the extremes of the range, compared with women. Women tend, on average, to do better in tests using verbal skills, while again on average, men tend to do better in visuo-spatial tests. The latter ability is important in many occupations usually predominantly male, such as scientific, engineering and architectural work.

Work that has been done on the ways in which thinking patterns develop tend to indicate some differences between male and female. For example, Bennet and Cohen, while emphasising the basic factor of the similarity between masculine and feminine thinking, which comes they suggest from the length of time a boy is under feminine control, produce from their sample of 1300 some broad contrasts. Briefly, they find that masculine thinking tends to be associated more with a desire for personal achievement while feminine thinking is associated more with a desire for social love and friendship;[41] that masculine thinking finds value more in malevolent and hostile actions against a competitive society, while feminine thinking finds value more in freedom from restraint in a friendly and pleasant environment.

Other studies lay more emphasis on the suggestion that differences in abilities between the sexes should rather be seen in terms of differences in the *distribution* of various modes of thinking or abilities common to both sexes. Yet it must be stressed that the nature-nurture controversy is relevant here also, and that attempts at precision in sex-related characteristics have to be seen against the background of the patterns of socialisation moulding an individual towards his or her sex role. Whereas as has been stated spatio-visual perception may be important in itself as a factor in career choice, equally important for a girl may be that her school regards science subjects as 'unfeminine', or the limited job-expectations her parents consider suitable for a daughter. A Unesco-sponsored study published in 1970 maintained that the educational opportunities of girls and women remain distinctly below those open to boys and men, quantitatively and qualitatively.[42] Cause and effect in these circumstances are more difficult to assign.

3. *The Occupational Sector*

Educational achievement is clearly one of the most important factors in determining an individual's position in the occupational sector. But the relationship of women's position in the occupational sector *vis-à-vis* men, to the question of women's participation in politics is by no means simple. Within the context of the minority approach,[43] women's position in the working world is significant. There are, in addition, other associations to be considered. If women's greater social isolation is a contributing factor in non-voting, or voting in a conservative direction, then the proportion of women (and especially married women) in employment outside the home becomes very significant. At a lower level of generality, the number of married women working may have one of two effects. Home commitments and a full-time occupation inevitably restrict time and energy for political activism or public life. This is a point which emerged in a survey of women councillors in a Midland Authority.[44] In contrast, studies (reported by MacKenzie) have shown that women who are employed in the middle years of life are more liable to take an interest in community work, and have more independence of political outlook. And when men are accustomed to women working and to the 'broader inter-relation of the sexes that follows upon this, they are more likely to be tolerant of women seeking roles beyond those traditionally accepted.'[45]

Moreover, if, as may be suggested, certain types of occupation circumscribe political activity (for example the bars to political activity for Civil Servants, or the prohibition of local government employees from serving as members of the employing authority) then there are negative implications inherent in the predominance of women in certain occupations such as primary school teaching and the clerical grades of the Civil Service. Similarly there is a significance in the sex ratio in self-employed occupations and the professions, e.g. directorships or consultancies, law practice, which are both more easy to combine with a political career, and more useful to cushion the lack of security involved in an elected status. Finally, the inclusion of women in the highest levels of the professional, industrial or financial world may indicate a social climate which considers women acceptable in the elite, or rather in the various elites. If the position of Member of Parliament is regarded as another proto-professional status, traditionally male, then the small numbers of women is not so surprising. It may be hypothesised that countries with a relatively substantial proportion of women in the higher ranks of traditionally masculine careers might be expected to have a correspondingly substantial proportion of women in the national political elite, and vice versa. While variations between countries make exact comparative data impossible, there seems to be some association (although not in the strictly statistical usage of the term) between the two indices, in the cases of America, Britain, USSR and France, for example.[46]

These, then, are some of the reasons for including some consideration of women's place in the occupational structure as part of the essential background to the larger study of women's political role. Much has been produced on women in employment in recent years,[47] so that only the main features as relevant to the major issue will be indicated.

To judge from the press on the subject of latch-key children (made topical by teachers' strikes, or fuel crises) and from some of the discussion on reactions to the issue of equal pay, the impression gained is that more women are working outside the home than at any time previously. Yet the most striking fact which emerges from any study of the sex composition of the labour force in this century is that the proportion of women has remained on the whole remarkably constant, amounting to around one-third of the total working population. Regional variations persist, in part dependent on the job opportunities that are available for female labour, male unemployment rates etc., and in part on sub-cultural differences, for example in attitudes to women working. But in this century, the proportion of women in the total labour force has not risen spectacularly.

In 1901, women formed twenty-five per cent of the total work force: today the proportion is around thirty-five per cent. What is much more significant than the size of women's participation is the changing composition as modified by the demographic factors already mentioned, and by factors such as changes in school-leaving age, and, more speculatively, by the coincidence of a decrease in working hours for men over roughly the same period.

In 1911, seventy per cent of all working women were under

thirty-four years of age. In contrast, by the mid-1960s the average age had increased such that around seventeen per cent of women working were under twenty, thirty-six per cent were aged between twenty and thirty-nine, and forty per cent between forty and fifty-nine. The proportion of married women of adult age working is about forty per cent of the female labour force, which in turn means that married women make up around one-fifth of the total labour force. With earlier marriage, the decline in the proportion of the unmarried women in the labour force is likely to continue. As Le Gros Clark has pointed out, 'The typical working woman of today is no longer the inactive and pliable girl who was so demonstrably filling in time until she got married; the typical working woman tends, on the contrary, to be a married woman in her middle life.'[48] Women's independent economic role is no longer exclusively confined to the pre-marriage years, but increasingly continues afterwards as well. The consequences of the recognition of a woman's likelihood to have two career periods in her life are considerable,[49] and may be exemplified in various social provisions, such as re-training, refresher courses and amended duty hours for married women doctors, all of which point to a revolution in attitude from the former marriage ban in the civil service and in teaching. Extension in the provision of re-training facilities throughout the working careers of men, necessary since the pace of technological development renders once-for-all initial training obsolete, should have positive effects for women also. Women returning to work after a gap for child-bearing and child-rearing will be at much less of a disadvantage than previously. Thus, while for nine women out of ten, adult life will still mean marriage, marriage need no longer be the sole and exclusive aim for a majority of women.

Of equal importance as the composition of the women's labour force is the location of women in the occupational structure. On the whole, the mass of women continue to occupy the positions demanding a lesser degree of skill, training and responsibility, with lower pay. Some occupations still remain essentially sex-typed, e.g. non-graduate teaching, secretarial and some clerical work, and nursing.[50] Scientific and engineering occupants are overwhelmingly male.[51] Since many women favour 'feminine occupations', entry into, and more particularly advancement in business, industrial or science fields still retain a pioneering connotation and meet the prejudice often aroused by the unusual. Even some apparent incursions of women into traditionally male fields conceal differences. In the police force women work shorter hours, do less night work, and have a separate career structure, such that while women hold high rank, there are no women Chief Constables.

It may be suggested that women tend to predominate in occupations where men had at no time been firmly entrenched, or in 'old' occupations which men had left, or from the extension of 'new' employment opportunities in white-collar or semi-professional areas of work. This pattern would include women's work in areas opened up by technology, from the 'lady typewriters' of the beginning of this century, or punch card operators and computer programmers of recent decades, to the social workers of an increasingly welfare-oriented society. Women, then, have not ousted the dominant male group from the occupational sector. In Great Britain, there are, technically, few areas closed to women since they have been admitted as full members of Lloyds in 1969,[52] licensed as race-horse trainers, allowed to ride in amateur races, with the prospect of professional rides in 1975, and are able since 1973 to become members of the London Stock Exchange.[53] For the Methodists, the Church of England and the Roman Catholic Church, however, the combination of the female and the priestly role is still not considered compatible.[54]

A clearer guide to women's position in the occupational structure than can be offered by numbers in particular occupations is the *level* at which women are employed. Generally, the proportion of women at each level of the occupation is in inverse relationship to the level of responsibility involved: the higher the responsibility, the fewer the women.[55]

One point which is made obvious in the table is the very slow rate of change for women's integration into certain professions and occupations dominated by men. In a little over thirty years, women's representation in the legal profession has barely increased by two percentage points. In the medical profession, the change from 1931 to 1951 was very much greater, but thereafter the rate of change slowed. Professional engineering also remains a male avocation. An example not included in the table may further illustrate the slowness with which change is accomplished. In 1962 complaints were made about the discrepancy by sex in the holding of senior positions in the BBC. About ten years later a study revealed a virtually unchanged situation.[56]

In America (which is often regarded as showing trends in advance of this country) there has been traced a relative decline in the number of women in occupations demanding lengthy training and in women taking higher degrees. This bears out the contention of Betty Friedan that women are deflected to easier options which are regarded as 'more

Table 11 Women in Selected Professional Occupations, 1931 to 1966[1]

Occupation	1931 Women as % of total	1951 Women as % of total	1961 Women as % of total	1966 Women as % of total
Judges and Barristers	2.6	2.7 }	3.5 }	5
Solicitors	0.7	2.6 }		
Medical Practitioners	0.9	15.5	15.6	18
Dental Practitioners	3.4	6.6	7.0	11
Nurses	90.1	89.2	90.2	91
Teachers	69.6[2]	60.5[2]	59.1	58
University teachers			12.5	13
Architects	1.1	4.2 } 1.8	2.3[3]	2[3]
Surveyors		0.5 }		
Civil, Structural Engineers	0.6	0.4	0.007	0.2
Chemists, Metallurgists	3.8	0.6	6.8	6
Social Welfare Workers	46.7	57.5	47.5	52

1. Derived from G.B., Registrar General, Census 1931, 1951, 1961, Occupation Tables; G.B., Registrar General, 10% Sample Census, *Economic Activity Table*, 2, part 1, p.50.
2. Including University Teachers.
3. Including Surveyors.

feminine.’[57]

The locus of women’s employment may perhaps best be illustrated by the example of the teaching profession. In teaching, the bulk of women’s contribution comes in the state sector, in primary schools. Over the years 1950–65 the percentage of full-time women teachers has been in the seventy-three to seventy-five per cent range at primary level, compared with a range of the order of forty to forty-six per cent for the same period in the state secondary system.[58] The head of a school with a mixed staff and pupils is usually a man, only occasionally is a woman appointed. And schools with an all-female staff tend to have a lower status.[59] At University level, women are still very much in a minority. It has been estimated that ‘the proportion of women academics has risen slightly during the century as more women have entered the Universities, but they still constitute a small minority of ten per cent who tend to concentrate in the lower ranks and in the faculties of arts and social studies.’[60] Women professors hold around two to three per cent of the total number of university chairs.

Similarly in the newly created social services departments of Local Authorities, of the first one hundred and fifty directors appointed only fourteen were women, despite women's slight preponderance in the occupation of social worker.

In terms of financial reward, women's smaller share of the higher level posts is underlined. Equal pay as a legal requirement has yet to be implemented, though in the Civil Service, teaching, and certain professions this equality has been established. Average weekly earnings in industry show a considerable disparity by sex,[61] a disparity which is, in the main, a reflection of the less skilled work done by the majority of women in industry. Beatrice Webb's hierarchical appraisal is not entirely outdated in principle today. Mrs. Webb's advice on filling a post is quoted as follows: 'to decide first what ultimate salary could be afforded and if that were £1,000 a year to look for an Oxbridge male graduate, if £500 for a non-University man, and if £250 for a competent woman.'[62]

In the higher earned-income groups there are far fewer women than men.[63] The type of explanatory approach propounded about the paucity of women in positions of the greatest responsibility and with the highest earning power has changed, over time, from single-factor arguments (male prejudice, feminine incapacity) to the realisation that a far more complex explanation is necessary. Today, role conflicts, the various and varying demands of the family at different stages in the life cycle, motivations and socialisation processes are all part of the total explanatory factors put forward. As the Rapoports point out, the dual *career* family (that is, one in which both husband and wife pursue exacting careers) is still a variant pattern, but one which may become more usual in time. Motivation plays a major part. The Rapoports report their research on the ambitions of graduates, which reveals that fewer women than men wanted to hold the highest or high positions.[64] Moreover, women's aspirations tended to decline as difficulties were encountered.

While in the present situation not many women may be highly motivated to seek highly responsible positions via cut-throat aggressive competition; this is perhaps attributable to the disabling effects of women's cultural background. A basic point here is that there seems to persist some degree of conformity to the traditional sex-division of labour, such that women's expressive role in the family may be seen as projected into the occupational structure. One useful way of looking at women's position in the occupational sector is in terms of Talcott Parsons' instrumental-expressive dichotomy.[65] Then, the fact that with the exception of certain areas such as social work or teaching, women are in occupations ancillary to those of men, not equivalent to them, as secretaries not executives, as nurses not doctors, is more readily understandable. A boy with (x) O levels may follow management courses, and become an executive: a girl with (x) O levels may become his secretary. Social work and teaching fit easily into the expressive area of the Parsonian dichotomy. Other (often amusing) examples may be seen in advertisements for Girl-Friday Personal Assistant or secretarial posts which seem to demand some kind of pseudo-maternal role function.[66] American sources tend to speak in terms of office wives. Otherwise the expressive role may be indirectly reflected in motivations for working, e.g. when it is primarily for the benefit of the family – better holidays, school uniforms etc. Even taking a job to get an interest may be explicable (or rationalised) in terms of 'not being a cabbage' that is in order to become a better, more interesting mother.

It seems still applicable, as Parsons argues, that the adult female role continues to be anchored in the internal affairs of the family, while the adult male role is primarily anchored in the occupational world.[67] Work that has been completed has, as yet, failed to reveal that the employment of the wife significantly alters the family power structure.[68] The status of married women is still largely a derived one, basically related to her husband's. Moreover, while women's move towards occupational equality has made considerable progress, a complex of factors exists that makes it unlikely that equality in the sense of identity will be complete. It is reasonable for the woman veterinary surgeon to specialise in small domestic pets, leaving to her male colleagues the more physically demanding work with the larger farm animals. That a woman tends to be excluded from higher management or is not accepted in the office of bishop is less readily explicable in these terms.

Notes

1. e.g. H. Gavron, *The Captive Wife*, London, 1966, part I; E. Sullerot, *Woman, Society and Change*, London, 1971; E. Dahlström, *The Changing Roles of Men and Women*, London, 1967; J. Mitchell, *Woman's Estate*, Harmondsworth, 1971, Ch. 6; C. Bird, *Born Female*, New York, 1968, Chapters 3 and 4.
2. T. Parsons and R.F. Bales, *Family, Socialisation and Interaction Process*, London, 1956, p.8.

3. J.A. Banks and O. Banks, 'Feminism and Social Change—a case study of a Social Movement', in G.K. Zollschan and W. Hirsch, *Explorations in Social Change*, London, 1964, p.549.
4. For example, cf. S.C. Lee and A. Brattrud, 'Marriage under a monastic mode of life: a preliminary report on the Hutterite family in S. Dakota', *Journal of Marriage and the Family*, 26, 1967, 512–20; J.W. Bennet, *Hutterian Brethren*, Stanford, 1967; V. Peters, *All Things Common*, Minneapolis, 1965.
5. cf. Milton Spiro, *Children of the Kibbutz*, first published 1958, Schocken, 1965, pp.16–17, where reference is made to the aim of the kibbutz to free women from economic dependence. There are, however, several forms of kibbutz, in which a woman may have varying amounts of productive work.
6. In terms of average age at marriage this has been a relatively slow decline. In 1901, the average age at marriage in spinsters was 25.6 years, in 1969 the figure was 22.7. The proportion of women marrying below the age of twenty has however risen considerably in this century, from 84 per thousand in 1901 to 290 per thousand in 1968 (cf. *Social Trends 1971*, London, HMSO, 1971, p.50). Lowering of the age of majority will no doubt effect a further reduction in age at marriage.
7. Of the marriages which took place between 1870 and 1879, the average number of live births per married woman was 5.8. By 1925 the figure was 2.2. The figure for marriages which took place in 1955–59 is now around 2.38, so that earlier age of marriage has not made a considerable difference. (Sources: for 1870–79, and 1925, Registrar General's *Statistical Review of England and Wales for the Year 1962*, London, HMSO, 1964, Part II, Table L, p.72; for 1955–59, *Social Trends*, 1971, London, HMSO, Table 4, p.49.
8. Source: op. cit. Table B2, p.10. Expectation of life, England and Wales. The differential by sex in life expectation is marked in most industrial societies.
   For the years cited in the text, the corresponding life expectancy for men is 40.4 years, 56 years and 68.8 years. Today in this country, it means that over the age of seventy, women outnumber men by the order of 29:16. The implications of this age distribution for voting behaviour are discussed above.
9. R. Titmuss, *Essays on the 'Welfare State'*, London, 1958, p.92. It is interesting to calculate that sixty or seventy years ago a mother might spend up to ten or twelve years of her life in pregnancies and nursing her children. Today the period may be as little as one and a half to two years, with smaller families and increasing use of bottle feeding.
10. J.A. Banks and O. Banks, *Feminism and Family Planning*, Liverpool, 1964, p.130.
11. T. Parsons and R.F. Bales, op. cit., p.16.
12. C. Wright Mills, *Power, Politics and People*, New York, 1963, p.340.
13. e.g. Britain: 1918; France: 1944; Russia: 1917.

14. e.g. M. Mead, *Male and Female*, London, 1950. A similar approach is that of Sullerot's 'Social Sex' concept, which defines women's place in society as much as 'biological sex'. Indices of social sex are not uniform in all cultures. cf. E. Sullerot, op. cit., p.8. A virtual synonym for 'social sex' is 'gender', a term that has psychological and cultural rather than biological connotations (A. Oakley, *Sex, Gender and Society*, London, 1972, p.159).
15. Extract from a lecture: reported in C. Bird, op. cit., p.xi.
16. L. Tiger, *Men in Groups*, London, Panther edition, 1971, p.40. The analogy runs throughout the work.
17. cf. S.L. Pressey and R.G. Kuhlen, *Psychological Development Through the Life Span*, New York, 1957, Chapter 2.
18. G. Myrdal, in E. Dahlström, op. cit., p.10.
19. Sir William Armstrong, answering questions at a meeting of the Women's National Commission, 9 January 1970 (*The Times*, 10 January 1970).
20. D. Riesman et al., *The Lonely Crowd*, New York, first published 1950. Doubleday-Anchor edition, p.37.
21. M. Komarovsky, *Women in the Modern World*, Boston, 1953; and K. Kammeyer, 'The feminine role, and analysis of attitude consistency', *Journal of Marriage and the Family*, 26, 3, August 1964, 295–305.
22. M-J and P-H. Chombart de Lauwe et al., *La Femme dans la Société*, Paris, 1964, p.39.
23. cf. A. Campbell et. al., *The American Voter*, 1960, who put forward data suggesting that education is the single most important factor in predicting voting and non-voting. cf. also S.M. Lipset, *Political Man*, London, 1960, Chapter 6; R. Lane, *Political Life*, Glencoe, 1959, pp.45–62; Feelings of political efficacy have been found to be associated with educational standards, cf. A. Campbell et al., *The Voter Decides*, Evanston, 1954, p.191.
24. For discussion of political socialisation cf. below p.160. In this connection, it is interesting (no more in view of the small numbers involved) that two schools occur more frequently than any others when looking at the backgrounds of women MPs. One of these schools produced 4 of the 29 women elected to Parliament in 1964.
25. There is some evidence (mainly from large comprehensive schools) that these subjects are latterly becoming slightly less sex-typed.
26. Committee on Higher Education, 'The Robbins Report', London, 1963, Appendix I, p.8.
27. Department of Education and Science, *Statistics of Education*, volume 3, London, 1970. Table 35, p.60.
28. op. cit., p.82.
29. ibid.
30. op. cit., Table 26, p.58.
31. Derived from *Statistics of Education*, vol.14, 1970, 'Teachers', Table 2, p.2.
32. B. Jackson and D. Marsden, *Education and the Working Class*,

London, 1962, p.228.
33. On the question of subject division, cf. K. Ollerenshaw, *Education for Girls*, London, 1961, p.118 ff.
34. Source: Statistics of Education, 1970, vol.2, 'School leavers', passim.
35. On the small numbers of women in applied and pure science cf. 'The Science Undergraduate', Oxford University Department of Education, Oxford, 1967; D. Hutchins, 'The Sexually Handicapped', *New University*, December, 1967, pp.16–20.
36. Around one-third of first degrees awarded in the UK in 1969–70 in social, administrative and business studies were awarded to women. cf. *Statisticsof Education*, 1970, vol.6, p.69.
37. It is difficult to be precise on the varied aspirations of the many facets of this 'movement', both in Britain and in the United States.
38. J. Newsom, *The Education of Girls*, London, 1948, p.116. Newsom stresses the 'need for a clearer realisation of this vital influence of women as women, of the fact which Rousseau was groping to express . . . that women civilize men and thus preserve civilization . . . . To work through others is not derogatory to human dignity than can even be fulfilled by attaining the minor political or professional successes, which in the past generation they have imitatively adopted from men as a criterion of social usefulness.' *op. cit.*, p.109.
39. cf. J. Hubback, *Wives who went to College*, London, 1957 p.137.
40. cf. the work of A. Oakley, *Sex, Gender and Society*, London, 1972, Chapter III; E. Maccoby 'Woman's Intellect' in S. Farber and R. Wilson (eds.), *The Potential of Women*, New York, 1963; A. Heim, *Intelligence and Personality*, Harmondsworth, 1970, Chapter 14.
41. E. Bennet and L.R. Cohen, 'Men and Women: Personality patterns and contrasts', *Genetic Psychology Monographs*, 59, 1959, 101–55.
42. cf. J. Chabard, *The Education and Advancement of Women*, Paris, Unesco, 1970.
43. cf. above p. .
44. cf. M.E. Currell, op. cit., Chapter 7.
45. N. Mackenzie, *Women in Australia*, London, 1963, p.135.
46. cf. above, p. .
47. There are many brief accounts available of women's participation in the labour force, eg. A. Myrdal and V. Klein, *Women's Two Roles*, London, 1963, Chapter 4; National Women's Advisory Committee, *Discrimination against Women*, London, 1968; M. Rendel et. al., *Equality for Women*, Fabian Research Series, 268 (1968); A. Hunt, *A Survey of Women's Employment*, London, 1968.
48. F. Le Gros Clark, *The Economic Rights of Women*, Eleanor Rathbone Memorial Lecture, Liverpool, 1963, p.7.
49. A. Myrdal and V. Klein, op. cit.; M.P. Fogarty et al., *Sex Career and Family*, London, 1971.

50. Psychiatric nursing, however, has not this feminine predominance, presumably as an inheritance from the custodial-type care formerly associated with severe mental illness.
51. cf. N. Seear et. al., *A Career for Women in Industry*'. London, 1964, p.92 ff, for her discussion of 'the scarlet thread of prejudice', which runs through her study, prejudice against putting women in positions of authority.
52. Of the first twenty-five women admitted, the majority were wives of established Lloyds' Members. Admission requirements include a £15,000 deposit, plus possession of resources of the same amount.
53. The first vote of members on women's entry failed in 1967. Successive votes showed a reduction in opposition to women's entry, but their entry was not carried. In 1972 members voted in favour of amalgamating all British Stock Exchanges. Women members of provincial Exchanges thus would become full members of the new organisation. In these circumstances, without further ballot, the Stock Exchange Council agreed to accept applications from women from 1973.
54. It would appear that the entry of women into the Church of England priesthood may not be deferred indefinitely. cf. 'The Ordination of Women to the Priesthood', a consultative document, London, Church Information Service, 1972.
55. M. Fogarty et. al., op. cit., p.20 ff.
56. Political and Economic Planning, *Women and Top Jobs*, Four Studies in Achievement, London, 1971, part 3, 'Women in the BBC', pp.157–219.
57. cf. *The Feminine Mystique*, Harmondsworth, 1965, Chapter 7.
58. OECD, Training, Recruitment and Utilisation of Teachers in Primary and Secondary Education, Paris, 1971, p.103.
59. cf. R.K. Hall, *Year Book of Education*, 1953, p.13.
60. A.H. Halsey and M.A. Trow, *The British Academics*, London, 1971, p.158; cf. also Report of the Review Body appointed by the Council of the University of Birmingham, (the 'Grimond Report'), 1972, in which part-time appointments for the married woman are proposed (p.115).
61. For example, median earnings (all occupations) in April 1970 were (in the 21–24 age-group), £22.9 for men and £15.1 for women. In the 25–29 age group, the figures were £27.0 and £16.7 respectively, G.B., Central Statistical Office, *Social Trends*, London, 1971, p.72.
62. Quoted in M. Cole, 'The Woman's Vote; what has it achieved?' *Political Quarterly*, 33, 1, 1962, p.79.
63. In contrast, the distribution of net wealth between the sexes reveals a different pattern, attributable to women's greater expectation of life. In 1970, the percentage of owners with assets covered by estate duty statistics valued at £25,000 to £100,000 were 2.5 and 2.8 respectively for males and females; and in excess of £100,000, the figures were respectively 0.3 and 0.4. (*Social Trends, 1972*; London, 1972, p.86).

64. M. Fogarty et al., op.cit., p.210 ff. cf. also R. Rapoport and R.N. Rapoport, *Dual Career Families*, London, 1971.
65. T. Parsons and R.F. Bales, op.cit., pp.14–15.
66. A classic advertisement of this genre was inserted in the national press in 1972. 'Evil tempered, over-worked, highly victimised Head of P.R. Department . . . needs cool, intelligent, understanding P.A. to look after him, protect him, and do most of his work for him . . . ability to chat up people like journalists vital, . . . and mix soothing cocktails. If you would like to learn all about P.R. and publicity the hard way and suffer from a masochistic desire to work yourself to death, ring me . . .
67. loc.cit.
68. e.g. R.O. Blood and R.L. Hamblin, 'The effects of the wife's employment on the family power structure' in N.W. Bell and E.F. Vogel, *A Modern Introduction to the Family*, London, 1961, pp.137–42.

Chapter 9 Why so Few? Towards Explanation

The unifying theme which underlies this study is the attempt to explore the possible factors which go to make up some kind of composite (and complex) answer to the question, 'Why are there so few women in politics?' The changes which have helped to determine women's status in society have been indicated, and something has been said of women's position in the educational and occupational sectors. The relevance of these positions to the ways in which women relate to politics has been suggested. But such stark outlines are insufficient of themselves to add much illumination to an understanding of women's political role. The study has raised more questions than it has answered. In this chapter, therefore, a consideration is made of some of the factors which may be construed as relating to woman's political role, notably her 'gladiatorial' role, as elected representative. Some of the factors may be seen as mediating women's entry into the political elite, some as militating against that entry.

The first factor to be examined is women's function as the child-bearing sex to which reference has been frequently made in the empirical work reported in this study. Next the process of political socialisation is discussed, from the perspective of a differential by sex. Possible positive factors will be considered, namely the relevance of conceptualisations as the 'politicised family', and 'male equivalence'. Then the validity and the implications of the characterisation of women as a minority group will be examined. In addition, a technical factor, that of voting systems, will be considered briefly. The presentation, then, cuts across some of the factors previously discussed, and draws together data scattered throughout the study. Finally the direction of essential future research in this area will be suggested.

1. *Women as the Child-bearing Sex*

The complex of factors associated with women's commitment to the family and the home as a result of the child-bearing function ranked fairly high on the list of reasons which women political activists suggested as accounting for the lesser political participation of women. There were, however, some indications that the primacy accorded to this factor as an absolute deterrent to political activism was being gradually eroded over time. While the data do not admit of statistical validation of this generalisation, impressionistically, at least, perceptions appear to be changing in a subtle way. The movement appears to be from the assertion as of fact, of child-bearing as a handicap to women's political activism, to women's being considered by others to be so handicapped by this identification. Yet the biological factor is likely to remain significant, despite the demographic revolution which has abbreviated the child-bearing-rearing segment of a mother's life cycle, and despite the effects of what may be called the domestic technological revolution in food preparation, and labour saving domestic equipment which have been diffused through all classes.

That the majority of women MPs has been married need not seriously detract from the argument that the pulls of family life are important in drawing women away from political life. Instead, it emphasises that those women who do aspire to political leadership are the exceptional, whose political ambitions and determination outweigh the considerable difficulties and sacrifices involved. It is also significant that women of the age group associated with maximum child-bearing, i.e. the under thirties, have rarely been MPs, though there is some indication that this tendency may be beginning to be eroded.[1] On the whole, though, women have tended to enter politics somewhat later than men. The later entry may, in addition, reflect to some degree at least the difficulty which a woman may experience in becoming well-known, and in achieving selection for a seat with a possibility of success. Late entry into the political arena is often regarded as a disadvantage in attaining office. As Guttsman points out, 'Seniority rather than age counts towards success in Parliament, and those who enter politics young have a greater chance.'[2] Yet as has been shown, women have achieved office in numbers more than commensurate with the size of their group in the House of Commons.

The question of women's family commitments means that it is perhaps wrong to consider women's participation in local level political activity with that at national level. For a woman to become a councillor makes demands on her time, which may vary with the size of the local authority. Demands may be made on her abilities, on her stamina, but prolonged periods of separation from home and family is not demanded. At national level, politics is increasingly becoming a full-time occupation. To become a Member of Parliament, with its requirements of partial residence in London, involves real separation from home and family for a woman member living in the provinces, and consequent extra financial demands, for domestic help and perhaps full-time care for the children. This is a sacrifice which many women may be unwilling to make. There is also the principle involved in the distinction between paying an adequate substitute to bring up her children, and being willing to delegate this responsibility.

The demands of the Women's Liberationists for provision of twenty-four hour nursery care may be relevant here, though not the whole answer, as already indicated. Similarly the implications of the commune[3] for women's political activism are interesting, though the movement is so small and so disparate as to make speculation hazardous.

2. *Political Socialisation*

Throughout this study, in seeking to explore the variations in male and female response to the political, and possible explanatory factors relevant to such variation, the notion of political socialisation has recurred. In considering women's lower rate of participation in the political elite, an obvious area to consider is the process by which the individual is inducted into the political culture, the way in which the individual is trained for his political role within the framework of the norms and values of the society in which he lives. This, in essence, is one of the many ways of defining the process of political socialisation.[4]

That there are continuities between childhood experience and attitudes and adult attitudes and behaviour is clear,[5] and therein lies the necessity to look at the indicators and prefigurations The relationships are complex. In considering the material presented here, it has to be stressed that the association between childhood learning and adult behaviour is not a simple one of cause and effect. Nor is political socialisation to be interpreted as a determinant or predictor of future behaviour. There are many variables mediating political behaviour, and while political socialisation tends to be more usually linked to the pre-adult years, the process is an on-going one throughout the life experience of the individual. And it is in adult life that many of the norms, values, and attitudes towards the political acquired in childhood are either reinforced or fade with the lapse of time. It must be stressed also that socialisation patterns to the male and female role generally may be equally significant as socialisation *vis-à-vis* strictly political objects. An early identification of the male with the dominating, ascendant role, and the female with the more passive, submissive role may have implications which impinge on the political sector.

These two themes are very similar to what Almond[6] has termed latent (or analogous) political socialisation, which includes personality development and the acquisition of general cultural values. The second of Almond's categories covers the explicit transmission of information, values and feelings relating to the inputs and outputs of the political system. The dimensions of this question, then, include whether the motivation in either teaching or learning is deliberate and intended, and whether the teaching or learning is of direct, explicit relevance to the political, or is only indirectly relevant to political objects.

The processes of political socialisation are then both complex and inter-acting. As in all learning situations, the process is mediated not only by individual levels of intelligence, but also by personality factors.

Generally, the existence of a differential between boys and girls in politicisation seems well-established, though the degree of difference reported in the literature varies. Hyman,[7] reviewing much early academic work in political socialisation, reported that girls show less interest in political matters than boys, and that girls have much the lower level of political information. More recent research has re-inforced, elaborated and refined these earlier findings. Greenstein in the New Haven study found that 'Whenever the questionnaire responses differentiated between boys and girls, the former are invariably "more political".'[8] Such findings are paralleled in other studies,[9] including a report of differential response by sex, from France.[10]

Variations between the sexes appear to exist both in level of interest,[11] and in knowledge of politics. It has been shown that at a cognitive level there are important differences between boys and girls, though age and type of school modified the differences.[12] Class differences appear to mediate also capacity and motivation for political participation.[13] Dowse and Hughes found that working-class girls were below the other groups in knowledge, in interest, and in degree of political efficacy.[14]

While it is easy to quote research-based sex differences in political orientation, it is more difficult to attempt to explain them. One mode of explanation lies in relating orientations to the agencies of political socialisation. Previous work has emphasised the centrality of the family.[15] Although in the five countries studied in *The Civic Culture* by Almond and Verba, men showed higher frequencies and intensities on nearly all the indices of political orientation and activity, yet different patterns for women emerged in America and Britain. In these countries, unlike the others, Almond and Verba found that women tended to be involved in the system of political communications. This involvement they attribute to the relative 'openness' of the American and British family. They suggest that in these two countries the family tends to be a part of the political system, that events and issues in the polity tend to be transmitted into the family via both marriage partners, and that political discussion tends to be frequent and reciprocal rather than male-dominated.

> Furthermore, we suggest that the problem of family life, the needs of women and children are more directly and effectively transmitted into the polity through this kind of politically open family . . . . We would suggest, too, that a family that is open to reciprocal discussion of political issues provides a type of political socialisation that enables children to develop *within the family itself*, a sense of political competence and obligation, and to learn to tolerate the ambiguities of politics and political controversy. From this point of view, politically competent, aware and active women seem to be an essential component of the civic culture.[16]

In more recent work, Hess and Torney attribute to the family an important but not central role.[17] Within the family its role in transmitting party preferences has been analysed by Campbell and his associates in terms of male dominance.[18] Yet in an interesting study by Jennings and Langton,[19] it was found that the mother's part in transferring party identification from like-minded parents had been underestimated. This is a fairly radical reassessment and deserves much more empirical work. Much more needs to be done also on reaction against family mores, such as in work on the political expression of adolescent rebellion.[20]

As the family has been displaced from centrality in the political socialisation process, so the function of the school has become increasingly stressed. At least three elements may be isolated: inculcation of political knowledge and the influence of attitudes and opinions through formal 'political' instruction; the function of the peer group; and the general climate and quality of school life. Unfortunately at the present stage of knowledge, data on sex differences are minimal. Therefore, only a short and necessarily crude outline can be attempted. The data comes mainly from American sources.

Briefly, research on the effects of that part of high school's curriculum concerned with politics has shown mixed results. The results of Langton's[21] study of nearly 1,700 twelfth-grade high school seniors offered strikingly little support for the impact of the curriculum. There has been no major research in this country which might indicate sex differences. Yet the teaching of 'civics' and political education has been sometimes suggested as a direct means of increasing women's political participation.[22]

The influence of peer groups and school climate have been considered analytically distinct in some work, and studied in association by others. The process is further complicated, since the influence of the peer group and school climate may be strengthened or modified by family socialisation in addition to personality development. Peer groups may have a sub-culture of their own, but they also teach the adult culture of which they are a part, reinforce the norms and social patterns of that society.

An interesting question arises from these research findings, briefly summarised here, that is of direct relevance to seeking to explain women's participation in politics. Hess and Torney's data suggest that though boys are more interested in political matters, yet girls learn earlier the *norms* of interest in current events and political issues as part of the good citizens' role. Hess and Torney attribute this to the fact that the influence of the school is most pronounced.[23] This contention would seem to have some support in the findings of Greenstein, that by the seventh or eighth grades, there is much less difference in the level of political interest between boys and girls. The distinction between girls' attitudes to the norms of political interest and their lower level of *active* interest is almost paralleled in certain findings of Easton and Dennis. The latter fail to find consistent differencesbetween boys and girls in their attitudes to the *norm* of political efficacy, though in other areas of political involvement girls foreshadow their roles as less politically-oriented adults.[24]

Easton and Dennis suggest that something happens between childhood and later adulthood that makes females become disenchanted with their earlier expected role in political life that they once shared with boys. It may be, it is suggested, that when, in succeeding years, it is gradually revealed to maturing girls that men's judgements do in fact command dominant attention and respect in the political sphere, a slow creeping disillusionment results.[25] They conclude that though women may rank somewhat lower on a political efficacy scale than men this does not justify the conclusion that women are any less supportive of the efficacy *norm* than men.

Again, Campbell provides a conclusion on more or less similar lines.[26] He maintains that moralistic values about citizen participation in democratic government have been bred in women as in men: what has been less adequately transmitted to the woman is a sense of some personal competence *vis-à-vis* the political world. In other words for girls there may be a self-perpetuating cycle, and girls appear to acquire quite early the belief that political activity is generally more suitable to the male rather than the female role.

If political socialisation is concerned with the emergence of those attitudes, norms and capacities necessary for active involvement in the political process, then it could be argued that we should look at the political socialisation of women as an example of the imperfect application, or at least incomplete application of that process, as compared to men. Within this context of a differential in political socialisation between the sexes, the concept of the 'politicised family' becomes more important, and it may be suggested counteracts the problems generated by 'incomplete' political socialisation.

3. *The 'Politicised Family'*

The term 'politicised family' has been interpreted by Marvick and Nixon as describing families in which the tradition of leadership and public service is handed on at the local level of political participation in the same way that the great political families have tended to produce national leaders from generation to generation.[27] In this study the term 'politicised family' must be understood as including both the national and the local levels. More usually the notion of families in which the tradition of leadership and civic responsibility was nurtured and sustained has largely been applied to those families prominent in national politics, e.g. the Churchill family, the Devonshire family or the Salisbury family.

A classic example from America may be seen linked to the name of Adams. John Adams, the second President, was a cousin of Samuel Adams, the 'American Cato' who devoted his life to American Independence and was a leader in the American Revolution. John Adams' eldest son, John Quincey Adams, was to become sixth US President. His grandson, Charles Francis Adams, was Secretary of the Navy in the Hoover administration. The political contribution of the family thus spanned two centuries.

Of such families in Britain there is no shortage of examples. In his analysis of the personnel of Parliament of the latter part of the eighteenth century, Namier was referring to very much the same type of family inheritance in the section of his book devoted to 'Predestination: The Inevitable Parliament Men.'[28]

More recently Guttsman, in a chapter entitled significantly 'The Influence of Kinship and Friendship,' points out that one-tenth of the Cabinet members in the period 1868–1955 were the sons of ministers, many of whom had themselves held Cabinet posts.[29] The proportion may not be high, but it must be remembered that these are the minister sons of ministers, and disregards other family influences and precedents, or other levels of participation in the political elite.

One of the great political families in Britain is the Devonshire family, which, in its considerable ramifications, has had a considerable influence on British political leadership over the years, so that in the 1960s both Harold Macmillan and Lord Boothby were connected, by marriage, as sons-in-law. Maurice Macmillan held office in the 1970 Heath administration. Examples are many, and a detailed account is unnecessary here.[30] It has been suggested that there are signs discernible that the Labour Party is beginning to develop its own dynasties by inter-marriage between family groups.[31]

The idea of the 'politicised family' includes various elements. First there is the way in which the child is shown the example of political activism, is shown that activity at whatever level is involved is accepted, acceptable, usual. Then the level of information which the child acquires is important, political subjects are discussed and the child lives in an atmosphere of politics. This exposure to the political, this learning and conditioning process, it may be suggested, is then a very important and sophisticated form of political socialisation, so that the child is inducted into an activist sub-culture. This may be of particular importance for the production of women political activists.

Examples of the politicised family background of some women political activists may be useful here. The Grey family produced outstanding public figures such as Lord Grey, famous in Reform Bill times, and Josephine Butler the campaigner for the repeal of the Contagious Diseases Acts. It is surely not mere coincidence that Countess Markiewicz, the first woman to be elected to Parliament, was the sister of Eva Gore-Booth, an ardent suffrage worker who had been tremendously active in the women's Trade Union movement. Octavia Hill, the social reformer, came from a family 'distinguished on both sides for public service'.[32] Mrs. Marion Greeves, the first woman Senator in Northern Ireland, was the daughter of George Cadbury and Dame Elizabeth Cadbury, a member of a family outstanding in public life in Birmingham. The wide family connections of Beatrice Webb are interesting. The wife of Charles Booth (author of the comprehensive *London Life and Labour*,) had as her cousins 'the nine Potter sisters who spread their enveloping wings over radical and socialist society at the end of the last century. The most famous was the eighth, Beatrice Webb'.[33] Her nephew was Stafford Cripps.

The incidence of the politicised family among women MPs and among candidates has already been indicated. Certainly the factor seems to be as important in the middle range, that of elected representative, as in the higher reaches of public service.

The notion of a family socialising its members in a particular direction, or providing precedents to a particular course of action, is not, of course, confined to the strictly political field. For example, a study of Co-operative Society activists, (i.e. those attending meetings and voting for the Society's Directors) found that the activist is 'more likely to have come from a Cooperative family and to have a wife or husband who is also a member'.[34] There is a link here also with the ascriptive element that persists in the occupational sector, where it can be shown that there is still a substantial remnant of family tradition in the professions.[35]

Guttsman sees the tradition of political service as acting not only as a spur towards success, but also as a lever in the process. 'In an attempt to reach the first rung on the political ladder, the tyro is often helped by the elder members of his family who are active in politics, and perhaps more subtly, by the veneration in which an ancestor may have been held.'[36] At a lower level, help given by family in terms of connections and contacts with the relevant sectors of political life. Another major component may be isolated in the functioning of the politicised family. This is environmental and socialising, so that in an atmosphere of family involvement in political life, and amongst political activists, the individual may emerge well-informed, with an expectation of activism as normal, and a highly-developed sense of political efficacy.

The advantages that the politicised family confers on its members clearly apply to both sexes, but it is suggested, here, apply differentially in the importance which they may hold for each sex. For women, the backing of such a family may help to counteract some of the factors which have been suggested as militating against women's participation in the higher echelons of political life. Women in political life may suffer from a lack of the network of casual connections which a man may build up through his business activities, and the 'pub and club' contacts which a woman rarely has. A man may be judged by his success in business enterprise as a convenient yardstick of assessment; a woman is less often in such a position. To some extent this is a handicap which can be offset by belonging to a family already well known, and as it were 'prejudged'. A woman is often more readily acceptable to the electorate if she bears a name known for public service, and as it were inherits good will and publicity. She has almost ready-made references and testimonials. Finally, it may be suggested, the 'educative' and socialising agency of the politicised family help to counteract women's lower sense of political efficacy.

4. *'Male Equivalence'*

Throughout history, it has usually appeared to be much more easy for a woman to gain acceptance in a power-wielding position which is ascriptive rather than achieved in character.[37] Even today, in an advanced technological society, it seems that a woman is much more readily accepted as hereditary monarch than she would be as Prime Minister or Archbishop. It is to be suggested here that factors related to ascription have mediated, and, to a significant though decreasing extent, continue to mediate women's entry into the political elite.

One such factor likely to confer substantial advantages on women seeking to enter, or *willing* to enter political life, is that which may be termed 'male equivalence'. This is a term which may, for the sake of brevity, be used to indicate a situation in which a woman is entering a particular position usually held by men, is considered to be acting primarily as a substitute for, as the equivalent to a man. This equivalence is usually to a husband, occasionally to a father, and very rarely to another male relative. If for some reason the man is not available, then the female equivalent replaces him. The crucial point is that the woman stands in a derived position, as an *alter ego* rather than solely in her own right. The woman is expected to carry on the man's work, move along more or less the same lines, acting almost as a projection of him. It is because of these expectations that the woman occupies this particular position. The implication, then, is an 'inherited' role, a carry-over from the male to the female, almost an imitative role.

Before discussing possible explanatory approaches, and, more important, the implications of 'male equivalence', it is necessary to consider the incidence of this factor over time and at various levels. This is not a distribution which is susceptible to sophisticated statistical procedures, as numbers are small. There are, moreover, grounds for suggesting that data on male equivalence may be underestimated: examples may go unreported.[38] Approaches which are made, invitations which may not be accepted, would probably, if known, considerably inflate the evidence for 'male equivalence'. Selection procedures for Parliamentary candidates are frequently private rather than publicised activities.

Bearing in mind the small numbers involved, the importance of male equivalence should not be exaggerated. Yet any study of women's role in politics cannot ignore the fact that male equivalence at national level has meant that the woman concerned fights a seat previously held by her own party. Her chances of success at first attempt are clearly enhanced, and furthermore the male equivalent usually fights a by-election. Then there is some evidence that though declining in importance, the male equivalence factor is a real and persistent one. As shown, elsewhere, the percentage of women MPs who entered Parliament as 'male equivalents' has declined over time, so that in the period from the end of the Second World War to the present only three out of a total of fifty-three women members had entered Parliament initially in this way. The number was higher on the Conservative side (two out of twenty-one) than among the Labour MPs (one of a total of thirty-two). The persistence of the *idea* of male equivalence may be illustrated, however, by instances from the 1970s. In correspondence in *The Times* in February 1970 were raised issues of much interest to political commentators. A letter from two eminent politicians alleged that Conservative Associations . . . like Louth 'arbitrarily refuse even to consider or interview women candidates'. Subsequent letter writers, though, revealed that *the first person to be invited to accept the Conservative candidature was the widow of the previous member (emphasis added)*.[39] In 1971, the sudden death of the Tory Minister Iain Macleod was followed by reports of the possibility of his widow following him in the Parliamentary Seat. Interestingly enough, Bernadette Devlin won her seat (Mid Ulster) at the first attempt from a Unionist woman candidate whose late husband had held the seat for the previous twelve years.

In local level politics, data on male equivalence may only be obtained by extensive fieldwork, complicated by women's change of name on marriage. For one large county borough, however, for which data has been obtained over a fifty-year period, has been collected, patterns of a decline over time similar to that nationally may be traced.

Elements of the equivalence factor may additionally be discerned in some few cases in the conferring of Life Peerages on women. Clearly there is a complex of interacting factors operating in this process. The fact that the widows of men active inpublic life have frequently carved out areas of activity for themselves is not unimportant. Nevertheless, even though husband and wife are not holding the same position successively, it seems reasonable to maintain that there are certainly elements here of male equivalence, when widows are given Life Peerages very shortly after the death of a famous husband. Examples as already mentioned, include the widows of Sir Winston Churchill, a Speaker of the House of Commons, two eminent politicians and a General Secretary of the Labour Party respectively.[40]

This pattern may, in some ways, be paralleled in the history of the Conservative Party organisation, in which as Guttsman has shown[41] that women in the elite have often been the wives or widows of the male elite of the same party. For example, Viscountess Bridgman, wife of the former First Lord of the Admiralty, was the first woman elected as Party Chairman. In 1954, Mrs. Henry Brooke succeeded Lady Kilmuir (wife of the former David Maxwell Fyfe) as Chairman of the Conservative and Unionist party organisation. There seems nothing strictly comparable to this in the Labour Party. In essence, however, a somewhat similar orientation may be discerned, though at a completely different level, is a recent example which appeared in the Honours List of Mr. Wilson after the 1970 General Election. In the list, the widow of Mr. Wilson's former principal private secretary was awarded a C.B.E., 'as a tribute to her husband', it was reported by one daily paper.[42]

Other examples may be adduced of male equivalence in various forms and in various locations. Is it merely coincidence that two of the first three women to be elected to the London County Council at its inception in 1889 (illegally, the courts were later to decide)[43] were the daughter of Richard Cobden and the widow of Lord Sandhurst?

Reference has already been made to the incidence of male equivalence in the early years of the Fabian Society.[44] Leaving aside the political and pressure group areas, there is also evidence to be found in other sectors of public life. In an analysis of the membership of four Regional Hospital Boards, (two Metropolitan and two provincial), it was shown that forty-three per cent of the women members were the 'wives, widows or daughters of peers, or distinguished medical men.'[45] Obviously it cannot be assumed that the figure of forty-three per cent represents, *in toto*, male equivalence as we have defined it. But a guess may be hazarded that something very much akin to the male equivalence factor operates here, and that male equivalence, as such, may be quite substantially represented in the figure quoted.

The elements of male equivalence in terms of political representation by women is not confined to Britain. In the immediate post-war period in France, when women were first enfranchised, a sizeable proportion of the women elected were the widows of men in the wartime resistance movement. The proportion of women elected (six per cent) has never since been equalled, and the proportion of 'male equivalents' declined also.

A study of women's representation in the US Congress reveals a situation of male equivalence far more explicit and overt than in this country. As far as election to the House of Commons is concerned women, 'equivalents' having obtained the candidature, go through the normal electoral process. In contrast, in America, Margaret Chase Smith (later one of the few women ever to run for President) was among those women who entered politics by means of the 'widow's succession': women were appointed by the governors of their state to the seats formerly occupied by their husbands. Most of the women entering Congress in this way completed their term but did not seek re-election. Margaret Chase Smith[46] was an exception to this pattern, a pattern which gradually changed over time. As Werner points out,

> During the first two decades after women won the right to vote, the majority of Congresswomen gained their seats not by their own efforts, by running as candidates and depending upon the popular vote, but via the road of 'widow's succession' . . . . Until 1949 most women had acquired their seats in Congress via the widow's succession, but this picture changed over the past fifteen years or so. Since 1949, the proportion of women who won their seats by their own efforts had steadily increased. By 1963, thirty-four Congresswomen had been elected. Of thirty-six who were appointed when a vacancy occurred, twelve were subsequently re-elected.[47]

It is interesting that this pattern of decrease in the incidence of widow's succession parallels the decrease in the incidence of male equivalence in Britain, and similarly there is evidence that elements of male equivalence persist.

One of the most striking examples of male equivalence was that of the late Mrs. Lurleen Wallace, who became Governor of Alabama in 1967, when her husband was not eligible to run for another term. Under the significant headline 'Mrs. Wallace will obey the boss', a British newspaper commented: 'That his wife is his surrogate was obvious during last year's electoral campaign.'[48] With the disablement of George Wallace during his campaign for the Democratic nomination in the 1972 presidential campaign, a somewhat similar situation with George Wallace's second wife seemed about to recur. In the event, however, this did not happen.

Other examples in the international field include the first woman Prime Minister in the world, Mrs. Bandaranaike of Ceylon who filled the post made vacant by her husband's assassination. The choice of Mrs. Indira Gandhi as Prime Minister, however, is not in this sense an instance of male equivalence, though the fact of her being Nehru's daughter is obviously not without considerable significance. A clear example of male equivalence is that of the late Miss Jinnah, who opposed Ayub Khan in the Pakistan presidential elections of 1965 and who became the focal point for all opposition elements as the inheritor of her brother's leadership of the Muslim League. Other examples could be adduced, mostly of women who are the first to hold positions formerly held only by men. The first woman deputy of the Lebanon, Myra Bustani, was returned unopposed in 1963 to fill the vacancy left after the death of her father.

The illustrations which have been brought forward, may, it is hoped, make clear that the essence of the male equivalence factor as the term is used in this study is qualitatively different from situations where the wife or widow of a politician comes into prominence in public life, but not in terms of occupying a position once held by her husband. These examples no doubt share something of the elements of male equivalence, it may well be that the woman reaches the forefront of certain activities at least in part because of her well-known name. The point may be made clearer if we contrast the position of Mrs. Bandaranaike with that of Mrs. Eleanor Roosevelt.

It is difficult to discuss the 'substitution', 'surrogate' elements of the male equivalence notion without the suggestion emerging of inferiority or second-best. Although motivations are difficult to probe, and generalisations on motivation dangerous, it is not, perhaps, unreasonable to suggest that the 'equivalent' is not so highly motivated as a candidate standing without the husband or father's precedent. On the positive side, however, the substitute has the advantage of shared or vicarious experience. The implications of male equivalence mean, at a minimum, that the woman is able to profit from the name, the goodwill accruing to her husband. Through her husband, she is known and has those friends and contacts which are most useful in initiating a political career. She has help in negotiating the major and primary hurdle, achieving acceptance. The implication of 'succeeding' to a role, 'succeeding' to a policy (for the woman is promoted in the expectation of forwarding known political views) does not, however, connote a secondary role, or inferiority. If, as has been noted elsewhere, the major problem for a woman seeking an activist political role seems to lie in the initial processes, notably at selection level for elected representatives, then male equivalence may merely help an able woman to 'cancel out' the disadvantages of her sex at this stage.

Lionel Tiger, in his work on male bonding, has explored a notion in essence very similar to male equivalence. After commenting that 'one common way in which females acquire high office is by being close and politically active relatives of senior politicians who die',[49] Tiger refers to party gratitude, pensioning off, etc., as only partial explanations for this phenomenon. Tiger believes that

> a more interesting if more fugitive process may be at work when

either professional politicians or electors or both give political posts to female relatives of deceased dominant males. In many vertebrate communities, females assume the status of their male mates; in primates the phenomenon is sufficiently closely related to small-scale human class structures for one ethnologist to propose that comparable mechanisms operate, in primates as well as humans. The suggested explanation is persuasive.

> Perhaps females possess the 'release' which stimulates people to follow them when they enbody or share the 'charisma' of dominance of a closely related male . . . Thus, that females only rarely dominate authority structures may reflect females' underlying inability – at the ethnological level of 'pattern-releasing' behaviour – to affect the behaviour of subordinates. However, this general handicap apparently can be overcome by those females who have obviously participated in the use of power through their closely related men. More than any other factor this appears to lend efficaciousness to females' otherwise ineffective political efforts.[50]

It may be, then, that male equivalence makes women candidates more acceptable to both women and men voters. A woman following her late husband in a particular parliamentary constituency may be seen to some electors as diverging less from the accepted stereotype of the feminine role than a woman standing for a seat with which she has no familial connection or precedent. To push the issue to extremes, in the first few decades after women's enfranchisement, male equivalence rendered totally irrelevant a response such as masculine protest, the ultimate in an extreme feminist orientation. Today, the situation has altered, but in this sort of context it may be argued that male equivalence may obviate the need for women in politics to be 'tough', a quality sometimes attributed to women in the political elite, and often commented on unfavourably by other women.[51]

5. *Women Characterised as a Minority Group*

On Louis Wirth's definition (though he did not apply the definition specifically to women) a minority group is seen as 'a group of people who, because of their physical or cultural characteristics are singled out from the others in the society in which they live for differential and unequal treatment, and who therefore regard themselves as objects of collective discrimination. The existence of a minority in a society implies the existence of a corresponding dominant group enjoying higher social status and greater privileges. Minority status carries with it the exclusion from full participation in the life of the society . . . A minority must be distinguishable from the dominant group by physical or cultural marks . . . They suffer from more than the ordinary amount of social and economic insecurity. Even as concerns public policy they are frequently singled out for special treatment; their property rights may be restricted; they may not enjoy the equal protection of the laws; they may be deprived of the right of suffrage and may be excluded from public office . . . Nor should it be assumed that the concept is a statistical one . . . The people whom we regard as a minority may actually, from a numerical standpoint, be a majority'.[52]

This definition, which has been quoted at length, is one of the earliest and fullest made. Whether derived explicitly from Wirth or not, the history of applying to women the criterion of minority status is a lengthy one. The list includes Gunnar Myrdal, who, in *The American Dilemma*,[53] considered the position of women and negroes in these terms, and Lionel Tiger for whom women are a minority group in analytical terms like negroes, Jews and immigrants.[54] Helen Hacker[55] was one of the first to apply the concept to the status of women, and more recently writers on Women's Liberation subjects have used this approach.[56]

The use of this conceptualisation is, then, hardly novel. Moreover, analagous approaches and assumptions are many. For example, there is Simone de Beauvoir's contention, 'Women have never constituted a closed and independent society: they form an integral part of the group which is governed by males and in which they have a subordinate place . . . hence the paradox of the situation: they belong at one and the same time to the male world, and to a sphere in which that world is challenged.[57] A somewhat similar assumption underlies Viola Klein's approach, when she sees women as an outgroup in a society whose standards are predominantly masculine. The outgroup tends to imitate and appropriate patterns and values from the dominant masculine society.[58] On the level of everyday speech, the minority situation seems to be accepted in such phrases as 'It's a man's world.'

The minority characterisation has to be tested against reality. In the terms of Wirth's definition, the minority's being singled out for the special treatment, and not enjoying the equal protection of the law, women's position needs to be carefully considered in at least two ways, discrimination against women, and positive discrimination in their favour over time. Historically, it is true that women have not enjoyed the protection of the law equally with men. The history of women's seeking equal custody and guardianship over their children has a long history. It runs from Caroline Norton's frantic efforts to obtain custody of her children, efforts which culminated in the Infant Custody Bill,

1839, through Annie Besant's losing custody of her children,[59] to the 1972 issue of inclusion of children on the mother's passport.

The legal status of women generally, it seems, has risen steadily over the past hundred or so years. One index of change lies in the development of family law to the benefit of the wife and mother. Such developments have formally ratified the changing moves of society over time. Even as women are no longer grouped with their children, felons, and the insane in their exclusion from the franchise, so they no longer count as minors legally, and their legal standing has improved such that they have rights in property, in nationality, in divorce, and a wife and mother has rights in the guardianship of her children, the location of the family home, and savings out of her housekeeping allowance.[60] In taxation, a single woman's dependant, e.g. an elderly parent, has now been recognised for tax relief.

Legally, then, little remains to be done to bring women into complete equality with men.[61] Yet, as suggested elsewhere, changes towards equality have been accompanied by conventions and statutes which protect women as a group, mainly in occupational terms. Positive discrimination, in protection of women from night work, dangerous or heavy industries, also reflects the 'special' position of women before the law. This is an area which is likely to be modified in future projected sex discrimination legislation. In certain instances, the inequalities that persist may not be the result of legal enactment, but occur because women, as a whole, may less frequently meet specific requirements than men. The obvious example here is that of jury service based on minimum property requirements. On the property qualification which was established in 1825, in the early 1970s still only around eleven per cent of those qualified as jurors were women. It was not until 1972 that a Bill was introduced which based jury service on eligibility to vote. Another example of the protective element is the fact that a woman juror may be still challenged simply because of being a woman. In 1965 The Magistrates' Association in a submission on jury service stated: 'We think it important that the majority on a jury should normally be of men, with the proviso that an accused woman should have the right to ask for a majority of women.'[62] And under the Sexual Disqualification Removal Act, of 1919, a judge is empowered to choose a jury of one sex. This power has been used recently in cases alleging the publication of obscenity.

An accused woman may have the right to ask for a majority of women on the jury, but there is much less likelihood of the accused being a woman than a man. There continues to be a considerable difference in the numbers of women and men found guilty of indictable offences. Criminality amongst men is of the order of six times as great as that of women.[63] And in a study of murder statistics from 1957 to 1968, it was shown that murder has always been a predominantly male crime and convictions of women amount to only one or two a year.[64] Interestingly the male dominance in criminality holds good in other societies. In Russia, for instance, the vast majority of convicted felons are men.[65]

Are women in a minority position today in terms of the economic institutions of society? First, the increasing economic independence of women must not be underestimated. The major factor here is the changing composition of the labour force, such that married women are no longer necessarily economically dependent on their husband for the whole of their married lives.[66] Instead wives tend to be economically dependent for a relatively short period of child-bearing and child-rearing. This is one important way in which the balance of economic power has shifted significantly since the era of suffragettes, and has carried with it implications for woman's importance as consumer; as exemplified in advertising directed specifically at her by the media. A further implication of one facet of the demographic revolution, that women have a greater expectation of life than men, is that women as widows may inherit controlling interests in shares, or hold directorships formerly held by their husbands or fathers.[67] Even so, in terms of earned income, women's percentage of the higher income groups is very much smaller than that of men.

Collective judgements on women *per se* are easy to substantiate, particularly in the occupational sphere, though with the equal pay issue tackled by legislation, and the whole question of women's equal access to hitherto male occupational preserves, to be the subject of future laws, the area is liable to change. Certainly it seems unlikely that legislation can, except in the very long term, change attitudes. Certainly in the discussion of anti-discrimination laws collective judgements abound, reminiscent of the tone of collective appraisal by employers, quoted in a study of career opportunities for women in industry.

Prejudice runs like a scarlet thread all through the pattern of this study: prejudice against putting women in positions of authority. Many managers and some of the women said explicitly that there was prejudice and gave historical and social reasons for it. Some went further and said there was a sound basis for the prejudice: women *are* unfit to manage . . .[68]

The minority status stereotype is also emphasised by the disproportionate publicity' syndrome, the amount of attention devoted by the media to a woman who is appointed to a post usually held by a man. This is a persistent trait,[69] and it is ironical that the very act of highlighting a woman's achievement, while superficially positive enhancement of the female's role, in fact serves to underline the 'special' status of women.

A parallel to the idea of collective judgements made about the minority group as objects is the notion of the group members regarding themselves very much as a collectivity, as separate. Do women regard themselves as a distinctive group, (albeit in Klein's terms as an out-group) with distinctive needs, distinctive attitudes, and a distinctive contribution to make? In Wirth's analysis it must be remembered, the subjective elements, the feelings of unfair treatment are stressed.

Supportive evidence may be drawn from the history of the feminist movement: the violence of the 'protest' when it seemed that the objects of the suffragists were not likely to be speedily achieved through peaceful legal pressure, the enlisting of the aid of some of the majority group to help the cause. Equally interesting, though rather more difficult to assimilate into the analysis, is the stance of Women's Liberation, in so far as it is possible to attribute a viewpoint to such an unstructured and amorphous grouping, loosely termed 'movement'. Yet since such women's activity is directed towards the effective change of women's position in society (however variously both change and position may be interpreted), collective judgements, on women by women themselves are many. Again elements of paradox are implicit; women by their stress on a disadvantaged status are emphasising the 'special' minority categorisation in their efforts to achieve change.

A further illustration of women regarding themselves as 'other', as 'different', as a collectivity of their own, may be found in women's tendency to form a single-sex organisations, the 'feminine ghettos'. Examples of sex-specific organisations may be found in the women's sections of political parties. Instances elsewhere include sex-segregated associations such as the WRVS, women's sections of other organisations, such as the connection between the Rotary Clubs and the Inner Wheel, women's sections of Friendly Societies, the women's Co-operative Guild. At a different level, there are the products of the 1960s, the Women Drivers' Association, the Ladies Only Bank which opened in Scotland in 1964 complete with a woman Bank Manager, or a publishing venture, directed by women, producing books with a feminine orientation.

To some degree, at least, this sex-segregation in institutions may correspond to some element of verzuiling, the formation of columns, blocks, in parallel organisations in society. The concept of verzuiling, Dutch in origin,[70] of a 'form of isolation of a society encapsulated within society', was considered by some commentators to have little application to the feminist movement of the Victorian age.[71] On this argument, the movement was deliberately organised to break down barriers between the sexes, rather than build them up. Yet today, there is further paradox. In one way, women's aims are towards removal of discrimination and towards increased integration in a male-dominated world. In another way, the 'special' position of women, in the minority sense, the women's pages in the press, TV programmes for women, surely reflects, albeit in some dilute form, elements of verzuiling. Finally some of the manifestations of the women's Liberal movement more nearly approximates to the verzuiling concept.

> People of the same faith, people with the same dream of a better world order, can through this proliferation of organisations prepare themselves regularly for it and in the meantime more easily sustain the period of waiting. Verzuiling is thus to be seen as a form of isolation within an existing society, the consequence of techniques employed to build up solidarity among the admitted by concentrating upon the ideological similarity and emphasising their lack of genuine dependence upon the enemy.[72]

Minority characterisation of women collectively seems amply justified, but how is this label of help in attempts at understanding women's political participation? Immediately there is a problem. Gouldner, writing in 1950, maintained that 'the minority conceptualisation is amply justified since there is no question of the subordination of women in the decisive institutions of contemporary life, political, economic and familial'.[73] There is a paradox here. Indices of women's political participation are, at one end and the same time, both cause and effect. Either it can be maintained that women are a minority, and as evidence their 'subordination' in contemporary political life may be adduced, or it may be argued that it is possible to move towards explaining women's political role by reference to their minority status generally. It is the latter possibility that is considered in this section.

The idea of membership of a minority group contribution to the phenomenon of abstention from voting has already been mentioned.[74] Then, in so far as a symbolic or even a microcosmic view of representation is taken, it has been shown that the notion of the representation of women as women, i.e. because of a distinctive contribution attributed to their sex, is a persistent one, though there seems to be evidence that this is declining.[75]

The ambivalence towards the success of a few of their members is often characteristic of the behaviour of certain ethnic minority groups, which Gouldner pointed out, is also applicable to women. The belief that women were unwilling to support other women in seeking entry to a Parliamentary career, occurred at intervals in empirical work. Jealousy of a successful woman by members of their own sex was often remarked on in 'off the record' examples. It was felt that some women were liable to dislike the prospect of seeing other women in a role which they would find themselves unable or unwilling to attempt.

It cannot be denied that the old-fashioned 'cartoon image' of the tweed-suited women, the aggressive organiser, who at least to some extent was camouflaging her femininity in order to compete with men, takes a very long time to be forgotten. The 'battle-axe' generation lingers as myth. A journalist posed the dilemma for a woman MP: 'If she plays it tough, she is accused of being unfeminine; if she behaves like a woman she cannot be trusted with a man's job'.[76]

The implications for political activity of sex-segregated associations merits attention. Associations intended to safeguard their members' interests, by their very isolation, may tend towards institutionalising inequality. The sex-segregated societies in the political parties, lacking autonomy and executive function, are explicable in historical terms, but what effects does this segregation have now? There seems to be a dichotomy here, between diverting very able politically aware women from a career in politics as an elected representative, and on the other hand, providing some sort of training ground preliminary to entering politics. This is not a point which can be easily quantified. Undoubtedly there are those whose political aspirations are satisfied within these associations where there is less competition for prestige positions. Yet the Women's Co-operative Guild seems unique in its functions. Not only has it been, and remains a force in education for women, mainly of the working classes, but it seems true to say that it acts as a recruiting ground in the Labour interest, both for local councillors, and for a proportion of women MPs. There seems to be nothing comparable on the Conservative side.

In summarising minority grouping in relation to women's political orientations, it is useful to refer to Lane's appraisal, 'The assignment of the ascendant power-possessing role to men and the dependant receptive role to women, has affected the area closely associated with gaining and wielding power.'[77] This is consonant with the notion of dominance from the majority and the lesser role of the minority, in this case women.

6. *Voting Systems*

Finally, a technical factor needs to be considered here, namely the method of voting employed in a given political system, and its relevance to women's representation. The essential division is that between the simple plurality, 'first past the post' method, and the variants of the Proportion Representation system. Clearly systematic investigation is needed, though it would be hazardous to expect any definitive answer to the question of which system 'favours' the election of women, since so many other, largely unquantifiable variables would have to be considered.

There are, however, some indications to be found in the limited data that is already available. Certainly there seems some association between the simple plurality system and the low levels of women's representation. This association as has been shown[78] seems to hold good in Britain, in France under the Fifth Republic's 'scrutin d'arrondissement' method, in West Germany, where women tend to enter the Bundestag via the Land lists, rather than by single member constituencies. In contrast, election to the Commonwealth Senate of Australia is by means of Proportional Representation, and as Norman MacKenzie has shown, it is apparently easier for women to be nominated and elected to the Senate than to other parliamentary seats. MacKenzie discusses the need for a party to balance its ticket to achieve maximum appeal, and the implications of more open competition for nomination in large constituencies.[79] Women, then, with other minority groups may well fare better on the party list system, when a party is trying to formulate its list to ensure the maximum electoral appeal. In this way, the selection process may be considerably less of a hurdle to women under this method of voting.

7. *The Direction of Future Research*

At various points in this study, reference has been made to the necessity for further systematic investigation in specific areas. It would be easy to draw up a list of the areas where the political scientist is on uncertain ground, where indicators, possibilities, subjective appraisals are more plentiful than empirically-based data and generalisation.

Most of these areas are associated with two major dimensions which may be seen as delimiting the investigation of women's participation in the political elite. The first dimension is that of women's role in society at large; the second dimension consists of the study of the role and the motivation of the political activist. Together these two dimensions may be regarded as the axes determining the observations on the graph of women's political activity.

In this study something has been said in summary form of the forces which have been involved in shaping the role of women since the nineteenth century. But despite the current salience of women's studies, at present, the remaining task is massive, and the research continuing rather than definitive. Without embarking on an exhaustive list, areas demanding investigation include the attitudes of both sexes to women in the higher echelons of the occupational structure, in so far as this may be relevant to, or parallel, the attitudes to women in the decision-making areas of the political sector. Also to be included is the voluntary activity universe. That there is an association between social activism and political activism has been realised for a long time. It has been established that those who are active in voluntary associations tend to be participant in politics.[79] The relevance of this relationship may be of particular importance for women. Work which has been done in America shows that 'women are more likely to serve on boards of agencies functioning primarily as expressive organisations than on essentially instrumental agency boards'.[80] Such a situation is obviously not strictly paralleled in this country. Further research along these lines might be illuminating.

In the educational sector more must be learned of parental attitudes to the education of boys and girls, and the differences of aspirations between them. In terms of the content of curricula, and the choice of available subjects, there is much to be investigated. Within such a framework, the content of subjects sometimes considered as comprising 'political education' may usefully fall.

Bridging the area between the social role and the political activist dimensions, political socialisation is a major field which demands investigation empirically on a mass scale. Only then could it be established whether the incomplete, imperfect socialisation of women which seems so persuasive an approach can be empirically validated.

It is clear that while the present study has paid some (limited) attention to women's role in society generally, and more to the women political activists' characteristics, reported motivations, etc., there has been no confrontation in depth of some of the questions underlying political activism as such. What are the elements in political life, in the local or national sphere that attract or repel. Much more needs to be known empirically of the key issues of motivations and job satisfaction. How do the satisfactions of voluntary work, for example, differ in demands and rewards? Within the context of a holistic study, the motivations of *all* councillors, *all* MPs, the motivations of women councillors and MPs may be seen in true perspective. Only then would it be possible to establish whether the sex difference operates as one variable among many such as age, class, level of education. Only then would it be possible to determine whether or not women emerge as a distinctive sub-group in the political arena.

Notes

1. cf. the younger group of women MPs entering the Commons in 1970.
2. W.L. Guttsman, op.cit., p.27.
3. G.R. Leslie, *The Family in Social Context*, London 1973, for example, includes sections on Women's Liberation and on communal living experiments.
4. It must be stressed that the section on political socialisation which follows is a very attenuated discussion of complex phenomena, limited to what is directly relevant to the theme of this study, and based essentially on the (partial) view of socialisation as training for a role. For sophisticated conceptual treatment of political socialisation, cf. for example, D. Easton, 'The theoretical relevance of political socialization', *Canadian Journal of Politics*, I, 2, June 1968; F. Greenstein, 'A note on the ambiguity of "political socialization", definitions, criticisms and strategies of inquiry', *Journal of Politics*, 32, 1970, 669–78.
5. e.g. a party identification acquired in childhood. For a discussion of continuities cf. R.D. Hess and J.V. Torney, *The Development of Political Attitudes in Children*, Chicago, 1967, p.6; J. Dennis and D. McCrone, 'Pre-adult development of Political Party Identification in Western Democracies', *Comparative Political Studies*, 3, 1970, 243–62.
6. G. Almond, 'A functional approach to Comparative Politics', in G. Almond and J.S. Coleman (eds.), *The Politics of the Developing Areas*, Princeton, 1960, p.28.
7. H. Hyman, *Political Socialization*, Glencoe, 1959.
8. F. Greenstein, *Children and Politics*, New Haven and Yale, 1965, p.115. The ages of the children ranged from nine to thirteen years.
9. e.g. R.N. Dowse and J. Hughes, 'Girls, Boys and Politics', *British Journal of Sociology*, 22, 1971, 53–67. The authors found, however, that the crude political differences between boys and girls were *not* very large.
10. C. Roig and F. Billon-Grand. *La Socialization politique des enfants: Contribution a l'étude de la formation des attitudes politiques en France*, Paris, 1968.
11. Greenstein, op.cit., and Dowse and Hughes, op.cit., report that girls recorded only a little less interest in politics than boys, and that

girls and boys were about equally likely to report discussing politics. Butler and Stokes, op.cit., report that 'even in the 1960s the interest which the men in our sample took in politics was greater: three-fifths of our women respondents said they had "not much" interest in politics, as against only one-third of our men' (p.72).

12. F. Greenstein, op.cit., p.116; R. Dowse and J. Hughes, op.cit.; P. Abrahamson, 'The differential political socialization of English secondary school students', *Sociology of Education*, 40, 1967, 246–74; R. Dowse and J. Hughes, 'The family, the school and the political socialisation process', *Sociology*, 5, (1), 1971, 21–45.
13. F. Greenstein, op.cit., p.94. Upper-status children exceed lower-status children in capacity and motivation for political participation.
14. R. Dowse and J. Hughes, *Political Sociology*, London, 1972, p.193.
15. H. Hyman, op.cit., p.69.
16. op.cit., p.398 ff.
17. R. Hess and J. Torney, op.cit.
18. A. Campbell et al., *The Voter Decides*, Evanston, 1954, p.206.
19. M.K. Jennings and K.P. Langton, 'Mothers versus fathers', *Journal of Politics*, 31, 2, May 1969, 329–57.
20. R. Middleton and S. Putney, 'Political expression of adolescent rebellion', *American Journal of Sociology*, 68, March 1963, 527–35.
21. Reported in K. Langton, *Political Socialization*, New York, 1969, p.98. cf. also K. Langton and M.K. Jennings, 'Political socialization and the High School civics curriculum', *American Political Science Review*, 62, September 1968.
22. e.g. by a few women Prospective Parliamentary Candidates.
23. K. Langton, op.cit., 'Peer group and school and the Political Socialization process', *American Political Science Review*, 61, September 1967, 751–8.
24. cf. D. Easton and Jack Dennis, 'The child's acquisition of regime norms: political efficacy', *American Political Science Review*, LXI, 1, March 1967, 25–38. The study covered 12,000 children, aged seven to thirteen; R.D. Hess, 'The acquisition of feelings of political efficacy in pre-adults', in C. Abcarian and J.W. Soule, *Social Psychology and Political Behavior, Problems and Prospects*, Columbus, Ohio, 1971, 59–78.
25. op.cit. Raising the school leaving age and reducing the qualifying age for voting could be expected to affect this situation, though this must remain, for the present, speculative.
26. A. Campbell et al., *The American Voter*, New York, 1960, p.484.
27. D. Marvick and C. Nixon, op.cit., p.210. On the American national level cf. S. Hess, *America's Political Dynasties*, New York, 1966.
28. Sir Lewis Namier, *The Structure of Politics at the Accession of George III*, first published 1928, second edition, London, 1957, pp.2 and 3.
29. W. Guttsman, op.cit., p.217.

30. cf. also Greaves, 'Personal origins and inter-relations of the Houses of Parliament since 1832', *Economica*, IX, 1929, 173–84; S. Haxey, 'Aristocracy in the House of Commons or the Modern Cousinhood', in his *Tory M.P.*, London, 1939, pp.116–75.
31. cf. A. Sampson, *Anatomy of Britain Today*, London, 1965, p.119.
32. cf. E. Moberly Bell, *Octavia Hill*, London, 1942, p.2 ff.
33. cf. N. Annan, 'The intellectual aristocracy' in J.H. Plumb (ed.), *Studies in Social History*, London, 1955, p.256. The whole essay is relevant here since the intellectual aristocracy is in close connection with other elite fields in political and public life.
34. G.N. Ostergaard and A.H. Halsey, *Power in Co-operatives*, Oxford, 1965, p.100.
35. For recruitment patterns in law, medicine, the Church and teaching, cf. R.K. Kelsall, 'Self-recruitment in four professions', in D. Glass (ed.), *Social Mobility in Britain*, London, 1954, pp.308–20; cf. also R.K. Kelsall, *Women and Teaching*, London, 1963, p.37. For American parallels, cf. the description of the professions as 'among the most hereditary of occupational categories' (W.E. Moore, *The Professions*, New York, 1970, p.66).
36. Guttsman, loc.cit.; for an American parallel, cf. A.J. Clubok et al., 'Family relationships, Congressional recruitment and political modernization', *Journal of Politics*, 31, November 1969, p.1036.
37. Obviously there are exceptions to this generalisation, as John Knox's gibes at the 'monstrous regiment' of women recall. Today the issue is also blurred by the restricted, honorific quality of constitutional monarchy.
38. On the death of Sir Mark Sykes, MP in 1919, his widow is reported to have refused the offer of the vacant candidature for Central Hull. Source: *Pall Mall Gazette*, reported in C. Sykes, *Nancy, the Life of Lady Astor*, London, 1972. After the sudden death of the Tory politician Iain MacLeod, it was reported that his widow was invited to stand in his stead.
39. *The Times*, February 17, 19, 21, 27, 1970.
40. i.e. Speaker Hylton-Foster, Hugh Gaitskell, Iain MacLeod and Morgan Phillips. In June 1973 when the widow of the assassinated Governor of Bermuda (and former Tory minister) was granted a life peerage. Lady Sharples is reported as being deeply conscious that it was a memorial to her husband (*The Times*, 28 June 1973).
41. op.cit., p.14.
42. *Daily Express*, 7 August 1970.
43. Women did not sit legally until 1907.
44. cf. p.12 above.
45. M. Stewart, *Unpaid Public Service*, London, Fabian Occasional Paper No.3, 1964, p.14 ff.
46. After twenty-three years as her husband's secretary, she 'succeeded' her husband in the House of Representatives, and was later to be the second woman to be elected to Senate.
47. Emmy E. Werner, 'Women in Congress, 1917–64', *Western Political Quarterly*, 19, 1, March, 1966, p.20 ff; cf. also W. Chafe,

The American Woman, New York, 1972, p.38.

48. *The Times*, 3 April, 1967.
49. L. Tiger, *Men in Groups*, London, 1969, p.73 ff.
50. op.cit., p.74.
51. Masculine protest implies the suppression of femininity and the imitation of male qualities, attitudes and in some cases, dress and appearance. On the 'toughness' issue, cf. below, p.   ; cf. also H. Deutsch, *The Psychology of Women*, London, 1947, Chapter 8.
52. L. Wirth, in R. Linton (ed.), *The Science of Man in World Crisis*, New York, 1945, Bobbs Merrill Reprints S-318, p.347 ff.
53. G. Myrdal, *The American Dilemma*, New York, 1944, Appendix 5.
54. L. Tiger, op.cit., p.69.
55. H. Hacker, 'Women as a minority group', *Social Forces*, 30, 1951, pp.60–69.
56. e.g. Kate Millett, *Sexual Politics*, London, 1969, p.55 ff.
57. S. de Beavoir, *The Second Sex*, London, Four Square, 1960, p.297.
58. cf. V. Klein, *The Feminine Character*, London, 1947, pp.171 ff., for a linking of the concepts of the 'out-group' and the literature on 'marginality'.
59. For the details of the Caroline Norton case, cf. A. Acland, *Caroline Norton*, London, 1948; for Mrs. Besant's case on losing custody of the children on the grounds of being morally unfit, after having published material on contraception, cf. T. Besterman, *Mrs. Annie Besant, a Modern Prophet*, London, 1934; A.H. Nethercot, *The First Five Lives of Annie Besant*, Chicago, 1960.
60. Women in Parliament have played a part in working towards these changes. For example, Mrs. Eirene White gave up her Private Member's Bill on Divorce, on the undertaking that a Royal Commission would be established in this area. From the Commission stemmed legislative amendment. It was Dr. Edith (later Baroness) Summerskill who achieved legislative recognition for a wife's share of the savings she had made from her housekeeping allowance.
61. Minor exceptions for example, are that a husband's signature is needed on a hire-purchase agreement; that women sometimes appear to have more difficulty in obtaining mortgages; that certain hotels and restaurants are able to refuse to serve a woman unaccompanied by a male escort.
62. Submission to the Departmental Committee on Jury Service, *Cmnd* 2627, London, HMSO, 1965.
63. *Criminal Statistics*, 1965, Introductory Note, Appendix II. In 1966, 86.5 per cent of those found guilty of indictable offences were men. (J.D. McClean and J.C. Wood, *Criminal Justice and the Treatment of Offenders*, London, 1969.) The offence most frequently committed by women is shoplifting. These figures are reflected in the statistics of women in prison and juvenile establishments. cf. G.B. Home Office, *Report on the work of the Prison Department*, Statistical Tables, Table C.2., p.6, *Cmnd* 4806, London, 1971.

64. G.B., Home Office, *Murder 1957–1968*, London, 1969, *passim*.
65. W.D. Connor, *Deviance in Soviet Society, Crime, Delinquency and Alcoholism*, London, 1972, p.152. Connor shows, from a sample of cases the Central Black Earth economic region, that men made up 88 per cent of convicted felons, a percentage which, he believes, is probably valid for the nation as a whole.
66. cf. p.148 above.
67. A function of women's longer life expectancy in the case of inheritance as widows.
68. cf. N. Seear et al., op.cit., p.92.
69. e.g. women joining the Stock Exchange (March 1967); the first woman president of NALGO, Britain's largest white-collar union, (June 1966); the first woman chairman of the Composers' Guild (May 1967).
70. J.A.A. van Doorn, 'Verzuiling: een eigentijds systeem van social controle', *Sociologische Gids*, 3, 1956, 41–9 ('a comtemporary system of social control').
71. J.A. Banks and O. Banks, 'Feminism and Social Change', in G.K. Zollschan and W. Hirsch (eds.), *Explorations in Social Change*, 1964, 547–69.
72. op.cit., p.551.
73. A.W. Gouldner (ed.), *Studies in Leadership*, New York, 1950, p.188.
74. cf. above, p.41.
75. cf. above, p.111.
76. G. Smith, 'Woman around the House', *Sunday Times*, 21 June 1964.
77. R. Lane, op.cit., p.212.
78. cf. Chapter VIII above.
79. W. Erbe, 'Social involvement and political activity', *American Sociological Review*, 29, 1, 1964; C.R. Wright and H. Hyman, 'Voluntary association memberships of American adults', *American Sociological Review*, 23, June 1958; H. Maccoby, 'The differential political activity of participants in a voluntary association', *American Sociological Review*, 23, October 1958. It is noted that councillors have wide voluntary association membership, and that a minority have many memberships, G.B. Ministry of Housing and Local Government, op.cit., volume II, 'The Local Government Councillor', London, 1967, p.185. cf. also N. Mackenzie, op.cit., p.276.
80. N. Babchuk et al., 'Men and women in social agencies: a note on power and prestige', *American Sociological Review*, 25, 1960, 399–403.

Appendix I

An attempt was made to contact any woman who was serving or had ever served as an MP at any time. The enquiry was begun as a piece of ongoing research in the 1960s when it seemed that much valuable information was being lost by the death of former women MPs. The original intention was to present material for analysis in two parts, roughly divided between those elected in periods I and II, and those serving in period III. Small numbers, reduced unevenly by death, old age or illness, made this impracticable. Reference has already been made to the increasing demands by research workers on the MP, and this factor tended to decrease the number of serving members contacted. With a heavy work load, and a timetable liable to be changed at short notice, arranging appointments is, of itself, time-consuming. In the event, fifteen Conservatives and twenty-five Labour members were included either by interview or by usable questionnaire.

Appendix II

(i) *1964 Enquiry*

The names of women already adopted as candidates were kindly supplied by the two major parties. In November and December 1963, letters were sent explaining the object of the enquiry and asking for the co-operation of those women candidates *who had not sat in the House of Commons previously*. The return could be made anonymously, though very few availed themselves of this option. With follow-up letters where necessary, a response rate was received of 84 per cent for the Conservatives, and 70 per cent for the Labour candidates, by January 1964. The survey, therefore, covered all those seriously nursing a constituency, in the event more than six months before the General Election. The number of candidates completing questionnaires comprised 58 per cent of those Conservatives and 80 per cent of those Labour women who subsequently fought the General Election (excluding any sitting members).

In general the questionnaires were completed very fully, with letters amplifying answers given. It seems that the subject was of great interest and that this increased the response rate.

(ii) *1973 Enquiry*

An attempt was made to replicate the 1964 study, once more in advance of the General Election. The project was deferred from 1972 since only one Conservative (never previously elected) had by then been adopted. Again with the generous co-operation of the two major parties, candidates were contacted. In September 1973 of the 27 Labour candidates, 81 per cent had completed questionnaires, and of the 11 Conservatives, 72 per cent had returned completed questionnaires. A further Conservative reply arrived too late to be included.

Again the respondents replied, on the whole, very fully, offering to supply further information if necessary. Again the level of interest was high.

The questionnaire used has not been reproduced here because the questions asked are quoted in full in Chapter V.

Appendix III

The selection of the late Miss Pitt (Dame Edith Pitt) presents an interesting divergence from the usual process of selection in the Conservative Party.

Miss Pitt, of working-class origins, had completed her full-time education at thirteen, and had graduated via night school and clerical work to become a factory welfare officer. Miss Pitt, in 1953, was a Birmingham City Councillor, well-known for her political and public work. Previous to the 1953 by-election, Miss Pitt had fought three seats in the Birmingham area unsuccessfully, but each time reducing the majority against her.

In the 1953 Edgbaston election, Miss Pitt and two male candidates were short-listed by the Selection Committee. The Executive Council decided on one of the male candidates. At the General meeting of the Edgbaston Conservative Association, when the candidate was presented for formal adoption, he was not accepted. The decision was reversed, Miss Pitt became the adopted candidate and won the by-election.

Source: personal communication from the late Dame Edith Pitt; cf. also Paterson, op. cit., p.68 ff.

Select Bibliography

Alexander, K.J.W., and Hobbs, A., 'What influences Labour M.P.'s?', *New Society*, 13 December 1962, pp.11–14.

Atholl, Duchess of, *Working Partnership*, Barker, London, 1958.

Babchuk, N. et al., 'Men and women in social agencies: a note on power and prestige', *American Sociological Review*, June 1960, pp.399–403.

Banks, J.A., and Banks, O., 'Feminism and social change – a case study of a social movement', in G.K. Zollschan and W. Hirsch, *Explorationsin Social Change*, Routledge and Kegan Paul, London, 1964, pp.547–69.

Banks, J.A., and Banks, O., *Feminism and Family Planning in Victorian England*, Liverpool University Press, Liverpool, 1964.

Barber, J.D., *The Lawmakers*, Yale University Press, New Haven, 1965.

Barnes, J., *A Woman's Place*, Conservative Political Centre, London, 1961.

Beauvoir, S. de, *La deuxième sexe*, Gallimard, Paris, 1949, 2 vols. Vol.1 published as *Nature of the Second Sex*, New English Library, London, 1963; vol 2 published as *The Second Sex*, Four Square, London, 1960.

Bennett, E.M., and Cohen, L.R., 'Men and women: personality patterns and contrasts', *Genetic Psychology Monographs*, 59, pp.101–55.

Bennett, E.M., and Goodwin, H.W., 'Emotional aspects of political behavior: the woman voter', *Genetic Psychology Monographs*, 58, 1958, pp.5–53.

Bilchai, V., *Solution de la question feminine en U.R.S.S.*, Political Editions, Moscow, 1959.

Blackburn, J., *The Framework of Human Behaviour,* Kegan Paul, London, 1947, cf. Chapter IV, 'Sex differences'.

Bloomfield, P., *Uncommon People*. A study of England's elite, Hamish Hamilton, London, 1955.

Bondfield, M., *A Life's Work*, Hutchinson, London, 1948.

Bonnor, J., 'The four Labour Cabinets', *Sociological Review*, 6, (1), 1958, pp.37–48.

Bowen, M., *The Fullest Rights*, Conservative Central Office, London, 1968.

Boyd, R.R., 'Women and politics in the United States and Canada', *Annals of the American Academy of Political and Social Science*, 375, January 1968, pp.52–7.

Braddock, J., and Braddock, E., *The Braddocks*, Macdonald, London, 1963.

Brookes, P., *Women at Westminster*, Peter Davies, London, 1967.

Brown, D.R., *The Role and Status of Women in the Soviet Union*,

Teachers College Press, New York, 1968.

Buck, P.W., *Amateurs and Professionals in British Politics, 1918–59*, Chicago University Press, Chicago, 1963.

Butler, D., and Stokes, D., *Political Change in Britain*, Macmillan, London, 1969; Penguin, Harmondsworth, 1971.

Campbell, A. et al., *The American Voter*, Wiley, New York, 1960.

Central Office of Information, *Women in Britain*, HMSO, London, 1960.

Chafe, W.H., *The American Woman*, Oxford University Press, New York, 1972.

Charzat, G., *Les françaises sont-elles des citoyennes*? Denoel Gonthier, Paris, 1972.

Chombart de Lauwe, P.H., *Images de la femme dans la société*, Editions Ouvrieres, Paris, 1964.

Clark, F.Le Gros, *The Economic Rights of Women*, Eleanor Rathbone Memorial Lecture, University Press, Liverpool, 1973.

Clubok, A.B. et al., 'Family relationships, Congressional recruitment and political modernization', *Journal of Politics*, 31, 4, 1969, pp.1035–62.

Cole, M., *The Story of Fabian Socialism*, Heinemann, London, 1961.

Cole, M., 'The woman's vote: what has it achieved?', *Political Quarterly*, 33, 1, 1962, pp.74–83.

Collis, M., *Nancy Astor*, Faber, London, 1960.

Courtney, J.E., *The Women of my Time*, Lovat Dickson, London, 1934.

Critchley, Y., 'Candidates: how they pick them', *New Statesman*, 5 February 1965.

Dahlstrom, E. (ed.), *The Changing Roles of Men and Women*, Duckworth, London, 1967.

Dawson, R.E., and Prewitt, K., *Political Socialization*, Little, Brown, Boston, 1969.

D'Eath, W., *Barbara Castle*, Clifton, London, 1970.

Dennis, J., 'Major problems of political socialization research', *Midwest Journal of Political Science*, 12, 1968, pp.85–114.

Dennis, J. et al., 'Political socialization into democratic orientations in four Western Systems', *Comparative Political Studies*, I, April 1968, pp.71–101.

Dennis, J., and McCrone, D.J., 'Pre-adult development of political party identification', *Comparative Political Studies*, 3, July 1970, pp.243–62.

Dicey. A.V., 'Woman Suffrage',*Quarterly Review* 210, no.418, January 1909, pp.276–304.

Dodge, N.T., *Women in the Soviet Economy*, Johns Hopkins Press, Baltimore, 1966.

Dogan, M., and Narbonne, J., *Les françaises face à la politique*, Armand Colin, Paris, 1955.

Dowse, R., and Hughes, J., 'The family, the school and the political socialization process', *Sociology*, 5, (1), 1971, pp.21–45.

Dowse, R.E., and Hughes, J.A., 'Girls, boys and politics', *British*

Journal of Sociology, 22, 1971, pp.53–67.

Dowse, R.E., and Hughes, J., *Political Sociology*, Wiley, London, 1972.

Duverger, M., *The Political Role of Women*, UNESCO, Paris, 1955.

Easton, D., 'The theoretical relevance of political socialization', *Canadian Journal of Political Science*, 1, 2, June 1968, pp.125–46.

Easton, D., and Dennis, J., *Children in the Political System*, McGraw-Hill, New York, 1969.

Easton, D., and Dennis, J., 'The child's acquisition of regime norms: political efficacy', *American Political Science Review*, 61, 1, 1967.

Easton, D., and Hess, R., 'The child's political world', *Midwest Journal of Political Science*, 1962, pp.229–31.

Eitzen, D.S., Status consistency and consistency of political beliefs', *Public Opinion Quarterly*, Winter 1972–3, pp.541–8.

Eulau, H. et al., 'Political socialization and political roles', *Public Opinion Quarterly*, 30, 1966–67, pp.569–82.

Fabian Study Group, *Womanpower*, Fabian Society, London, 1966.

Figes, E., *Patriarchal Attitudes*, Faber, London, 1970.

Fogarty, M. et al., *Sex, Career and Family*, Allen and Unwin London, 1971.

Freeman, J., 'The Women's Liberation Movement: its origins, structures, and ideas', in H.P. Drietzel, *Family, Marriage and the Struggle of the Sexes*, Macmillan, New York, 1972, pp.201-16.

Freedman, M.B., 'Changes in six decades of some attitudes and values held by educated women', *Journal of Social Issues*, 17 1961, pp.19–28.

Freemantle, A., *This Little Band of Prophets. The story of the Gentle Fabians*. Allen and Unwin, London, 1960.

Friedan, B., *The Feminine Mystique*, Gollancz, London 1963; Penguin Harmondsworth, 1965.

Fulford, R., *Votes for Women,* Faber, London, 1957.

Gavron, H., *The Captive Wife*, Routledge and Kegan Paul, London, 1966.

Geshwender, J.A., 'Continuities in theories of status consistency and cognitive dissonance', *Social Forces*, 42, 2, 1967, pp.160–71.

Glazer-Malbin, N., and Waehrer, H.Y., *Woman in a Man-Made World*, Rand McNally, Chicago, 1972.

Gouldner, A.W. (ed.), *Studies in Leadership*, Harper, New York, 1950.

Great Britain, House of Commons, *Special Report* from the Select Committee on the Anti-Discrimination (No.2.) Bill, Session 1972–73, 6 June 1973, London HMSO.

Greenstein, F.I. (issue editor), 'Personality and politics: theoretical and methodological issues', *Journal of Social Issues*, XXIV, 3, July 1968, whole issue.

Greenstein, F.I., *Children and Politics*, Yale University Press, New Haven, 1965.

Greenstein, F.I., 'A note on the ambiguity of 'political socialization; definitions, criticisms and strategies of inquiry', *Journal of Politics*, 32, 1970, pp.969–78.

Greer, G., *The Female Eunuch*, Paladin, London, 1971.

Gripp, R.C., *The Political System of Communism*, Nelson, London, 1973.

Hacker, H.M., 'Women as a minority group', *Social Forces*, 30, 1951, pp.60–69.

Hamilton, M.A., *Remembering my Good Friends*, Jonathan Cape, London, 1944.

Hamilton, M.A., *Uphill all the Way*, Jonathan Cape, London, 1953.

Havel, J.E., *La condition de la femme*, Armand Colin, Paris, 1961.

Henderson, P., *William Morris, his Life, Work and Friends*, Thomas and Hudson, London, 1967.

Hess, R.D., 'The acquisition of feelings of political efficacy in pre-adults', in C. Abcarian and J.W. Soule, *Social Psychology and Political Behavior*, Columbus, Ohio, 1971, pp.59–78.

Hess, R., and Torney, J.V., *The Development of Political Attitudes in Children*, Aldine Publishing, Chicago, 1967.

Hobman, D.L., *Go Spin, you Jade*, Watts, London, 1957.

Hornsby-Smith, P., 'The second sex? Wanted: the will to lead', *Punch*, 9 May 1962.

Hunt, A., *A Survey of Women's Employment*, Government Social Survey, HMSO, London, 1968.

Jacob, H., 'Initial recruitment of elected officials in the U.S.: a model', *Journal of Politics*, 24, 4, 1962, pp.703–16.

Jennings, M.K., and Langton, K.P., 'Mothers versus fathers: the formation of political orientations among young Americans', *Journal of Politics*, 31, 2, May 1969, pp.329–57.

Jennings, M.K., and Niemi, R.G., The division of political labour between mothers and fathers', *American Political Science Review*, 65, 1971, pp.69–82.

Jennings, M.K., and Niemi, R., 'Family structure and the transmission of political values', *American Political Science Review*, 62, March 1968, pp.169–84.

Jephcott, P., *Married Women Working*, Allen and Unwin, London, 1962.

Johnston, J., *A Hundred Commoners*, Herbert Joseph, London, 1931.

Kamen, H., 'Women and revolution under Alexander II', *History Today*,XV, June 1965. pp.400–08.

Kamm, J., *Hope Deferred: Girls' Education in English History*, Methuen, London, 1965.

Kamm, J., *Rapiers and Battleaxes*, Allen and Unwin, London, 1966.

Kammeyer, K., 'Sibling position and the feminine role', *Journal of Marriage and the Family*, 29, 1967, pp.494–9.

Kelsall, R.K., *Women and Teaching*, HMSO, London, 1963.

Klein, V., *The Feminine Character – History of an Ideology*, Kegan Paul, London, 1946.

Kornberg, A., and Thomas, N., 'The political socialization of national legislative elites in the United States and Canada', *Journal of Politics*, 27, 1965, pp.761–74.

Labour Party, The, *Discrimination Against Women*, The Labour Party, London, 1972.

Lane, R.E., *Political Life*, Free Press, Glencoe, Illinois, 1959.
Langton, K.P., and Jennings, M.K., 'Political socialization and the high school curriculum in the United States', *American Political Science Review*, 62, 1968, pp.852–67.
Lee, J., *This Great Journey*, McGibbon and Kee, London, 1963.
Lee, S.C., and Brattrud, A., 'Marriage under a monastic mode of life: a preliminary report on the Hutterite family in South Dakota', *Journal of Marriage and the Family*, 29, 1967, pp.512–20.
Lennon, L., 'Women in the U.S.S.R.', *Problems of Communism*, July–August 1971, pp.47–58.
Lenski, G.E., 'Status crystallisation, a non-vertical dimension of social status', *American Sociological Review*, 19, 1954, pp.405–13.
Lipset, S.M., *Political Man*, Heinemann, London, 1960.
McCarran, M.P., *Fabianism in the Political Life of Britain*, Heritage Foundation, Chicago, 1957.
McCarthy, M., *Generation in Revolt*, Heinemann, London, 1953.
Maccoby, E. (ed.), *The Development of Sex Differences*, Stanford University Press, Stanford, California, 1966.
MacKenzie, N., *Women in Australia*, Angus and Robertson, London, 1963.
Magas, B., 'Theories of women's revolution', *New Left Review*, 66, March–April 1971, pp.69–96.
Mann, J., *Woman in Parliament*, Odhams Press, London, 1962.
Manning, L., *My Life in Education*, Gollancz, London, 1972.
Marreco, A., *The Rebel Countess:* The life and times of Constance Markievicz, Weidenfeld and Nicolson, London, 1967.
Marvick, D. (ed.), *Political Decision Makers*, Free Press, Glencoe, Illinois, 1961.
Matthews, D.R., *The Social Background of Political Decision Makers*, Doubleday, Garden City (USA), 1954.
Mattfield, J.A., and Van Aken, C.G.S., *Women and the Scientific Professions*, M.I.T. Press, Cambridge, Massachusetts, 1965.
Mezey, M., 'Ambition theory and the office of Congressmen', *Journal of Politics*, 32, 1970, pp.563–9.
Michel, A., and Texier, G., *La condition de la française d'aujourd'hui*, Gonthier, Geneva, 1964.
Michel, A., *La sociologie de la famille*, Mouton, Paris, 1971.
Milbrath, L.W., *Political Participation*, Rand McNally, Chicago, 1965.
Millet, K., *Sexual Politics*, Hart-Davis, London, 1971.
Mitchell, D., *The Fighting Pankhursts*, Cape, London, 1967.
Mitchell, J., *Woman's Estate*, Penguin, Harmondsworth, 1971.
Morgan, D.R., 'The women's campaign', *Parliamentary Affairs*, 21, 1967–68, pp.182–8.
Muggeridge, K., and Adam, R., *Beatrice Webb: a Life*, Secker and Warburg, London, 1967.
Myrdal, A., and Klein, V., *Women's Two Roles*, Routledge and Kegan Paul, London, first published 1956, revised edition 1968.
Nethercot, A.H., *The First Five Lives of Annie Besant*, University of Chicago Press, Chicago, 1963.

O'Neill, W.L., *The Woman Movement*; feminism in the United States and England, Allen and Unwin, London, 1969.

Parsons, T., and Bales, R.F., *Family, Socialization and Interaction Process*, Routledge and Kegan Paul, London, 1956.

Patai, R. (ed.), *Women in the Modern World*, Free Press, New York, 1967; Collier Macmillan, London, 1969.

Paterson, P. *The Selectorate*, MacGibbon and Kee, London, 1967.

Picton-Turbervill, E., 'Myself when young', in Countess of Oxford and Asquith, *Myself when Young*, Muller, London, 1938, pp.313–60.

Political and Economic Planning, *Women and Top Jobs*, Allen and Unwin, London, 1971.

Prewitt, K., 'Political socialization and leadership selection', *Annals of the American Academy of Political and Social Science*, 361, 1965, pp.96–111.

Raeburn, A., *The Militant Suffragettes*, Michael Joseph, London, 1973.

Ranney, A., *Pathways to Parliament*, London, 1965.

Richards, P.G., *The Backbenchers*, Faber, London, 1972.

Roig, C., and Billon-Grand, F., *La socialisation politique des enfants*: contribution a l'étude de la formation des attitudes politiques en France, Paris, Cahiers de la Fondation Nationale des Sciences Politiques, Armand Colin, 1968.

Rose, R., Class and party divisions: Britain as a test case', *Sociology* , 2, 1968, pp. 129–62.

Ross, J.F.S., *Elections and Electors*, Eyre and Spottiswoode, London, 1955.

Ross, J.F.S., *Parliamentary Representation*, Eyre and Spottiswoode, London, 1948.

Ross, J.F.S., 'Women and Parliamentary elections', *British Journal of Sociology*, 4, 1953, pp.14–24.

Rossi, A., 'Equality between the sexes: an immodest proposal', *Daedalus*, 93, (2), 1964, pp.604–52.

Rowbotham, S., *Women, Resistance and Revolution*, Allen Lane, Penguin Press, London, 1972.

Rush, G., 'Status consistency and right-wing extremism', *American Sociological Review*, 32, 1967, pp.86–92.

Rush, M., *The Selection of Parliamentary Candidates*, Nelson, London, 1969.

Schlesinger, J.A., *Ambition and Politics*. Political careers inthe United States, Rand McNally, Chicago, 1966.

Schmitt, D.R., 'An attitudinal correlate of the status congruency of married women', *Social Forces*, 44, (2), 1965, pp.190–95.

Seear, N. et al., *A Career for Women in Industry*? Oliver and Boyd, London, 1964.

Smith, G., *When the Cheering Stopped*, Hutchinson, London, 1964.

Spiro, M.E., *Children of the Kibbutz*, Schocken, New York, 1965.

Stassinopoulos, A., *The Female Woman*, Davis-Poynter, London, 1973.

Stewart, M., *Unpaid Public Servants*, Fabian Occasional Paper, 3, Fabian Society, London, 1964.

Sullerot, E., *Woman, Society and Change*, Weidenfeld and Nicolson, London, 1971.

Sullerot, E., *La vie des femmes*, Gonthierm, Paris, 1965.

Summerskill, Baroness, *A Woman's World*, Heinemann, London, 1967.

Sykes, C., *Nancy; The Life of Lady Astor*, Collins, London, 1972.

Tanner, L.B , *Voices from Women's Liberation*, Signet Books, New York, 1970.

Thompson, L., *The Enthusiasts*, Gollancz, London, 1972.

Tiger, L., *Men in Groups*, Panther, London, 1971.

Toole, M., *Mrs. Bessie Braddock, M.P.*, Robert Hale, London, 1957.

Tsuzuki, C., *H.H. Hyndman and British Socialism*, Clarendon, Oxford, 1961.

Van Loon, R., 'Political participation in Canada: the 1965 election', *Canadian Journal of Political Science*, 3, 1970, pp.376–99.

Veblen, T., 'The barbarian status of women', *American Journal of Sociology*, 4, 1898, pp.503–14.

Wandor, M. (ed.), *The Body Politic*, Writings from the Women's Liberation Movement in Britain, Stage One, London, 1972.

Watson, P., 'Is woman nigger?, *New Society*, 6 May 1971.

Werner, E.E., 'Women in Congress 1917–1964', *Western Political Quarterly*, 19, (1), 1966, pp.16–30.

White, E., 'Intelligence, individual differences and learning: an approach to political socialization', *British Journal of Sociology*, 20, March 1969, pp.50–68.

Wilkinson, E., 'Marion', (Dr. Marion Phillips, M.P.,), *The Labour Magazine*, 10, February 1932, pp.460–61.

Note:

The discussion of women's political role necessarily impinges on many areas and disciplines. In order to prevent the bibliography from becoming unwieldy, many references including historical and comparative material, and literature on feminism, women's suffrage activities and Women's Liberation movements have had to be omitted.

Index

Adamson, Mrs J. L. 66
Almond, G. 38, 160-61
Anti-Discrimination Bill 1
Apsley, Lady 64
Armstrong, Ann 126
Asquith, Margot 14-15
Astor, Lady 36, 60
Atholl, Duchess of 60, 61
Atkinson, J. W. 90
Australia 34, 43, 125, 179
Austria 125
Aveling, Eleanor Marx 11, 19*n*

Bacon, Baroness (Alice) 33
Bandaranaike, Sirmavo 122, 131-2, 170, 171
Banks, J. A. and O. 135
Bennet, E. 145
Benney, M. 42, 44
Bentham, Ethel, 10, 12
Besant, Annie 12, 174
Birk, Baroness 33
Blondel, J. 38
Bondfield, Margaret 10, 30, 32, 59, 60, 61
Braddock, Bessie 70
Bridgman, Viscountess 169
Brooke, Emma 13
Brooke, Mrs Henry 169
Bustani, Myra 171
Butler, D. E. 44
Butler, Josephine 11, 165
Buxton, Lady Noel 63

Campbell, A. 46-7, 162, 163
Castle, Barbara 30, 32, 35, 70
Chartism, 10, 18
Charzat, G. 42-3
child-bearing 135-8, 158-60
Clarion, The 9
Clark, F. Le Gros 148
class 7, 32; and Womens' Liberation 115-16, 118-19; of M.P.s 55, 62
Cohen, L. R. 145
Communist states 122, 127-9, 133*n*
Conservative M.P.s (women): attitudes to number of women M.P.s 84-6; attitudes to the job 82-3; background 76-7; marital status 78; reasons for becoming an M.P. 79-82; specialisations 88
Conservative Party 15, 53-73 *passim*. 132*n*, 164-5; candidates 26-7, 96-7, 101-3; support for 44-5; women in top positions 168-9
Contagious Diseases Acts 11
Cooper, Duff 15, 21*n*
Co-operative movement 97, 166, 178
counter-culture 119
Crewe, Marchioness of 15
crime 174-5
cross national comparisons 122-34

Dalton, Mrs F. R. 63
Davidson, Viscountess 33, 63-5
de Beauvoir, S. 173
de Lauwe, Chombart 140-41
demographic changes 136-8, 147-8, 153*n*
Dennis, J. 163
Devlin, Bernadette, 168
Devonshire, Duchesses of 9, 14
Dicey, A. V. 2
Dickenson, Lord 65
Divorce Act (1969) 1
Dowse, R. N. 161
Duverger, M. 5, 38, 42, 87

Easton, D. 3, 114, 163
economic dependence of women 175
Edelman, M. 15
education 141-6, 180; and socialisation 162-3; curriculum 141-4; higher 142-5; level of 40, 41; of M.P.s 55, 62, 73; of Parliamentary candidates 102
elections: landslides 65-7; success of women in 27-8 *see also* franchise, extension of *and* voting
elites 6
Equal Pay Act (1970) 1
exploitation of women 118-19

Fabian Society 12-13, 20*n*
Fairfield, Letitia 13
family 136-41, 152; and socialisation 161-6; commitments, effect on political activity 158-60; influence of, on politicians 57, 64, 69-70, 71-2*n*, 77, 80, 104
femininity 1
feminism 4, 84, 116-17, 120; and social change
Figes, Eva 138
Finland 43
Firestone, Shulamith 118
Ford, Isabella 10
France 38, 123-4, 147, 169, 179
franchise, extension of 2, 4, 18*n*, 19*n*; political activity before 7-17 *see also* voting
Friedan, B. 149-50
Furtseva, Yekaterina 128-9

Gandhi, Indira 122, 130, 170
General and Municipal Workers, National Union of 10
Germany, 43; Federal Republic 124-5, 179
Gladstone, W. E. 8
Glasier, Kathleen 9, 10
Gore-Booth, Eva 8, 165
Gouldner, A. W. 177, 178
governments 28-32, feminine type jobs in 31; women in 60-61, 66, 70-71, 124, 125
Greenstein, F. 161, 163
Greeves, Marion 165
Guttsman, W. 159, 164, 166, 168-9

Hacker, H. 173
Hamilton, M. A. 36
Hardie, Keir 46
Hart, Judith 70
Hess, R. D. 162-3
Hobby, Oveta C. 126
Holland 125
Horsburgh, Baroness 30, 66
House of Lords 32-3, 168
Hughes, J. 161
Hyman, H. 161

images (of women) 140-41
Independent Labour Party 9
India 122, 130
influence, womens' 34-7
Israel 122, 130-31
Italy 43, 125

Jackson, B. 143
Jeger, Lena 35
Jennings, M. K. 162
Jinnah, Fatima 170
jury service 174

Kammeyer, K. 154
Keir, Cazalet 66
Kilmuire, Lady 169
Klein, V. 173, 176
Komarovsky, Mirra 140

Labour M.P.s (women): attitudes to number of women M.P.s 84-6; attitudes to the job 82-3; background 76-7; disadvantages of being 86; marital status 77-8; specialisations 87-8; reasons for becoming an M.P. 79-82
Labour Party 4, 9, 15, 23, 53-73 *passim*, 105; cabinets 29-32; candidates 26-7, 96-7, 101-3; National Executive 12; organisation 37; sympathy to women 46-7; voting for 44
Lancelot, A. 41
Lane, R. 38, 178
Langton, K. 162
Laski, H. 44
Lasswell, H. 90
law relating to women 173-5
Lawrence, Susan 12, 58, 59, 61
leadership, qualities of 86
Lebanon 171
Lee, Baroness (Jennie) 33, 64, 66
legislation 34-5
Liberal Party 8, 15, 26
life peerages 32-3, 168 *see also names of life peers*
Lipset, S. M. 40, 44
local government and politics 8, 12; M.P.'s experience in 69, 76; Parliamentary candidates' experience in 102-3
Londonderry, Marchioness of 15
Lynd, R. and H. M. 45

McArthur, Mary 10
Mackenzie, N. 34, 43, 125, 146, 179
Macleod, Baroness 33
'male equivalence' 33, 58-9, 63-4, 80-81, 167-72; motivations for 171-2
Mann, Jean 32, 109
Markiewicz, Countess 54, 165
marriage 136-41, 153*n*; and politicians 54-5, 61, 67, 101

Marsden, D. 143
Marshall, T. H. 34
Martyn, Caroline 10
Marvick, D. 164
Marxism 118
Maud Report, Committee on the Management of Local Government 6
Mead, M. 138
Meir, Golda 122, 130-31
Melbourne, Lady 14
Members of Parliament (women) 18-28, 74-92; *1918-28* 54-61; *1929-44* 61-6; *1945-70* 66-71; age at election 56, 61-2, 67; attitudes to the job 82-3; career appraisal 78-83; class 55, 62; contribution of, to politics 86-8; family commitments 78, 158-60; job satisfaction 87-91; marital status 54-5, 61, 67, 77-8; offices held by women 60-61, 66, 70-71; opinions on number of women M.P.s 84-5; perceptions of womens' role 83-91; pre-election expertise 55-7, 62-3, 69, 75-8; proportion of women as 28; qualities needed for 88-9; reasons for becoming 79-82, 92*n*, service of 60-61; womens' organisation of 36
middle classes: and Parliamentary candidates 102; Fabian women 13; in the Labour Party 23; over-representation of among M.P.s 56, 62, 68, 71*n*
Millet, K. 114
Mills, C. Wright 138
minority group, women as a 172-9
Mitchell, J. 117, 119
mobility, social 46; of M.P.s 55, 62
Morley, Edith 13
Morris, May 11
Morris, William 11
Morten, Honor 13
motivation 120, 180-81; career 151; of women M.P.s 59, 89-91; of Parliamentary candidates 105-7
Myrdal, G. 139, 173

Namier, Sir L. 6
National Labour Women's Advisory Committee 96
National Organisation of Women 117
nationalised industries 34
New Zealand 125
Newsom, J. 144-5, 155*n*
Nixon, C. 164
Norton, Caroline 173
Norway 72*n*

occupations 43, 129, 130, 146-52; before election to Parliament 55-7, 62-3, 67-8; communication type 56-7, 68, 75-6, 91*n*, 102 effect on political activity 146-7; level of 148-52; male dominated professions 149-50; number of women in 147-8; of Parliamentary candidates 102; re-training for 148; teaching 150
organisations, single sex 176-8

Pankhurst, Christabel 36
Pankhurst, Emmeline 10
Parliamentary candidates 26-8, 85, 93-113; advantages and disadvantages of being a woman 108-9; age of 101; attitudes to women M.P.s 109-12; characteristics of 97-103; Conservative 99, 100-101, 104, 107, 110, 113*n*, Labour 98, 100-101, 104-10, 113*n*; majorities faced by 98-101, 105; marital status 101, 104-5; motivation 105-7; pre-adoption experience 102; selection processes 28, 93-7
Parsons, T. 14, 135, 138, 151-2
participation 1-2
pay, equal 1, 139-40
peer groups 162-3
Perkins, Frances 126
personality 160
Philips, Baroness 33
Philipson, Mrs Hilton 58
Phillips, Marion 10, 12
Pike, Miss Mervyn 35
Pitt, Dame Edith 188
political activity: defining 3-4, 104; lack of women engaged in 158-85
political efficacy 41, 163, 166, 172
political generations 45
political parties 51*n*, 122-32 *passim*; organisation 37; selection of candidates 93-7 *see also* Conservative Party *and* Labour Party
'politicised family' 164-6
power motivation 90, 114
prejudice *see* sex discrimination
pressure groups 4, 10-13
priesthood 149, 156*n*
Private Members Bills 35
public bodies 34, 169

Rapoport, R. and R. N. 151
Rathbone, Beatrice 64

Rathbone, Eleanor 59
Reeves, Pember 13
religion 45-6, 149, 156*n*
Renger, Annemarie 125
representation 36-7
Riesman, D. 138, 140
Robbins Report, Committee on Higher Education 142
Rokkan, S. 46-7
role 136-41; and the family 136-8; perceptions 83-91, 109-12
Roosevelt, Eleanor, 171
Roper, Esther 8
Rose, R. 23, 31, 34
Ross, J. F. S. 27, 28, 56
Rowbotham, S. 119
Royal Commissions 33, 49*n*
Runciman, Viscountess 58

SCUM 118
Salisbury, Countess of 9
scandal 16
schools 162-3
Seear, Baroness 33
sex: differences 145-6, 161; discrimination 95, 109, 174-5; roles 136-41, 145
Shackelton, David 8
Sharp, Baroness 33
Sharples, Lady 33
Shaw, George Bernard 12
Shield, The 11
Shinwell, Lord 8
single sex organisations 176-8
Smelser, N. 117
Smith, Margaret Chase 170
Smith, Thorley 8-9
Snow, C. P. 15
Snowden, Viscount (Philip) 12
Social Democratic Federation 11, 20*n*
socialisation 145-6, 180; political 160-64
Socialist League 11
Socialist Woman 115
Socialist Woman Manifesto (1972) 118
Spencer Churchill, Lady 33
Sri Lanka 122, 131-2
Stacy, Enid 10
status: inconsistency 40; sensitivity to 46-7; socio-economic 40-41
Stock Exchange 149, 156*n*
Stokes, D. 44
Suffragettes 60, 116, 176
Summerskill, Baroness (Edith) 16, 28, 32, 33, 66, 184*n*
Summerskill, Shirley 70
Sweden 38, 126-7, 139
Switzerland 125

teaching profession 150
Thatcher, Margaret 32, 35, 70, 73*n*
Tiger, L. 139, 171-2, 173
Tingsten, H. 38
Titmuss, R. 137
Torney, J. V. 162-3
trade unions 4, 10, 18, 76
Tweedsmuir, Lady 70

U.S.A. 16, 72*n*, 125-6, 147, 161; 'male equivalence' in 169-70; Womens' Liberation in 117-19
U.S.S.R. 127-9, 147

values 3, 117, 160-61
Veblen, T. 45
Verba, S. 38, 161
Veroff, J. 90
verzuiling 177
Vickers, Dame Joan 35
Victoria, Queen 2
voluntary organisations 180
voting 37-47; in France 123; in Germany 124; in Sweden 126-7; non-voting 38, 177-8; social factors in 43-4; systems 179; tendency to conservatism 42-5, 52*n*; turnout 38-40

Wallace, Lurleen 170
Wardle, Lena 11
Warwick, Countess of 15, 20-21*n*
Webb, Beatrice 12, 151, 165
Wells, H. G. and Catherine 12-13
Werner, E. E. 170
White, Baroness (Eirene) 33, 35, 10, 184*n*
Wilkinson, Ellen 16, 30, 32, 59, 60, 61
Williams, Shirley 70, 73*n*
Wilson, Mrs Woodrow 16
Wintringham, Mrs K. 58-9
Wirth, L. 172, 176
Woman Power 36
women: as a minority group 172-9; as elected representatives 22-8, 53-73; attitude to political careers 178; attitude to women candidates 47; differences to men 6-7, 47,

145-6; in office 28-32; influence of 34-7; symbolic representation of 31
Womens' Co-operative Guild 178
Womens' Liberation Movement 1, 3, 44, 114-21, 176; class composition of 115-16; conceptualisation of 116-20; in Britain 114-16; objectives 115; reform or revolution 117-19; size of 115-16
womens' party (idea of) 36
Womens' Trade Union League 10
work *see* occupations
working classes 42, 71*n*; and Womens' Liberation 116; their position compared with women 18-34 *passim*

Yugoslavia 128

54572

DATE DUE

30 505 JOSTEN'S